Demand, Prices and the Refining Industry: A Case-Study of the European Oil Products Market

ROBERT BACON
MARGARET CHADWICK
JOYCE DARGAY
DAVID LONG
ROBERT MABRO

Published by Oxford University Press
for the Oxford Institute for Energy Studies
1990

Oxford University Press, Walton Street, Oxford OX2 6DP

Oxford New York Toronto
Delhi Bombay Calcutta Madras Karachi
Petaling Jaya Singapore Hong Kong Tokyo
Nairobi Dar es Salaam Cape Town
Melbourne Auckland
and associated companies in
Berlin Ibadan

Oxford is a trade mark of Oxford University Press

OIES books are distributed in the United
States and Canada by PennWell Books, Tulsa, Oklahoma

British Library Cataloguing in Publication Data
Bacon, Robert, 1942–
    Demand, prices and the refining industry :
    a case-study of the European Oil Products Market.
    1. Europe. Petroleum industries & trades – serials
    I. Title II. Oxford Institute for Energy Studies
    338.2'7282'094

ISBN 0–19–730010–3

Typeset by Oxford Computer Typesetting
Printed in Great Britain
by Bookcraft Ltd, Bath, Avon

Preface

The Oxford Institute for Energy Studies completed in 1989 a large study entitled *Petroleum Product Prices: A Case Study of the European Market*. The complete report on this study runs to seven mimeographed volumes and for reasons of length is not amenable to publication in its entirety. This book of essays brings together analysis and results relating to the main aspects of the study: the behaviour of demand for petroleum products in Europe, the structure of European refining and the patterns of investment and disinvestment in refining, the characteristics of capacity utilization in refining and of the marginal refinery yield, the determinants of product price movements and their relationship to crude oil price behaviour and finally the characteristics and change over time of petroleum product taxation in Europe. The first chapter provides a summary presentation of the findings, a synthetic view of their relationships to one another and a brief discussion about future developments.

The analysis and findings in the essays collected here relate to the major concerns of oil companies operating in Europe, oil-producing countries interested in expanding their activities downstream in Europe, governments and organizations of states, and the oft-forgotten final consumers. We read these concerns as follows.

Oil companies' concerns are largely about the profitability of refineries and other downstream activities. Refining margins in Europe have been very low, and often negative, since the early 1970s, and the exceptions to this pattern have been both rare in their occurrence and of short duration. Although considerable restructuring took place over the period 1976–88, largely through investment in upgrading plant and closure of refinery sites and distillation capacity, the economic performance of refineries is still unsatisfactory. Oil-producing countries with downstream investment in Europe, and those that are contemplating such investment, are likely to have similar concerns. European governments and international organizations probably share the natural concerns of final consumers in their countries about maintaining access to secure supplies at competitive prices. We do not address the issue of supply security directly, which appears to have lost its relevance, at least for the medium term. There is a glut of crude oil supplies on the world market, and there is no immediate constraint on the supply of products, given the considerable volume of excess capacity in European refining and the openness of Europe to international trade in petroleum products. While immediate concerns about the security of oil supplies may be dismissed, two other important concerns remain: that of governments about competition and that of final consumers about competition and taxation.

The structure of the refining sector in Europe has distinct competitive features that have become more marked in recent years. Indeed it is argued by some that the final markets for petroleum products are not perfectly competitive in all European countries. Furthermore, the poor economic performance of refining in Europe is eliciting demands for trade protection which, if heeded by governments, will inevitably push up product prices. European governments are unlikely to succumb to such protectionist pressures, although petroleum product imports may be effectively restricted in the future by the introduction of more stringent product specifications.

Finally, the taxation of petroleum products in Europe raises issues of interest to final consumers. Not only are taxes on some products, particularly gasoline, heavy in most European countries, but they have also been consistently raised even in periods of falling crude oil prices. Governments usually justify this fiscal policy on grounds of security of supply: one major objective of OECD countries' governments is to limit their energy consumption and their dependence on imported oil. Consumers may legitimately ask whether security is being bought at the right price or whether they are being unduly burdened by governments for reasons of revenue, rather than security. If the various tax harmonization proposals made by the EEC are adopted and implemented, they will cause petroleum product prices to change significantly in the final markets of most European countries during the 1990s.

The book is addressed to all those in industry and governments who are continually puzzled by the behaviour of petroleum product markets, the apparently erratic movements of their prices, the complexities of refining economics and of the investment/disinvestment decisions in refining. It is also addressed to economists interested in the application of their discipline to the problems of the largest industry in the world.

The essays in this book have been written by individual authors and published under their respective names. These authors, however, have worked together and with others under the direction of Robert Bacon as a team researching the issues covered here. Each one of them owes much to all others and is happy to acknowledge this debt.

Robert Mabro

Acknowledgements

This study on which the present book is based was carried out by a research team led by Robert Bacon and consisting of Margaret Chadwick, Joyce Dargay, David Long and Robert Mabro. Hugh Quick and Peter Beck were consultants to the team. Philip Barton, Richard Harvey, Kaye England and Edward Flemming provided indispensable help.

The study was sponsored by the Benefactors of the Institute, namely British Gas, British Petroleum, Cosmo Oil, Dubai Aluminium, Elf-Aquitaine, ENI, Enterprise Oil, Kansai Electric Power Company, Neste Oy, the Olayan Group of Companies, Osaka Gas Company, Petróleos de Venezuela, Repsol, the Royal Ministry of Petroleum and Energy (Norway), Shell International Petroleum, Sun Company, Tokyo Electric Power Company; and by other companies and institutions – Britoil, the EEC, Exxon, Kuwait Petroleum International, Mobil, Ruhrgas, Statoil, Texaco and Veba. We take pleasure in thanking warmly all those who contributed to the project through research, writing, advice, the supply of information, ideas, staff and financial resources.

Contents

Tables

Figures

Abbreviations

API	American Petroleum Institute
ARA	Amsterdam, Roterdam, Antwerp
b/d	barrels per day
BP	British Petroleum
bpcd	barrels per calendar day
CCU	Catalytic cracking unit
CDU	Crude distillation unit
CFP	Compagnie Française des Pétroles
c.i.f.	cost, insurance and freight
CMEA	Council for Mutual Economic Assistance
CPEs	Centrally planned economies
CRF	Catalytic reforming unit
DWS	Durbin–Watson statistic
EEC	European Economic Community
EIA	Energy Information Administration (USA)
ENI	Ente Nazionale Idrocarbari
FIFO	First in, first out
f.o.b.	free on board
GDP	Gross domestic product
GPW	Gross product worth
HCU	Hydrocracking unit
HDS	Hydrodesulphurization unit
HDT	Hydrotreating unit
HVU	High-vacuum distillation unit
ICI	Imperial Chemical Industries plc
IEA	International Energy Agency (OECD)
IMF	International Monetary Fund
INPC	Irish National Petroleum Corporation
KPC	Kuwait Petroleum Corporation
LIFO	Last in, first out
LPG	Liquefied petroleum gas
n.a.	not available
NGLs	Natural gas liquids
OECD	Organisation for Economic Co-operation and Development

OJS	Oelwerke Julius Schindler GmbH
OLS	Ordinary least squares
ÖMV	Österreichische Mineralölverwaltung AG
OPEC	Organization of the Petroleum Exporting Countries
PDVSA	Petróleos de Venezuela SA
RDP	Refinería Dominicano de Petróleo SA
SEE	Standard error of estimate
t/d	tonnes per day
THC	Thermal cracking unit
VAT	Value Added Tax
WOCANA	World outside Communist areas and North America

1 Petroleum Products in Europe: Demand, Refining and Price Behaviour

Robert Mabro and Robert Bacon

A main purpose of this chapter is to present in a synthetic form the main findings of the research project which gave rise to this book. These findings relate to the behaviour of petroleum product prices in Europe and to important determinants of this behaviour, namely demand and the economics of refining (supply). Another purpose is to identify and briefly discuss issues that may significantly influence the future development of refineries and petroleum products in Europe. The analysis of past developments and past behaviour in the essays published here naturally raises interesting questions about future performance. The aims of this chapter are therefore interrelated.

In this overview we analyse the main economic features of demand for petroleum products in Europe, their supply (and more precisely the throughput of the refining sector), the industrial structure of European refining, international trade in products and the patterns of crude oil acquisition by refiners. We then present our findings on the behaviour of margins and of three types of price relationships: (a) the own-price differentials of particular products in the various European spot markets; (b) the relationship between an aggregate measure of product prices (the gross product worth) and crude prices; and (c) the relationships between the prices of the various petroleum products. We then provide a short synthesis in which the main findings are highlighted and related to each other and briefly discuss the future.

1.1 Demand

The two main features of the behaviour of petroleum product demand in OECD Europe in recent years were the remarkable change to the overall trend of rising demand that had lasted from the late 1940s to the early 1970s, and the equally significant change in the composition of that demand. The high rates of growth in oil consumption that persisted over this remarkable, probably unprecedentedly long, period of twenty-five years were followed by virtual stagnation between 1973 and 1979, and by a marked decline in demand between 1979 and the mid-1980s. A low point seems to have been reached in 1985, and figures for 1986 and 1987 indicate that a recovery has recently been taking place. Table 1.1 presents data for total product demand in OECD Europe.

Table 1.1: Total Demand for Petroleum Products in OECD Europe. 1973–87. Million Tonnes of Oil Equivalent.

1973	705.56
1974	663.47
1975	622.01
1976	667.95
1977	653.93
1978	679.41
1979	691.58
1980	645.91
1981	592.48
1982	566.39
1983	552.54
1984	555.98
1985	546.60
1986	568.29
1987	571.50

Note: Product demand is calculated as: production plus imports minus exports minus marine bunkers minus stock changes.
Source: OECD/IEA, *Quarterly Oil and Gas Statistics*, various issues.

As is well known, these trends in petroleum product demand are related to two factors: first, the sharp decline in the rate of growth of primary energy consumption in the period following the events of 1973; and, secondly, significant inter-fuel substitution against oil. These energy trends, in turn, are due to:

(a) an initial increase in the price of energy relative to the prices of other commodities, factors of production and services in the European economy;
(b) an increase in the price of oil relative to the costs of supplying other primary fuels;
(c) a decline in the rates of growth of the European economies;
(d) the energy policies pursued by governments, through price and non-price instruments, to reduce both the total consumption of energy and the share of oil in the consumption fuel mix;
(e) changes in economic structure involving a shift away from energy-intensive industries (some of which began before 1973);

(f) the building up of nuclear capacity in the 1960s, which then came on stream in the 1970s independently of the oil price rise.

It is interesting to note that the combined effect of all these forces on the fuel mix was to reduce the share of oil from nearly 60 per cent in 1973 to less than 44 per cent in 1987 (see Table 2.1 below). The share of nuclear rose dramatically from 1.4 to 11.0 per cent between these two years, and that of gas from 10.3 to 16.1 per cent. Coal, however, behaved differently: its share fell from 20.6 per cent in 1973 to 19.6 per cent in 1987 but the rapid decline that had begun at the end of World War II and accelerated in the 1960s was largely arrested by the oil price increases of 1973 and 1979.

The shift in the composition of demand for the various petroleum products was towards middle and light distillates and away from the 'black end' of the barrel, i.e. heavy fuel oil. This was because the scope for inter-fuel substitution against oil is much more significant in its uses as a burning fuel than in the transport sector. In general, the scope for substitution seems to decrease as one moves through the product spectrum from the heavy to the light fractions. Hence the marked decline in the consumption of heavy fuel oil, the less steep decrease in the use of middle distillates, and the positive, albeit very small, rate of growth of gasoline demand in the 1980s (see Table 2.2 below).

The changes in the aggregate demand for oil and in the demands for the individual products conceal important differences in the behaviour and structure of demand between countries and economic sectors at any point in time, and for any country or sector in different periods. Modelling the demand for the various products gives some insight into the responses of demand to changes in income and prices, and reveals some of the differences between them (see Chapter 3 below).

Demand responses can be measured as price and income elasticities. Average price elasticities in OECD Europe are low in the short term (one year) for all petroleum products. In this respect there is no significant difference between gasoline at one end of the product spectrum and heavy fuel oil at the other end. However, as might be expected, the price elasticities of all products reach higher values in the medium term (five years), and in the long run the elasticities for the different products diverge. The greater ease of substitution for heavy fuel oil than for gasoline is reflected in its higher (long-run) price elasticity. The income elasticities of all products have higher numerical values than the corresponding price elasticities in the short run, and tend to increase in value over time (except for the income elasticities of fuel oils used in industry).

The fact that in the short term the price elasticities of the demands for petroleum products are both low and smaller than their income elasticities indicates that the observed drop in demand after the shocks of 1973 and 1979 was largely due to a reduction in the rate of economic growth (which was due in part to increases in the crude oil price and in part to other factors).

The full demand response to a given price or income change does not occur instantaneously, but spreads over a period of years. One main reason is that energy is not consumed directly but only as a result of consumers' use of vehicles, plant or appliances, so that the full demand adjustment is constrained by the durability of capital goods. Thus the speed of adjustment seems to be higher for gasoline and gas oil than for heavy fuel oil, because cars and domestic boilers have a shorter economic life than fuel oil-using plant in industry. This is the only generalization that can be made about the speed of adjustment of demand to oil price changes in Europe. Considerable variations in the results for individual countries preclude us from drawing general conclusions on other aspects of the demand response to price and income changes.

Large differences between countries were also found in our estimates of price and income elasticities, and we found it difficult to explain them in terms of differences in the economic, technological or institutional features of the countries concerned. Thus the behaviour of oil demand, and of the parameters that define demand responses to changes in income and price, can not be assumed to be similar in different countries, so that the results of aggregate analyses that estimate demand elasticities on the basis of aggregate data for a whole continent, or for the world as a whole, are unlikely to hold for demand in any individual country.

In order to understand fully the behaviour of petroleum products demand in Europe in the period after the price shock of 1973, it is important to study the development of taxation on the various products. Throughout Europe petroleum products attract substantial taxation. Increases in the tax payable are passed on, at least in part, to the final consumers through higher prices, thus affecting their demand for petroleum products. Petroleum taxation in Europe operated during the period studied in such a way as to ensure that any percentage increase in crude oil prices (or more precisely in 'refinery gate prices') was reflected by an equal percentage increase in retail prices, usually within one year. In other words the final consumer was not cushioned against the effects of crude oil price increases but, on the contrary, made to feel their full impact. Although the price elasticity of demand was found to be small in the short run for most products, the responses of absolute demand to the big crude oil price increases of 1973 and 1979 were significant because prices to final consumers were made to rise at high rates.

The relationship between changes in crude oil prices and tax rates was not symmetrical. Tax rates were increased when crude prices rose but were not reduced when prices fell in 1986 and thereafter. On the contrary several European governments pushed up tax rates on some products in 1987. This counter-price tax behaviour prevented European demand for petroleum products from responding fully to lower crude oil prices.

The general behaviour of petroleum product demand in Europe after the price shock of 1973 can be explained by a combination of four factors. First, the relatively high income elasticities suggest that the impact of the recessions of 1974–5 and the early 1980s on the demand for petroleum products was considerable. Secondly, the low price elasticities mean that the proportional impact of any small price change on demand would be relatively small. The price increases of 1973 and 1979–80 were very large and fully passed on to the final consumer through increases in taxation. Although the proportional effect on demand was small (because of the low elasticities) the absolute impact was significant (because of the high rates of price increase). Thirdly, the long lags in the adjustment of demand to price changes mean that the impact of a price increase continued to be felt several years after the rise had taken place. Fourthly, the counter-price tax policies of European governments ensured that falls in crude oil prices were not fully translated into increases in petroleum product demand. In short, recession and taxation policies, in combination with the crude oil price increases of 1973 and 1979–80, choked off product demand in Europe in the years following these oil shocks. Crude oil prices began to fall in 1982, but the positive impact of this on demand was mitigated by a number of factors. Taxation policy was one of these. Another factor was the adverse effect of earlier price increases, which continued to be felt several years after the oil shocks because of the long adjustment lags involved. Paradoxically these adverse effects were still being felt in 1985–8, a period of falling prices.

1.2 The Supply of Products from European Refineries

The considerable changes to the growth trend and the composition of demand for petroleum products after 1973 had a significant impact on the structure of the European refining industry. Adjustments had to be made. There was disinvestment – the closure of some refinery sites and reductions in distillation capacity at some surviving sites – in response to the decline in demand; and at the same time there was investment in upgrading capacity because of the need to adapt the refining structure to the change in the composition of demand.

Some idea of the extent of these adjustments can be gained by comparing data for 1976 and 1986, as detailed in Chapter 4 below. It is interesting to note that the majority of closures occurred from 1982 onwards, which indicates that the industry took a long time to decide on closures. Oil companies did not disinvest after the price shock of 1973; and they did not even disinvest in the immediate aftermath of the second price shock of 1979. This is slightly surprising considering that there was considerable surplus refining capacity in Europe in the mid-1970s even *before* oil demand began to decline. The reluctance to disinvest was therefore very deep, and was probably due to a combination of the following factors:

(a) The expectation that a resumption in the growth of demand for oil products would inevitably occur a few years after the shock (this expectation may have been encouraged by signs of recovery in 1976 and 1979);
(b) The high costs and the political difficulties involved in closing refineries;
(c) The classical oligopolistic stalemate which inhibits every player from moving first, lest rival players take advantage of this first move (the company that closes some of its refineries first increases the potential market share of those rivals who are holding back).

These factors delayed decisions to close or retrench for almost seven years; but by 1981 it must have become so abundantly clear to any refinery owner that closures were unavoidable that the disinvestment trend began. The result of refinery closures and other disinvestment decisions was to reduce crude distillation capacity from 20,527 thousand barrels per calendar day (bpcd) in 1976 to 14,496 thousand bpcd in 1986, and catalytic reforming from 2,535 thousand bpcd to 1,790 thousand bpcd.

Our model of refineries' survivals and closures, which is described in detail in Chapter 5 below, correctly predicts the fate (open or shut) of 85 per cent of the 174 refineries considered. More specifically, the model predicts that forty-one refineries out of the fifty-four that actually shut should have done so and that 109 out of the 120 that actually remained open should have done so.

Twelve refinery characteristics were found to be significantly associated with the open/shut decision. Other things being equal, a refinery had a greater probability of remaining *open* if it was: (a) located in the the Mediterranean area (rather than in North West Europe), (b) located near the coast, (c) attached to a product pipeline, (d) associated with a petrochemicals plant; or if it had: (e) bitumen or (f) lubricants production (or indeed production capacity for any special product), (g) catalytic reforming capacity, (h) thermal treating capacity, (i) catalytic cracking or hydrocracking plant. Survival was inversely related to: (j) the total volume of crude distillation capacity in Europe available to the refinery's owner and (k) the volume of distillation capacity available to its owner in the country where the refinery was located. Finally (l), the owner's integration upstream or further downstream, increased the refinery's chances of survival.

The probit model was also used to predict which of the 1986 survivors were candidates for closure in the next few years, being as it were the 'weakest' in the surviving set. This was achieved by giving the various refineries 'scores' calculated on the basis of the criteria (a) to (l), and ranking them in descending order. If we form a view on how much capacity may still have to close, then such an estimate of surplus capacity may be used to identify a cut-off point on the ranked list of refineries. This would reveal which refineries still need to be closed. Finally, a comparison of refineries' scores estimated on the basis of the 1976 values of the parameters with their scores computed for 1986 values shows: (a) that virtually every refinery had a higher score by 1986 than it had in 1976; and (b) that the ranking of refineries involved significant reordering between 1976 and 1986, so that the comparative competitive strengths of the surviving refineries changed a great deal during this period.

As mentioned earlier, the closures of refineries and reductions of distillation capacity at surviving sites were accompanied by investment in upgrading plant and new technology. The quantitative significance of this parallel trend can be appraised from Table 1.2. A large proportion of refinery sites in 1986 (fifty-two out of 120) were upgraded, and most others benefited from some investment to replace or modify existing units. Whichever way one looks at the data, it becomes evident that investment was a major feature of European refining in the past 10–15 years.

Investment and disinvestment – two developments that are at the same time opposite in character and complementary – combined to change the capacity structure of European refining in a radical manner. We define capacity by the type of yield that can be produced in a refinery, and we distinguish topping, simple, semi-complex and complex capacities.

Table 1.2: Capacity of Upgrading Plant in Europe. 1976 and 1986.
Thousand Barrels per Calendar Day.

Plant Type	Volume		% Change
	1976	*1986*	
Continuous Catalytic Reforming	–	389	n.a.
Thermal Cracking	500	1,528	206
Thermal Coking	61	80	31
Delayed Coking	97	177	83
Catalytic Cracking	986	1,647	67
Hydrocracking	60	247	309
Flexicoking	–	30	n.a.

Table 1.3: Comparison of Capacities by Type of Yield in Europe. 1976 and 1986.
Thousand Barrels per Calendar Day.

Yield by Type	Volume		Change in 1976–86	% Change
	1976	*1986*		
Topping	3,319.2	1,806.8	−1,512.4	−45.6
Simple	10,581.4	3,307.0	−7,274.4	−68.7
Semi-complex	1,192.3	2,025.9	+833.6	+69.9
Complex	5,433.9	7,355.8	+1,921.9	+35.4
Total	20,526.8	14,495.5	−6,031.3	−41.6

Table 1.3 shows the changes in the structure of capacity by type of yield that occurred between 1976 and 1986. In absolute terms the total reduction in capacity between these two years was 6,031 thousand bpcd, consisting of an overwhelmingly large reduction in simple capacity (7,274 thousand bpcd) and in topping, which were partly compensated by increases in semi-complex and complex capacities.

The important observation, however, is that these major developments did not completely eliminate surplus refinery capacity in Europe. It is difficult, of course, to assess accurately how much excess capacity there actually is, for a variety of reasons. First, surplus capacity relates to demand, which is notoriously variable. Installed capacity must meet peak demand and cater for breakdowns, accidents, maintenance periods, etc. Any measure of surplus capacity that compares installed capacity with *average* demand will, by definition, overstate the true amount of excess capacity. Secondly, capacity can be defined in many different ways and from different standpoints. The designer of a plant will tend to define it in terms of some technical optimum; a production engineer in terms of average actual performance; and an economist according to some criterion of economic efficiency. Thirdly, the measurement of capacity under any definition is beset by problems because assumptions and judgements have to be made about the technical characteristics of the plant, the type of crude used, the composition of the input (crude/NGLs/feedstocks), the institutional mode of operation, the prevailing economic conditions, etc. ... , and more importantly because of the heterogeneity of plant and types of capacity to be found in individual refineries and in the industry as a whole. How should we compare, for example, a situation in which crackers are used at 90 per cent of capacity and distillation units at 80 per cent with a situation where crackers are used at 95 per cent of capacity and distillation units at 70 per cent?

We use rather rough measures of capacity utilization (because more sophisticated concepts are not easily amenable to measurement). The simplest measure, and naturally the most misleading, is the ratio of *crude oil* throughput to technical capacity as reported by refinery owners. This is often calculated by using, for example, the *BP Statistical Review of World Energy* data on capacities and throughputs. These computations would put the capacity utilization rate in Europe in 1987 at 70 per cent. This is clearly an understatement because throughput should include NGLs and product feedstocks as well as crude oil. Usually NGLs go through the distillation plant where they will occupy a larger volume than equivalent quantities of crude; and feedstocks such as fuel oil often pass through distillation but get virtually a 'free ride'. Our own estimate of capacity utilization uses a weighted aggregate of crude/NGLs/feedstocks with weights of 1.0, 1.3 and 0.3 respectively. This gives an estimate of 74 per cent for the capacity utilization rate in European refining in 1987. An independent estimate, obtained on a confidential basis from an oil company, for the EEC region (which can be taken as an approximation for OECD Europe) puts the utilization rate at 78 per cent in 1987.

It is interesting to note that all the available data, irrespective of sources and methodology, agree on the broad features of changes in the rates of capacity utilization over time. They all show that surplus capacity reached a maximum in either 1981 or 1982, began to decline as a percentage of total capacity in 1983, and continued to fall, although at a diminishing rate, until 1987, the most recent year for which data are available. Finally, they all agree that there is still surplus capacity in Europe but differ in their estimates of its extent.

Surplus capacity and low (or negative) profitability in refining cause some industrialists to lobby for protection against imports of petroleum products into Europe. In this context, it is relevant to ask whether surplus refining capacity would disappear if Europe closed its borders to extra-European trade. The ratio of inland demand to refining capacity was 0.85 in 1986 and probably 0.86 or 0.87 in 1987; the banning of imports would have improved the rate of capacity utilization from 0.74 to 0.86 in 1987. It would not have eliminated the whole surplus but would have brought the rate of utilization so close to full capacity as to cause, from time to time, the emergence of bottlenecks.

1.3 The Industrial Structure of European Refining

The impact of excess capacity on the profitability of an industry depends to some extent on its market structure, that is on whether the industry is dominated by a monopoly (or an oligopoly) or consists of a large number of firms operating in a competitive set-up.

Excess production capacity need not impair the profitability of a monopolist (nor that of a powerful oligopoly), because the dominant firms will 'freeze' the surplus capacity at their disposal. They are able, by definition, to regulate production in order to realize a preferred price; and this simply means that they themselves determine the volume of capacity that is kept idle.

The impact of excess capacity on profitability is radically different in a competitive market. Initially, the capacity overhang will depress prices as firms attempt to increase their production and their total revenues, and this causes the least efficient firms in the market to incur losses. Losses trigger a self-correcting mechanism, however, because the less efficient firms are eventually forced to exit. Total capacity in the industry is thus reduced, and demand and supply are ultimately brought into a balanced relationship. The profitability of the industry is thereby restored to the benefit of the survivors, i.e. those firms that were initially more efficient or better able to sustain financial losses.

There is no doubt that the refining industry in Europe displays some of the features of a competitive market. First, the number of participants is fairly large. Secondly, the main input (crude oil) and the main output (petroleum products) are both actively traded in markets where powerful forces of supply and demand are at play. Given these features, we would expect the competitive pressures in this market to wipe out excess capacity fairly rapidly, perhaps over a period of four or five years. We would expect them to eliminate a number of small players and to increase the degree of market concen-

tration over time, and consequently the market power of the survivors. In these circumstances, big firms usually survive better than
small firms. Large firms are often able to finance a loss-making
activity by diverting profits from other activities (say, from their
upstream interests or from profits made in wholesale/retail distribution). Because of their greater access to financial resources, large firms
are in a better position than small ones to invest in upgrading capacity
and new technologies, and these investments should further enhance
their competitive advantage over the small firms.

Actual developments in the European refining sector did not follow
this pattern, however. As mentioned earlier, there was a reduction in
capacity, but the response lag was unduly long. Significant refinery
closures began in 1982, eight years after the first oil shock; and there
was still excess capacity in European refining in 1988, fourteen years
after the shock.

More surprisingly, we found that, although a number of refinery
owners at the smaller end of the ownership distribution exited
altogether from the scene between 1976 and 1986, there was a larger
number of new entrants during this period, and that the entry point
was not always at the small end of the size distribution of refineries.

Finally, we found that the degree of market concentration in European refining *decreased* between 1976 and 1986, as is apparent from
Table 1.4, which shows how the share of each of the four principal
refinery processes held by the ten largest owners (in each case)
declined between 1976 and 1986.

A more sophisticated measure of market concentration is the Herfindahl index, H, the inverse of which, 1/H, can be interpreted as the
number of equal-sized firms that would be equivalent in terms of
concentration to the actual number of different-sized firms in a market. This is also shown in Table 1.4. The larger this number, the lower
the concentration or the smaller the market power wielded by each of
the firms. The changes in the values of 1/H between 1976 and 1986

Table 1.4: Shares of Top Ten Owners and Inverse Herfindahl Indices (1/H) for
European Refining, by Plant Type. 1976 and 1986.

Plant Type	% Share of Top Ten Owners		Inverse Herfindahl Index	
	1976	1986	1976	1986
Crude Distillation	67	63	14.98	18.38
Catalytic Reforming	71	65	13.67	16.89
Thermal Cracking	93	64	4.39	17.04
Catalytic Cracking	82	71	9.20	14.98

reveal a decrease in market concentration, since in all cases 1/H was higher in 1986 than in 1976, and in some cases significantly higher.

The important issue, therefore, is why recent developments in European refining have been at odds with the normal behaviour of competitive markets. In other words, why is it that capacity adjustments were so delayed that market concentration decreased instead of increasing and the refining industry attracted new investors whose entry into this business between 1976 and 1986 more than compensated for the exit of small owners?

In our judgement the explanation for these unexpected phenomena is to be found in the *dualistic* structure of refinery ownership in Europe. European refineries are not owned by a large number of private firms of different sizes as the competitive model implicitly assumes. It consists rather of two main groups:[1]

(a) Large privately-owned companies, including all the traditional majors (the Seven Sisters and CFP-Total) and several big US independents;
(b) State-owned oil companies, mostly European but now including an increasing number of national oil companies belonging to the oil-producing countries.

In 1976, the first group owned some 61 per cent of refining capacity in Europe, and the second group some 17 per cent. By 1986, the share of the first group had shrunk to about 48 per cent and that of the second group had increased to some 29 per cent. The share of other types of owners – chemical companies, independent Italian and Greek refiners, banks and a motley collection of private interests – remained virtually unchanged at about 22–23 per cent.

The majors, because of their size, their historical attachment to the virtues of vertical integration, and their ability to finance refining losses with cash flows from both marketing and upstream operations, were in a position to resist retrenchment for a long while. They had to give in eventually, and on a rather big scale, because the staying power of other refinery owners with smaller interests proved to be considerable. This was simply because the second group of refinery owners consisted of state-owned companies, which were not vulnerable to the normal economic consequences of commercial losses, as these could be covered in one way or the other by the state. They were

---

[1] We ignore, for the sake of simplicity, the set of small private owners in the Mediterranean region.

able to resist retrenchment more stubbornly and for longer than the majors. In some instances government policies encouraged expansion for strategic or other objectives even when the investment was expected to have negative financial returns. This was, and still is, the peculiarity of the European refining scene. Although some national oil companies reduced their distillation capacities to some extent, many others – in Spain, Portugal, Greece, Turkey, Norway and Sweden – expanded their interests. None of the national oil companies left the business altogether: on the contrary there were new entrants during the period 1976–86, in particular the national oil companies of some oil-producing countries.

The normal outcome of the competitive model – the exit of small owners, the reduction in the share of middle-size firms and a *relative* expansion of the large companies – did not apply in the case of European refining. The share of the big companies declined, that of the state-owned companies (mostly in the middle of the range of ownership distribution) increased, and that of the smaller entities remained virtually unchanged.

Other things being equal, this state of affairs would be expected to have adverse effects on profitability because the trimming of capacity that is normally brought about by competitive forces did not take place rapidly and fully. The ownership structure in Europe ensured a high rate of survival and delayed the shedding of capacity. In the USA, in contrast, the reduction of capacity was faster, and the remaining excess capacity in 1988 was a smaller percentage of the total than in Europe. This was partly because of differences in ownership structure: the national oil companies have only negligible interests in the USA.

1.4 International Trade

There are other features of competition in European refining that deserve analysis. The markets for the main refining output, petroleum products, and for the main refining input, crude oil, have both become very competitive. The refining industry is squeezed, as it were, between two sets of markets in which prices respond flexibly to small and big shocks, where fairly efficient arbitrage removes distortions (and therefore the opportunities for some to make abnormal profits), and competition erodes margins.

The situation in the product market may be briefly described as follows. First, the European product market is an *open* economy. International trade in products is virtually unhindered, and European refiners are therefore subject to the competition of refining centres outside Europe. There is competition in Europe itself between domestic and non-European refiners, and some degree of competition in the world at large between European product exports and the product exports of other refiners.

It is useful to analyse the pattern of international trade in petroleum products in Europe. Table 1.5 presents OECD data for 1987. We note first a statistical discrepancy between the total exports and imports of OECD European countries to and from each other. Theoretically these two numbers should be equal, since the exports of, say, the UK to France are identically the imports of France from the UK; but differences in reporting lags, the re-routing of shipments initially intended for one country to some other destination, discrepancies between bills of lading and actual receipts, statistical errors and other factors cause the two aggregates to be different. We see, for example, that the imports of OECD Europe from OECD Europe amounted to 110,265 thousand tonnes in 1987, while the corresponding exports amounted to 122,243 thousand tonnes. For the purpose of calculating shares of imports and exports from different sources and for different destinations and their ratios to other aggregates, we have adjusted the figures in Table 1.5 by splitting the difference between reported imports of OECD Europe from OECD Europe and the corresponding reported exports.

Table 1.5: OECD European Imports and Exports of Petroleum Products. 1987. Thousand Tonnes.

Source/ Destination	Reported Imports	Reported Exports	Adjusted Imports	Adjusted Exports
OECD Europe	110,265	122,243	116,254	116,254
USA	6,252	12,482	6,252	12,482
Total OECD	116,778	135,705	122,767	129,716
OPEC	29,889	2,235	29,889	2,235
CPEs	45,855	706	43,855	706
Others	11,339	12,388	11,339	12,388
Total	201,861	151,034	207,850	145,045

Source: OECD/IEA, *Quarterly Oil and Gas Statistics*, Fourth Quarter 1987.

Table 1.6 shows the percentage shares of OECD European imports/exports by source/destination (calculated on the basis of the 'adjusted' figures in Table 1.5) for 1987, and Table 1.7 shows the corresponding figures when intra-OECD European trade is excluded from the calculations.

Table 1.6: Percentage Shares of Major World Regions in Total OECD European Trade in Petroleum Products. 1987.

Source/Destination	Imports	Exports
Intra-OECD Europe	56	80
USA	3	9
Other OECD	–	0.5
Total OECD	(59)	(89.5)
OPEC	14	1.5
CPEs	21	0.5
Other non-OECD	5	8.5
Total non-OECD	(40)	(10.5)
Total	99	100

Table 1.7: Volumes and Percentage Shares of Major World Regions in Extra-OECD European Trade in Petroleum Products. 1987. Volumes in Thousand Tonnes.

Region	Imports		Exports		Net Imports	
	Volume	%	Volume	%	Volume	%
USA	6,252	6.8	12,482	43.4	−6,230	−9.9
OPEC	29,889	32.6	2,235	7.8	27,654	44.0
CPEs	43,855	47.9	706	2.4	43,149	68.7
Other	11,600	12.7	13,368	46.4	−1,768	−2.8
Total	91,596	100.0	28,791	100.0	62,805	100.0

This pattern is very revealing. In 1987, OECD Europe as a whole was a gross importer of 207,850 thousand tonnes, representing some 40 per cent of net consumption, which is estimated at 517,927 thousand tonnes; but a very large proportion of the import/export trade in products was intra-European. This indicates that the European refining sector had closely-knit links across European borders. A considerable volume of transactions continually took place between subsidiaries of the same corporate groups, refiners, traders and other agents. More importantly, the concentration of refineries in such centres as Antwerp, Rotterdam, Sicily and Genoa generated significant intra-European trade.

Extra-European imports were a smaller proportion of the total (40 per cent). Net imports into Europe (i.e. the difference between extra-European imports and exports) amounted to some 62.8 million tonnes of products in 1987, representing some 12 per cent of net consumption. These data exclude refinery feedstocks, of which Europe is a net importer, and therefore understate the degree of import dependence of the European refining industry.

Europe imported products from two main sources: the CPEs, which accounted for almost 48 per cent of extra-European imports in 1987, and the OPEC countries, which accounted for some 33 per cent. Exports, which constituted a much smaller volume, were mainly to the USA (some 43 per cent of total extra-European exports in 1987) and to a mixed group of nations consisting mainly of developing countries in Africa and Asia (some 46 per cent).

We now turn to the economic characteristics of European trade in petroleum products with the CPEs, OPEC and the USA (the three major trade partners) and note three important differences.

First, the trade between Europe and the USA partly reflects arbitrage between Rotterdam and New York: hence the two-way movement of exports and imports. To the extent that this arbitrage is efficient, this physical trade provides a solid economic link between Europe and another major world market in petroleum products. Small and large shocks that cause price movements in Europe are thus transmitted to the USA; similarly Europe responds fairly swiftly to price movements in the USA. The ability to shift products physically between the two regions without hindrance and in both directions underpins arbitrage operations that take place on spot and futures markets in Europe and the USA. It is worth noting, however, that European exports to the USA usually exceed European imports from this region. This reflects a domestic imbalance in the USA between the demand for and production of petroleum products, which is met in part by European exports.

Secondly, European trade in products with the CPEs and the OPEC countries consists largely of imports. European exports to the CPEs are insignificant and exports to the OPEC region fairly small. The economic nature of this trade is fundamentally different from that of trade with the USA. The CPEs and the national oil companies of OPEC countries are more concerned with placing given quantities of products in Europe than with price arbitrage between Europe and their internal markets. In this sense, the CPEs and OPEC's export refiners are price takers. The Soviet Union's decisions on oil exports to the West, mainly to Europe, are determined within tight production and allocation constraints (the planned allocations of oil produced in the Soviet Union to domestic consumption, the CMEA countries, and the developing countries) by balance-of-payments considerations, as is clearly shown by Nissanke, 1987.[2] Export refiners in the OPEC region set their production at levels consistent with technical rather than economic optimization. In other words, their output is determined by physical constraints and not by the prices ruling in their export markets. These prices are taken into account, however, in the allocation of whichever quantity is produced among the various export markets, namely Europe, the USA and the Far East. The quantities supplied to Europe by the CPEs and the OPEC countries are therefore the result of exogenous factors and decisions. These quantities do vary, but not in response to the cost/price parameters that influence the production decisions of European refiners.

The European market thus involves two types of agents with marked differences in economic behaviour. The CPE/OPEC exporters place given quantities in Europe and take the ruling price; whereas the European refiners try to optimize their production on the basis of price expectations which are rarely fulfilled. The production decisions of European refiners and the exogenous export decisions of the CPE/OPEC refiners constitute the short-term supply curve, and as such have a determining influence on prices. Since the quantities exported by the CPEs and the OPEC countries can be construed as a first, but variable, load on the market, it follows that European refiners do not know exactly what these quantities are going to be. They can neither assume that they will necessarily increase when prices go up and decrease when prices fall, nor expect the opposite in all circumstances. They cannot encroach easily on this first and variable slice of the market taken by the CPEs and the OPEC exporters; a share which, as argued above, is not very price sensitive. European refiners are therefore, in a certain sense, residual suppliers to the European market. Some of the interesting implications of this are: (a) that European refiners absorb *all* the shifts in demand even though they are not the sole suppliers to the European market; and (b) that the CPEs and OPEC exporters depress the general price level of petroleum products in Europe to some extent simply because their supplies are not price sensitive.

Thirdly, European trade in products with regions other than the USA, the CPEs and the OPEC countries falls into two categories: imports from non-OPEC producers and exports to several developing countries. The former display the same economic features as exports from the CPEs or OPEC; the latter probably reflect transactions

[2] In Chadwick *et al*, *Soviet Oil Exports: Trade Adjustments, Refining Constraints and Market Behaviour*, Oxford University Press for the Oxford Institute for Energy Studies, 1987.

between affiliates of integrated companies and direct exports to developing countries suffering from imbalances between domestic production and consumption.

The conclusion is that product imports from the CPEs and the Third World producers (OPEC and non-OPEC) constitute an important category of European oil trade in terms of both quantitative significance and economic behaviour. Because of its unusual characteristics, trade in products with these regions has created *physical* links between them and the European refining industry. This becomes more evident when imports of refinery feedstocks are taken into consideration.[3] European net imports of virgin naphtha from the CPEs and oil-producing countries (partly for the production of gasoline) account for a large proportion of total naphtha supplies.[4] Further, because the main suppliers of imported naphtha are not very price sensitive, it can be argued that a strong structural link now exists between the CPE/OPEC oil product export industries and European refiners. This state of affairs has both short- and long-term implications. In the short term, unanticipated variations in supplies from these sources, even when small, can have significant price effects. This is because the short-term demand curve is fairly inelastic and the import component of the product supply curve in Europe is itself inelastic. In the long run, the European refining industry needs to adjust its capacity and the pattern of its supplies through investment or disinvestment in response to developments in the CPEs and in the OPEC region. These long-run adjustments are difficult to make efficiently, however, because information on likely developments in the CPEs is usually unsatisfactory and incomplete.

To sum up, the European market is not a self-contained system. There are strong economic links through price arbitrage between North West Europe and the USA and slightly weaker links through the Mediterranean with the Gulf market, and at one remove with Singapore. There are 'physical' links through price-insensitive imports of final products and refinery feedstocks between the European refining industry and the export refiners of the CPEs and the OPEC countries. Price determination is affected in the short run by these relationships. Production decisions are influenced by information or guesses on CPEs and OPEC exports. Finally, investment plans that determine long-term supply patterns need to take into account expected developments in the CPEs and in the OPEC region because the European refining system is in effect the residual, even though the largest, supplier of the European market.

---

[3] These cannot be analysed accurately because trade statistics do not always distinguish them from final products.

[4] In 1987 net imports represented 58 per cent of net naphtha consumption.

1.5 The Acquisition of Crude Oil by Refiners

We now turn to the critical issue of crude oil purchases. The cost of producing a barrel of petroleum products consists largely of the acquisition cost of crude. The petroleum market is at present very competitive and involves a considerable number of transactions effected under a variety of trading instruments. In theory, competitive markets equalize prices, which means that they remove all price gaps that do not reflect genuine differences in costs. In fact, crude oil prices move flexibly on spot, physical forward and futures markets, and arbitrage seems to operate between markets, competing away some price gaps that do not relate to cost differentials; but arbitrage fails to remove all market imperfections and price distortions, and crude oil is often acquired on different terms and at different prices by different refiners. The main imperfections relate to institutional factors – different types of contracts, property rights, fiscal regimes, etc. – and to uneven distributions of bargaining power among both buyers and sellers. First, the prices of crude obtained under equity arrangements and crude purchased in arm's length transactions usually differ by either a smaller or a greater margin than is warranted by the competitive return on the producers' equity.

Secondly, crude oil exchanged under long-term contracts (or, more exactly, within the framework of long-term relationships between a buyer and a seller) is likely to be priced differently from oil sold in spot transactions. This difference is supposed to reflect, depending on market conditions, the value to a buyer or a seller of a secure transaction. Paradoxically, there are odd situations where the term price involves a premium in a buyers' market when it should be sold at a discount, or where it involves a discount in a sellers' market instead of a premium. In any case the differential is unlikely to reflect exactly the economic value of the security that term contracts afford sellers in a glut or buyers in times of shortage.

Thirdly, vertical integration creates an internal market in which the crude oil price is often different from the corresponding price in the external market. Although the opportunity cost of oil transferred from the upstream to the downstream branch of an integrated concern is the market price, a different value may be imputed to oil transferred internally. The reasons are varied and may include, depending on circumstances: fiscal optimization, subsidy of particular assets, administrative convenience, etc.

Fourthly, the bargaining abilities and power of different economic agents are far from uniform, and vary not only between agents but also over time. In a sellers' market, this producer manages to obtain a better price from one buyer than that producer; and in a buyers' market, this company manages to buy at a more favourable price from this producer than from that one. Competition does not eliminate these temporary and sometimes fortuitous advantages but transfers them, now and then, from one player to another, causing prices to spiral downward in a glut and upward in times of tight supplies.

For these and other reasons, different refiners do not acquire crude oil at the same price (even after allowing, of course, for quality and other real differences). The effects of this important distortion on suppliers' margins and prices differ fundamentally depending on the existence or absence of surplus capacity in refining.

If there is no excess capacity, the company that happens to obtain crude at a lower price than its competitors will simply make more profits. By definition, this company cannot increase its output of refined products. The aggregate supply of products is not affected and, since the balance of the market is not disturbed, prices remain unchanged. In this context the fortunate company that acquires crude on better terms than others increases its profits (both unit and total profit) and becomes an intra-marginal producer. Other things being equal, the additional profit accrues for as long as the company retains its advantage on the crude oil market.

If there is excess capacity, the company that happens to obtain crude at a lower price than its competitors will be able to increase its production, say by q_1. Total supplies will increase by a certain amount q_2 (smaller than q_1 if the supply curve rises). This means that other refiners, taken together, reduce their production by the difference $q_1 - q_2$. However, the increase in total supplies disturbs the balance in the market and lowers product prices. In this context the refiner that enjoys a cost advantage in the crude market is likely to make higher total profits (thanks to the increase q_1 in its production). However, depending on the size of the crude cost advantage relative to the change in product prices, this margin may change in either direction. Other refiners lose volume and suffer from reduced margins; and their total profits decline therefore on two counts. Other adjustments may take place in this case. The fall in margins may lead some marginal refiners to exit from the industry altogether. In this case, other refiners with excess capacity will increase their output, thus partly compensating for the withdrawal. Product prices will also rise, but not necessarily back to their initial level. Exit restores some of the profitability in favour of survivors and increases the profits of the refiners with the initial advantage in the crude market even further.

The important conclusion is that preferential access to crude by some refiners will only affect the output and margins of their less fortunate competitors if those who acquire crude on better terms have surplus capacity at their disposal. The quantitative significance of these adverse effects will depend on the size of this surplus capacity (relative to the total) and on the elasticities of the supply and demand curves.

What matters in this story is not the identity of the refiner that is able to acquire crude on cheaper terms, but the excess capacity at the disposal of this refiner. The oil industry tends to worry about refineries owned by producing countries and refineries involved in processing deals with producers. But this concern is too narrow. Vertical integration enables any company that wishes to do so to subsidize its downstream operations with transfers of crude oil at a discounted price from the upstream sector. Netback arrangements have effects similar to, and sometimes worse than, processing deals. Finally, and more importantly, the uneven distribution of bargaining power and bargaining opportunities and the continual change over time of the pattern of these opportunities cause differences in crude acquisition costs to arise all the time in the world market. Companies are always looking for bargains. The name of the supply game today is 'look constantly for the best opportunity'. There may be immediate arbitrage in paper markets, but physical purchases of oil from producing countries are agreed bilaterally on the basis of pricing formulae which are rarely identical at any point in time. The same buyer obtains oil at different prices from various producers and the same producer sells oil at different prices to various buyers. Market-related pricing formulae are more likely to create these differences than to equalize acquisition costs. Of course these bargaining games do not favour the same players consistently. The company that succeeds in obtaining crude oil on advantageous terms today may fail to do so tomorrow, but tomorrow another company will succeed; and so goes the merry-go-round.

The implications of this analysis are as follows. First, since any company that acquires oil on advantageous terms can cause damage to the profitability and production of other refiners if it has excess capacity at its disposal, and since the major oil companies have large amounts of surplus capacity, it follows that they can in turn do more damage to the profitability of the industry when they compete against each other for crude oil bargains than can the small independent who secures a processing deal. As mentioned earlier, all companies attempt to obtain the best possible terms for their crude oil purchases, playing now Iraq against Saudi Arabia, and now Mexico against the Gulf producers. By definition, there is always a winner in this game where only relative positions matter; and therefore a potential for continuing damage.

Secondly, the effects of downstream integration by producing countries on the profitability and performance of European refining depend crucially on whether a refinery purchased by the producing country would otherwise have been scrapped or kept in use either by its previous owner or by others. The real issue is therefore not that 'the producers are moving in' but 'what would have happened to the capacity they acquired if they had not moved in'. The impact of downstream integration by producing countries relates to the *total* capacity of the producing country's refinery if this refinery would otherwise have been scrapped, or to the *difference* between the rate of utilization under the new owner and the rate that would have obtained if the refinery had not been sold to a producing country and kept in use. The same approach applies to any assessment of the impact of processing deals.

This analysis shifts the focus from a partial problem (downstream investments of producing countries), which seems to dominate many commentators' discussion to the point of obsession, to a much broader one (significant and widespread imperfections in the crude oil market), which has not received sufficient attention.

1.6 Margins and Prices

Considering our analysis of the demand for and supply of petroleum products in Europe, it is not surprising that the average refiner's margin (defined here as the difference between the price of a barrel of crude and the revenues obtained from the corresponding barrel of refined products) was either negative or small for most of the period under study. The unfavourable conditions were:

(a) The stagnant or declining demand for products, particularly fuel oil, caused by the price shocks of the 1970s, whose effects on final consumers were magnified by taxation and, at times, by the appreciation of the dollar *vis-à-vis* European currencies;
(b) The persistence of excess capacity in European refining;
(c) Competition in product markets from the Soviet Union and OPEC countries, that is from exporters with a price-inelastic supply curve;
(d) Imperfections of the crude oil market, largely due to differences in property rights and bargaining power, which are responsible for divergences in the acquisition prices of crude, the main cost element in refining.

Our data on the values of the difference between the gross product worth (GPW) of the refined barrel and the crude oil price are presented in Table 7.5 below. The following remarks are essential to the correct interpretation of these data.

First, the lack of accurate information on refining costs over the whole of the period covered prevented us from calculating the 'true' margin. Our data refer to GPWs (net of fuel used by the refinery) minus crude oil costs (f.o.b. price plus freight). To arrive at estimates of more meaningful concepts of the margin it would be necessary to deduct either the variable refining costs or the variable and fixed (other than capital) costs. In 1988 variable costs in Europe were probably of the order of $2.0–2.5 per tonne for a simple configuration and $3.4–4.0 per tonne for a complex configuration. In 1982, according to a survey of some forty European refineries, provided to us on a confidential basis, these costs were of the order of $1.0–1.2 per tonne for simple and $1.6–1.8 per tonne for complex refining. Comparison of dollar refining costs in one period with costs in another, or of costs in one country with costs in another, are very difficult to make, because of the significant changes in the exchange rate of the dollar over time and differences in purchasing parities among countries. Most costs are incurred in local currencies while estimates of refinery margins are made in dollars. In today's conditions refining costs are no longer a negligible proportion of the gross margin (GPW minus crude price) and, in this respect alone, exchange rate variations can make a significant difference to the profitability of refining.

Secondly, the set of yields used to calculate the GPW of the refined barrel in the present study may not be typical of European refining. Some companies told us that the yields we used are more favourable for the semi-complex and less favourable for the simple configuration than is usually the case. If this is true, then the differences between the gross margins for simple and semi-complex refining should be smaller than those shown in Table 7.5 below, and the differences between semi-complex and complex margins larger. We are unable to determine which set of yields is truly representative of European refining, and the debate on this issue must remain open. The important point is that yields differ not only between refineries of the same type, but even for the same refinery depending on a host of changing circumstances.

Thirdly, there are aspects of refining that are relevant to profitability but which cannot be easily taken into account in the estimate of the margin. The most notable of these is the production of special products. Another important aspect is flexibility, and in many instances this may favour the semi-complex configuration.

We conclude therefore that, other things being equal, the true margin is smaller than would appear from our data because of the exclusion of certain costs. Estimates of the margin are affected by a number of factors, particularly yields. However, the sensitivity of estimates should not be exaggerated. To give one example, small differences in the shares of the various middle distillates in the total yield of a barrel have a negligible effect on the estimates of the GPWs. The sensitivity to variations in the share of fuel oil in the total yield would be greater because of the large gap between the prices of fuel oil and middle/light distillates taken as a group.

Finally, margins are not very good indicators of profitability, partly for the reasons mentioned above, and partly because profits are determined by the *total* volume of operations and not by *unit* revenues and costs.

With these provisos in mind, we shall now discuss our results on gross refining margins. We found that the mean GPWs were always ranked in increasing order from topping to simple, semi-complex and complex; and therefore that the mean estimates of the gross margins (GPW minus crude oil price) were ranked in the same manner. This indicates that the merit order of refining technologies generally remained the same.

Our data show that the difference between the gross margins obtained from semi-complex and complex configurations was very small when Arabian Light (the typical crude in 1976) was used in the computation as the representative input; but that this gap was much larger when Ninian (the closest type of crude to the average used in Europe in 1986 in terms of its API gravity) was taken to be the representative input. As indicated earlier, there are some disagreements on these findings; if they are correct they imply that investment in complex refining (relative to semi-complex) was not attractive in 1976, but that its relative attractiveness had increased by 1986.

A further finding is that on average neither topping nor simple refining covered crude costs during the period 1976–86. Taking other costs into account darkens the picture further. These results are robust: the mean values of our estimates of gross margins for topping and simple refining are unlikely to change from negative to positive through the use of alternative sets of yields. We also found that during this period semi-complex and complex refining covered crude costs on average. However, the estimated value of the gross margin for semi-complex refining is small and would become smaller or even negative if average yields were actually less valuable than the sets used in our computations. Allowing for refining costs would probably make the margin on the semi-complex configuration either negligibly small or perhaps even negative.

Finally, it appears that the gross margins for all types of configurations were variable. The coefficients of variation were large but the standard ranges were not very wide; which implies that the fluctuations, although strong, were not particularly abnormal except during periods of severe disruption (November 1980–January 1981 and February–April 1986).

The relationship between GPWs and crude prices (our gross margin) lies at the heart of understanding how the general level of product prices is determined. If the behaviour of this margin were very stable it would suggest that some adjustment mechanism was at work bringing the supply and demand for products into such a relationship as to preserve some margin over the price of crude. Clearly, the behaviour of the margin is not stable when the periods considered include temporary but severe shocks. It is not stable in the short-to-medium run, in which no fundamental adjustments to the volume or technology of refining capacity can complete their course.

It is, however, worth asking whether the relationship between GPWs and crude prices is stable in the long run, and finding the conditions under which such stability obtains.

In order to address this issue it is important, first, to identify the type of refining configuration that is to be regarded as the marginal or incremental technology. We found that during the 1980s virtually all European net demand for products could have been met by the extant complex and semi-complex capacity. It would not have been necessary to run refineries with simple or topping configurations save in exceptional circumstances (e.g. in 1986). Given the merit-order ranking of technologies, it follows that complex refining capacity would always be used in full, and that demand in excess of the volume met by complex capacity would be supplied from semi-complex capacity. In this sense, semi-complex was the marginal refining configuration (see Chapter 6).

In a competitive market, market forces ensure that in the long run the economic performance of the marginal capacity will be such as to keep revenues (here expressed as the GPW) in line with costs (the crude oil price). We tested the hypothesis that, for semi-complex refining, a change in the crude oil price was correlated in the long run with an equal change in the GPW of the refined barrel. The dynamic model used for this test performed well. The long-run relationship between changes in the crude price and the corresponding changes in the GPWs of the semi-complex barrel was very nearly one-to-one, the goodness of fit was high, and the average error was small. Omitting from the data those months when, for exceptional reasons, it was evident that semi-complex refining was not in fact the marginal technique significantly reduced the average error of estimate. There was no evidence of systematic misspecification of the model; and the factors behind the errors of estimation did not appear to be systematic or predictable.

Our hypothesis that semi-complex refining was generally the marginal technique receives further support from the findings that the long-run relationships between changes in crude oil prices and GPWs were less than one-to-one for topping and simple refining, and greater for complex configurations.

We are thus confronted with two results which, put together, reveal conflicting characteristics of the economic processes at work. The one-to-one long-term relationship between changes in crude prices and GPWs for the marginal refining technique is strong evidence that product markets are competitive, and that they rapidly, though not instantaneously, produce all the necessary price adjustments. The fact that semi-complex refining does not appear to be profitable in the long run (the gross margin is small and the net margin, even without allowance for capital costs, either close to zero or negative) suggests, however, that these competitive markets are failing in an important respect. They are not forcing unprofitable concerns out of the industry at the rate that would be required to eliminate the long-run losses made by the marginal refiner. These results support those of our earlier analysis of the pattern of exit and entry in European refining, which appeared to contradict the normal competitive outcome. We explained that the reluctance to exit was related to (among other factors) the high costs involved, the ownership structure of European refining, and strategic considerations.

Although the gross product worth of semi-complex refining remained tightly bound to crude prices, the prices of the individual products did not move in unison. Relative product prices, whether measured by their absolute differentials or expressed as ratios, moved over time in ways that contrast with the fairly stable behaviour of the overall product/crude oil price relationship, and which make this behaviour even more remarkable than we thought at first. It is clear from Figure 8.1 below that the behaviour of the twelve-month moving average price of the four distillates was markedly different from the behaviour of the corresponding fuel oil price. In general, the distillate prices tended to move together. The ratios of distillates prices to fuel oil prices behaved in a highly cyclical manner but did not show any long-term trend over the period as a whole. The variability of product prices relative to each other deserves special investigation. An understanding of the variation of relative product prices may provide useful insights into the operation of product markets and the economics of refining.

Because GPWs are so closely linked to the relevant crude prices, it might be thought that the variation of product prices relative to one another is constrained. The close link of the GPW with the crude price suggests that any wild movement in the price of some products (say distillates) relative to crude must be compensated by another wild movement of the opposite sign in the price of another product (say fuel oil), and that there must therefore be a limitation on prices swinging far apart from each other. We observed, however, that the variability of relative product prices was considerable: the constraint on potential variation probably exists, but does not appear to bind the fluctuations within a narrow range.

The variability of product prices can be expected to depend on demand conditions, stock levels, the supply of crude and some seasonal factors. A dynamic model involving these variables or convenient proxies and allowing for adjustment time-lags was therefore constructed, and applied to a set of price ratios: the 'average' price of distillates to the fuel oil price; and the relative prices of all distillates to each other.

The model was particularly successful in explaining the variation in the distillates/fuel oil price ratio, as it was able to relate virtually 90 per cent of this variation to the factors included in the equation. Although all these factors (demand, stocks, crude throughput and seasonality) turned out to be significant, relative stock levels played an overwhelming role in explaining variations of this price ratio. When the stock levels were relatively high, only small price shifts occurred; by contrast, low stocks were associated with large price shifts.

The importance of the role played by stocks confirms the view that the product supply structure is fairly rigid. In other words, the ability of the refining industry to change the output mix in the short run is extremely limited. This would not be surprising in the case of the single refinery; but one would have thought that a large refinery system, closely knit together by flows of transactions, open to international trade, and enjoying the room for manoeuvre given by surplus capacity, would display greater flexibility. The important result on stocks suggests that information on the levels of product stocks is critical for short-term predictions of product price movements.

Other results of the model are also of interest. The behaviour of the demand variable is consistent with the finding that the supply side is rigid in the short term. Higher *relative* demands are met by higher price ratios. Similarly, an increase in refinery throughput reduces the ratio of distillates to fuel oil in total output, and brings about a price adjustment, again reflecting supply rigidities. Finally, seasonal variables appear to have a substantial impact on relative prices in the model, which is an important result because the price ratio is not itself seasonal. The seasonality of demand induces changes in stocks but there is no corresponding price cycle. The markets thus appear to smooth out oil prices against seasonal fluctuations in demand, a strong indication of their ability to perform in a flexible and competitive manner.

The model has much less to explain in the case of inter-distillate price ratios because the variations, as mentioned earlier, are small. The main difference between the behaviour of the inter-distillate and distillates/fuel oil price ratios is that supply adjustments are more important for the former than the latter. In other words, supply rigidities in refining affect the ability to vary the distillates/fuel oil output mix than the relative proportions of the different distillates. However, this may be partly due to the greater magnitude of actual demand shifts between fuel oil and distillates than among the distillates. Because prices bear the burden of adjustment in the distillates/fuel oil case they tend to adjust more rapidly than in the inter-distillate case. Where prices have more work to do, they seem to do it more quickly.

The results of all models support the view that product price ratios tend not to be constant. There are both short- and long-run aspects to this issue. In the short run, the impact of shifts in relative demand on price ratios may be dampened by stocks. However, when the stocks of the product for which demand has increased become depleted, the burden of adjustment falls to a considerable extent on the price ratio. On the other hand, inventory behaviour has at times amplified swings in relative product prices. In 1978 a large run-down of the stocks ratio was followed by a large relative price rise later in the year; in 1984, the high levels of distillates stocks relative to fuel oil were followed by a large fall in the relative price of distillates.

Relative product prices have important implications in the long run. In this context the long run refers to the period in which investment/disinvestment decisions are made. With hindsight, we can see that the general trend of the 1974–88 period was one of a rise in the distillates/fuel oil demand ratio despite the tax-indexation of gasoline, whose retail price rose faster than that of fuel oil. The demand shift towards the lighter end of the product barrel called for an investment response involving the upgrading of refineries and the closure of crude distillation capacity. It is interesting to note that the behaviour of the distillates/fuel oil price ratio during this period was not consistent with the direction of the demand shift. Short-term shocks caused by inventory behaviour or events such as the UK miners' strike on occasions reduced the distillates/fuel oil price ratio. Even if investors dismissed these movements as reflecting short-term or temporary occurrences (even if of long duration), the cycles in relative prices remained confusing and failed to provide clear and consistent signals of the need to upgrade or close refineries. Furthermore, there were changes in the relative size of the advantage of having semi-complex rather than simple refining configurations, which confused perceptions further.

There is no doubt, therefore, that short-term movements in relative product prices are a misleading basis for long-term economic decisions. This is a common failing of markets which, however flexible and competitive, do not allow long-term forces and trends to dominate the day-to-day determination of prices. Of course, one can always recognize the impact of long-term developments on the historical behaviour of prices *ex post*, but price movements today are of little use in signalling what these future developments should be. The investment decision depends on expectations about future returns on costs which may be, but need not be, closely related to current price behaviour.

1.7 A Synthetic View

The fundamental characteristic of the petroleum product industry in Europe in the period of our study was the *co-existence* of very competitive product markets, competitive but imperfect crude oil markets, and a fairly rigid supply structure.

In the period from the late 1970s to date, product markets underwent remarkable developments with the mushrooming of new trading instruments for spot, physical forward and futures transactions. New trading 'centres' emerged that extended the scope of the traditional Rotterdam market. Arbitrage is now taking place rather efficiently between the different European centres such as the Mediterranean and Rotterdam; and arbitrage also operates rather smoothly between product markets in North West Europe and in New York. These market relationships between Europe and the USA are underpinned by a small amount of physical trade in products operating in both directions. Within Europe, the movement of products between countries is extremely significant, suggesting that there is active trading and considerable competition.[5] Finally, Europe is an open economy subject to competition from other refining centres, particularly in the

---

[5] Intra-European trade in products is estimated at some 116 million tonnes in 1987 representing 22 per cent of total consumption in that year.

CPEs and in the OPEC region. In short, the European (spot) product market is very competitive, partly because of its internal structure and its own development, and partly because of its links to other markets and other refining centres in the rest of the world. Outside shocks are transmitted to Europe, and the existence of excess refining capacity in other regions would have an impact in Europe through these links even if European refineries succeeded in closing their own surplus capacity. Both external and internal shocks, whether significant or small, cause product prices to move rapidly and flexibly. There appears to be a highly sophisticated market mechanism, which reflects changes in crude prices in spot product prices, and reflects changes in the relative demands for products or in total refinery throughput in significant movements in relative product prices.

These active, flexible and strongly competitive product markets intermediate between a supply system that is marred by significant and troublesome rigidities and a demand structure that is constrained in the short term by the small values of the price elasticities, but which is subject to important shifts in the longer run because of divergences in the long-term behaviour of these elasticities.

The rigidities that affect the refining structure are of two types. In the short run they relate to the facts that refinery output is a joint product and that technology does not permit great variations in the output mix of a particular set of plants. In the long run, the rigidity of the refining industry in Europe manifests itself in long delays in the adjustment through disinvestment to significant shifts in demand. Hindrances and delays have been caused in the period since 1973 by a host of factors.

First, at the time of the first price shock in the mid-1970s European refining was already suffering from surplus capacity that was due to previous expansion by companies vying with one another in the downstream sector and to exogenous factors such as earlier political decisions to develop nuclear power. Secondly, the majors, always caught in oligopolistic stalemates, initially believed that the impact of the price shock on demand would be temporary, and when they recognized later on that demand was badly hit they still delayed the shedding of distillation capacity in the hope that others would exit before them. By 1982 it had become clear, however, that closures were inevitable. Thirdly, high exit costs and a strong belief that refining is an essential part of the vertically integrated structure also delayed the necessary adjustments. Fourthly, and more importantly, the ownership structure of the refining sector in Europe involves national companies that are able to sustain losses (or to survive profitably owing to government policy) and large international companies that are able to subsidize the downstream with profits made elsewhere. This again slowed down the disinvestment process; and in some instances caused perverse responses such as expansion by national oil companies at a time when the economics of refining called for significant reductions in capacity. By 1988, the adjustment process, which involved both upgrading (to cope with changes in the composition of the demand barrel) and closures (to cope with the stagnation of overall demand), was well advanced but not complete.

The combination of a rigid supply structure with a very competitive product market means that the response to shifts in relative demand *in the short term* can only come from external supplies (international trade), stocks or price changes. Europe is open to international trade in products but its main suppliers – the CPEs and some OPEC countries – are themselves supply constrained. Little relief can be expected from these sources, which are often the cause of short-term shocks rather than the origin of moderating influences. Stocks therefore have to cope with changes in demand until they are either depleted or built up to high levels. When these points are reached, the adjustment burden has to be carried solely by changes in relative product prices.

A flexible and competitive product market does not always send correct price signals *for the long term* and is not necessarily of help in eliciting an appropriate long-term response. There is of course the problem of supply rigidities, particularly of those relating to the ownership structure. These rigidities – or more specifically the abilities of large privately owned companies to finance losses in one sector for strategic or other reasons, and of national oil companies to expand in spite of losses through public sector subsidization – hinder the normal long-term outcome of competitive processes, which is to the elimination of losers and the restoration of the profitability of survivors within a reasonable period of time. However, whether rigidities exist or not on the supply side, most markets usually fail to signal long-term trends in a meaningful way because of the myopia of the economic agents involved and the imperfection of arbitrage between current and future transactions. Considering these hurdles, it is remarkable that long-term adjustments – however unsatisfactory – have taken place in European refining to the extent observed.

Another important component of the picture is the market for crude oil, the main input of the refining industry. From the early 1980s onwards, this market became very competitive and developed in terms of both the *volume* of transactions and the *diversity* of trading instruments available to all the economic agents involved. Yet, different types of property rights, different modes of access to primary supplies of crude oil, and differences in bargaining power *vis-à-vis* producers mean that crude oil of the same specification is acquired at different prices and on different terms by different refiners. This has a depressing effect on prices if the refiner that acquires crude on relatively advantageous terms has surplus capacity at its disposal. The problem here is not related exclusively to the entry of the national oil companies of producing countries into the European refining industry.[6] In fact, any refiner with temporary access to cheap crude and with excess capacity ends up by depressing product prices. In other words, virtually everybody does so, and the greatest damage is done by those who have the largest volumes of surplus capacity.

An industry burdened with excess capacity, where exit is constrained, where the market for the main input (crude oil) is imperfect and thus allows different buyers to acquire the commodity at different prices, and where the market for its products is very competitive, can only incur losses. All these forces bring the weighted average price of products close to the level of the crude oil price, the cost of the main input. The incremental technology, which we now find to be semi-complex refining, barely makes a positive margin in the short run and incurs losses in the long run (when allowance must be made for capital costs). Inferior technologies, even if maintained in existence either because of high exit costs or because of favourable factors (production of special products, for example), make a loss on the refining of a plain barrel of oil. Complex refining is perhaps the only sector that is profitable in the long run.

Improvements in the economic performance of European refining involve further investment in upgrading capacity and disinvestment from distillation capacity, better inventory policies (as these are essential to price stabilization), and greater price transparency in the crude oil market. These remedies are not all available to the industry. The problems of European refining are not all of European origin. They are not all problems that the individual refiner can solve through changes in its performance and policy. Some of the problems are structural – the imperfections of the crude market, the peculiarity of the composition of refinery ownership, the trade links with supply centres where export policies have more to do with quantities than with price and cost parameters – which simply means that they cannot be removed by economic forces on their own without the support of policy.

---

[6] They can price crude to themselves in any way they like, but their actions will only depress the product market if the refinery capacity they acquired would otherwise have been reduced or scrapped.

1.8 Issues for the Future

European refining faces in the ten or fifteen years ahead a world in which a number of important parameters will change as a result of economic, political and institutional developments. Investment/ disinvestment decisions are more likely to be related to a company's assessment of these developments than to misleading price signals given by competitive but imperfect oil markets. The prospects for improved profitability depend partly on whether a correct anticipation of future developments will elicit the appropriate economic responses.

The first issue worth considering is demand. The conventional wisdom in Europe today is that oil demand will probably increase in the remaining years of this century, but that the rate of growth will be small. This view is founded first of all on conservative forecasts of economic growth, and hence of the prospects for a rise in primary energy demand, and secondly on the belief that the potential for conservation and the substitution of other fuels for oil is not yet exhausted. Extrapolation of the trend of the past fifteen years is, however, dangerous. Important new factors are beginning to emerge and their possible effects must be either assessed, or at least kept in mind. The period of low oil prices that started in 1986 may well continue for many years to come. It is becoming increasingly evident that the present structure of the crude oil market will not be easily amenable to cartelization until the mid-1990s at the earliest, and perhaps not before the end of the century. The reasons are that: (a) there are too many crude oil producers in the world; (b) too many producers are not members of OPEC; (c) significant non-OPEC countries such as the UK and the Soviet Union are strongly disinclined to participate in concerted producers' actions; and (d) OPEC countries are unable to agree and, more importantly, to implement consistently and effectively a production programme when the demand for their oil is well below their full production capacity.

A long period of low international oil prices may well increase petroleum demand in Europe by more than is suggested in most forecasts. This does not mean, however, that demand will be allowed to run away. Governments are likely to respond, sooner or later, to low crude oil prices in international markets by compensatory increases in taxation on petroleum products sold domestically. The fear of renewed dependence on oil imports from the Middle East, which has not yet disappeared despite the recent experience of secure supplies, could well produce such a reaction.

Political considerations are likely to protect the nuclear industry in many European countries, and we do not believe that pressures for decommissioning plants or for stopping investment in projects already under way will succeed. In any case, the long life of nuclear generating plant and the long gestation of projects mean that decisions cannot be easily reversed. This implies that the demand for fuel oil is unlikely to receive a boost in the next decade from a reduction in nuclear energy supplies arising from environmental concerns. The effect of these concerns will probably be felt over a much longer period.

Another important determinant of demand is economic growth. New developments such as the establishment of the EEC internal market in the early 1990s may usher in a period of enhanced economic growth. Liberalization in the Soviet Union may increase East–West trade and lead to stronger economic links between OECD Europe and the countries of the Communist bloc, with a favourable impact on economic growth. The success of anti-inflationary policies pursued in the late 1970s and 1980s by the governments of most OECD countries may well have laid the foundations for a new period of sustained economic growth. If this turns out to be the case, then the levels of demand for both primary energy and oil in particular will rise in the next decade at a higher rate than is expected by the conventional wisdom, but not to the same extent as they would if their main determinants (price and income) were allowed to operate freely. The favourable impact on demand of low crude oil prices and high income growth will probably be checked by fiscal and other policy measures because of security concerns.

A second issue of interest is the impact on the European refining and downstream sectors of the EEC's move towards a single internal market in the early 1990s. One aspect of this issue is the tax harmonization proposals. The proposals, which would apply to a very large part of the total European market, have two components. It is proposed that the harmonization of excise duties across the Community will leave the *average* level of this element of taxation unchanged; while the approximation of VAT rates will narrow the band within which petroleum products are presently taxed (but this may well imply that the average VAT rate charged will change). Because the harmonization proposals have been drawn up product by product, and not country by country, the implication of the initial set of proposals is that certain countries (e.g. Germany) would find their taxation rising on almost all petroleum products while others (e.g. Greece) would face a fall across the board.

The willingness of governments to accept such proposals is very uncertain. Those with a great need for revenue from indirect taxation (e.g. Greece) would not be happy to see such a substantial reduction, while others with a strongly anti-inflationary bias (e.g. Germany) would be unlikely to be happy with such a large (albeit once-for-all) rise in the cost of living. However, the proposals for tax harmonization have to be seen as a whole. Even though countries may 'lose' on petroleum products they may 'gain' elsewhere, so a compromise may be struck that will have important ramifications for the refining industry in all European countries.

The approximation of VAT rates covers a much wider range of products, and involves important changes to social policy (e.g. the abolition of 'zero rating' on certain items in the UK). Thus it is likely to be a highly contentious issue, and any compromise is likely to widen the tax bands within which governments will have discretion to choose their rates. The actual outcome of these negotiations is unpredictable, depending partly on each country's attitude to the concept of the European Community. The tax shifts involved may be of such a magnitude that, even at the very low price elasticities we have assumed, the shifts in both the overall level and the composition of demand for products in some countries will greatly alter the prospects for the refining industry. In some cases the relative competitiveness of different fuels may also be radically changed and countries with easy access to alternative fuels will see a further restructuring of their energy industries.

A second aspect of the EEC internal market relates to petroleum product specifications. There is already a tendency, resisted by some European countries but encouraged by others, to alter these specifications for environmental reasons. Thus, the move towards lead-free petrol is steadily gathering pace. This is changing the nature of the gasoline required from the refining industry as a higher octane level is needed to compensate for the lower level of additives. At present, the consumption of lead-free gasoline accounts for only a small part of the total market, but this will rapidly grow. The requirement for higher octane levels will inevitably depress the yield of gasoline to the refiner, or else require investment, since there is no evidence that consumers will be willing to buy the same quantity of lead-free petrol at higher prices than they pay at present for premium gasoline. It is proposed that taxes on lead-free petrol will be lower, but this is unlikely to offset fully the extra cost of making it. It is likely that either the market as a whole will shrink or refiners will be forced to accept lower margins (which would not be sustainable in such a competitive environment) as a result.

At the same time other restrictions are gradually being adopted. The move towards lower sulphur emission in refining (and a lower sulphur content in products) will have similar effects on the costs of meeting those restrictions, and will also reduce the margin, which can be recovered only by a rise in prices and a fall in supply brought about by further exit from the market.

In both cases certain types of refinery will be *relatively* well placed to deal with shifts that affect some parts of their market more than others. As was already the case in the period 1976–86, the ability to produce lubricants or other special products, which are least affected by the introduction of tighter specifications, and the ownership of some favourable local facility (giving an intra-marginal profit) will continue to be important factors in determining survival.

These are tendencies that now exist independently of policies that may be proposed in the context of the European Community's single internal market. An attempt to impose identical product specifications on all EEC countries would induce, if successful, important changes in the refining industry's structure, and may transform the pattern of international trade. The introduction of tough specifications would pose serious problems to exporters in the CPEs and open the way for a long-term shift of trade relationships in favour of the USA and against Eastern Europe. The attempt to introduce uniform specifications will succeed only if countries with inferior specifications agree to raise their standards to the more demanding levels already adopted by their more advanced partners. In this case harmonization will only be possible if it brings everybody to the *highest* common denominator; but this very condition makes it unlikely that harmonization will obtain immediately. At best, a long transition period will be required. For these reasons we discount the importance of this issue.

A third issue with some technical and economic implications for the future of European refining is the supply of crude oil. North Sea production as a whole will reach a peak in a few years' time (at present the small decline in UK production is being more than compensated by increases in Norway), and will then begin to fall rapidly. European refiners will then have to look elsewhere for supplies, and a change in the average API gravity of available crude is likely to be felt. The expected long-term trend is one of a heavier crude oil barrel and a lighter demand barrel of refined products. Such a shift in the pattern of crude supply would have several effects. It would put pressure on distillates prices which would in turn make investment in technologies with a higher distillates yield more attractive. However, the investment response is typically slow and one may well witness a significant change in the price ratio of distillates to fuel oil lasting for a while.

Finally, the issue that is as important for the future as it consistently appears to be in the present is the probable behaviour of crude oil prices. In the discussion of demand above, we assumed that crude oil prices are likely to remain fairly low for a number of years ahead. The behaviour of crude oil prices has implications for economic variables other than demand: it may for example directly or indirectly affect refiners' margins and relative product prices. We expect crude oil prices, in the foreseeable future, to display considerable volatility. Given that product prices are closely tied to crude oil prices, this volatility will undoubtedly spread to products. Volatility is likely to be greater for middle distillates than for other products. It is also possible that the price of distillates relative to fuel oil will rise initially under the impact of falling crude oil prices (hence causing an increase in refinery throughput and bringing on stream topping capacity with a high fuel oil yield), and then decline if the lower fuel oil prices stimulate demand for this easily-substitutable product. This cyclical price behaviour might send incorrect signals for long-term investment decisions. Like many other factors, such behaviour has a destabilizing impact. European refining, like other industries, is likely to move in the long run from one unbalanced situation to another.

Finally, an issue of some importance is whether European governments will follow the UK's lead in privatizing their national oil companies. This is a question about possible future developments, not a policy recommendation. The question is important because privatization would help the competitive process to reach its normal outcome: the elimination of the weak in favour of the survival of the fittest. It would eventually lead to a reduction in European refining capacity, which is the necessary condition for improved profitability.

To sum up, our inevitably speculative views about the future are: (a) that demand will rise by more than is expected by the conventional wisdom in European circles but by less than is hoped for by OPEC; (b) that refining will be affected by the EEC's drive for a single internal market to a larger extent than is anticipated by most oil companies; (c) that low and volatile prices are a feature of the product market that will not disappear in the medium term, and that this volatility may well persist in the longer term even if the price level rises; and (d) that margins and profitability will eventually be restored through further capacity reductions and investment in upgrading plant. In this latter respect privatization of national oil companies, or tighter financial restrictions by governments on their public sector enterprises, would hasten the pace of retrenchment. Paradoxically, the industry may overshoot the equilibrium target and Europe could find itself short of refining capacity in a few years' time, through a combination of factors such as higher-than-anticipated demand and faster-than-expected disinvestment. The world of excess capacity and low margins that we have analysed and described in this study may well give way, sooner than expected, to a different state of affairs.

2 Trends in the Demand for Petroleum Products

Joyce Dargay

As is well known, total oil consumption increased steadily and rapidly up until the oil crisis of 1973–4. The period after 1973 has witnessed a considerable change in this pattern: not only has oil consumption decreased, but far greater fluctuations in demand are also apparent. The trends in consumption have not been identical for all oil products, however; nor have they been so for all European countries. Both the growth rates of the 1960s and early 1970s *and* the responses to the oil price shocks of 1974 and 1979 varied considerably amongst products as well as across countries. The differences in adjustment to higher oil prices have primarily to do with the differing possibilities for substitution of other energy sources, which vary not only for different products, but also according to their different uses. Where alternative energy forms were available for a particular use – e.g. gas or electricity for residential heating, nuclear power for electricity generation – the demand for the oil product previously used (in this case fuel oil) declined considerably. Conversely, where there was no viable substitute – e.g. gasoline or diesel for road transport – the response to higher prices was far smaller.

In this chapter, the development of the demand for oil since the early 1960s is investigated, both for Europe as a whole and for sixteen individual countries. As well as the total demand for individual oil products – gasoline, fuel oils, etc. – the consumption of these products in different sectors of the economy – industry, residential, transport and electricity generation – is discussed. In order to improve our understanding of how changes in oil consumption have been accommodated by the energy system, total energy demand and the consumption of other energy sources – coal, gas, etc. – are also analysed. All data used are taken from OECD publications.

2.1 The Share of Oil in Primary Energy Consumption

To put the trends in total oil consumption over the past twenty-five years in a wider perspective, it is helpful to view their development in the context of total primary energy consumption, including that of other forms of energy. Some relevant information is given in Table 2.1, which shows the total primary energy requirements in the European OECD countries for five selected years during the period 1960–87. The table shows, for each primary energy source, its consumption in million tonnes of oil equivalent, its average annual percentage changes for selected periods, and its share in total requirements.

First, we see that total energy use increased over the entire period, but that its rate of growth declined considerably from 1973 onwards. During the 1960s, total energy use rose by 5.5 per cent per annum. Oil, gas and nuclear all increased at a far higher rate, but the latter two were still of only marginal significance. The growth rates for hydro and solid fuels other than coal were lower than those for total energy, while coal consumption actually decreased. The most significant developments in energy consumption patterns during this decade

Table 2.1: Primary Energy Consumption in OECD Europe. Shares in Total Energy Consumption and Average Annual Rates of Growth.[a] Selected Years, 1960–87. Volumes in Million Tonnes of Oil Equivalent.

	Coal	Other Solid	Oil	Gas	Nuclear	Hydro	Total Energy
Energy Consumption							
1960	337.5	13.9	186.1	10.4	0.5	48.5	596.7
1970	273.8	14.1	590.8	63.2	9.9	69.2	1,020.9
1973	242.8	20.8	705.6	121.0	16.5	72.3	1,179.1
1980	253.9	24.3	645.9	180.2	47.8	87.7	1,240.2
1987	257.9	29.9	571.3	211.6	144.9	98.4	1,314.4
Average Annual Growth in Energy Consumption							
1960–70	−2.1	0.1	12.2	19.8	33.9	3.6	5.5
1970–73	−3.9	13.9	6.1	24.2	18.7	1.5	4.9
1973–80	0.6	2.2	−1.3	5.9	16.4	2.8	0.7
1980–87	0.2	3.0	−1.7	2.3	17.2	1.7	0.8
Shares in Energy Consumption							
1960	56.6	2.3	31.2	1.7	0.1	8.1	100.0
1970	26.8	1.4	57.9	6.2	1.0	6.8	100.0
1973	20.6	1.8	59.8	10.3	1.4	6.1	100.0
1980	20.5	2.0	52.1	14.5	3.9	7.1	100.0
1987	19.6	2.3	43.5	16.1	11.0	7.5	100.0

Note: (a) Since the data in this table are for *primary* energy consumption, the figures given here for oil consumption include refinery fuel, refinery losses, etc., and are therefore not comparable with the data on *final* oil product consumption given elsewhere in this chapter.

were the continuing substitution of oil for coal, the introduction of nuclear power and the increasing role of natural gas. A continuation of this process was evident in the early 1970s. However, the growth in total energy consumption was somewhat slower, and the annual increase in oil consumption was about half that of the 1960s. After 1973, the growth in total energy consumption was appreciably re-tarded. The absolute decline in oil use played the most significant role, but even the consumption of natural gas increased at a much lower rate than previously. During this period, the decline in the use of coal noted for the previous decades was reversed, while nuclear and hydro maintained similar growth rates to those experienced earlier. Table 2.1 clearly shows that only the consumption of nuclear energy increased at a rapid rate over the entire period studied.

These differences in the rates of growth of consumption of different energy sources over the period changed the composition of European primary energy consumption considerably. In 1960, coal and oil clearly dominated, with shares of over 56 and 31 per cent respectively. The substitution of oil for coal, which began in the 1950s, continued during the 1960s, reversing the relative positions of these two fuels. By 1970 oil accounted for nearly 58 per cent of energy use, while coal's share had declined to slightly less than 27 per cent. The dominance of these two fuels is evident up until 1973, when only 20 per cent of primary energy requirements were met by all other sources combined. The oil price rises of the 1970s, in combination with the growth of the nuclear power industry, led to a substantial diversification of energy consumption. By 1987 oil's share had fallen to around 44 per cent, and coal's to around 20 per cent, while the share of all other energy sources combined rose to over 36 per cent. The increases in the use of gas and nuclear power were primarily responsible for this change, while the shares of hydropower and 'other solid' fuels remained more-or-less constant over the entire period. In summary, the decline in oil consumption evident since the early 1970s was accompanied by a slow-down in the growth of total energy demand and was partially compensated by a rapid increase in the importance of gas and nuclear power.

2.2 Final Consumption of Oil Products

Against this background, we now return to the major issue of interest – the development of total demand for oil and of demand for the individual oil products. This is clearly illustrated in Figure 2.1, which shows total final oil consumption (including consumption of fuel oil in electricity generation), as well as the consumption of individual

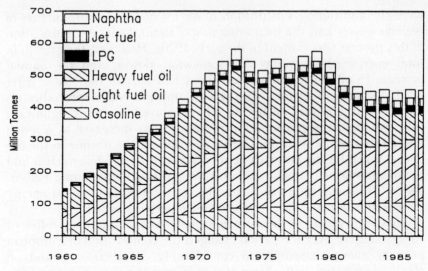

Figure 2.1: Final Consumption of Oil Products in OECD Europe. 1960–87.

petroleum products, in the OECD European countries for the period 1960–87.[1] We see that the growth trend of the 1960s was sharply broken by the oil crisis in 1974. Consumption fluctuated considerably during the next five years but always remained well below the peak of 1973. Following the second oil price shock of 1979, demand steadily declined, finally levelling off in 1983. Although a slight increase may be noted following the 1986 oil price collapse, its effect appears to have been rather small.

It is apparent that not all petroleum products behaved identically, and this is illustrated more clearly in Figure 2.2, which shows the consumption of the individual petroleum products over the period separately. We see that the use of each product rose steadily up until 1973. The oil price increases of the 1970s broke this trend, but their effects on the individual products varied substantially from case to case. The demand for heavy fuel oil decreased most significantly, with the greatest decline occurring during the period after 1979. The demand for light fuel oil fell in 1974, but reverted to an upward trend soon afterwards, only to fall again after 1979. The picture for gasoline is very different. Clearly, the growth in demand was retarded by the price rises, but demand continued to increase over the larger part of

---

[1] Here, and in the remainder of this chapter, 'OECD Europe' refers to all the European OECD countries except Iceland, Luxembourg and Turkey.

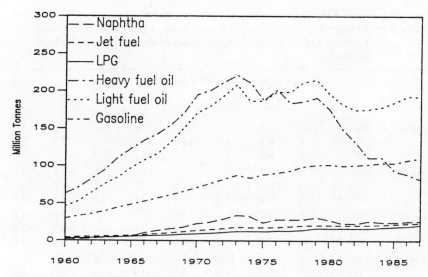

Figure 2.2: Final Consumption of Oil Products in OECD Europe. 1960–87.

the post-1974 period. Of the minor products, only the demand for naphtha and kerosine (not shown in the figure) actually declined after 1973.

The trends in consumption of the individual oil products are shown in Table 2.2, which gives their average annual percentage changes for the periods 1960–70, 1970–80 and 1980–87 for OECD Europe as well as for the individual countries. Comparing the figures for the various countries we find that the general pattern of development is rather similar. Total oil demand increased by well over 10 per cent per annum during the 1960s in all countries with the exceptions of Norway, Sweden and the UK, where the rates of growth were appreciably lower. During the 1970s, its rate of growth decreased to well under 5 per cent per annum in all countries except Greece, Portugal and Spain; while absolute declines occurred in Belgium, Denmark, Sweden and the UK. All countries except Norway, Portugal and the UK show an absolute fall in final oil consumption during the 1980s. Although it is not apparent from these data, most of the decline in the growth rate of consumption occurred in the earlier part of the decade. In nearly all countries, demand increased between 1985 and 1987.

It is apparent from Table 2.2 that the consumption of all products rose considerably during the 1960s in all countries (with the exception of kerosine in some cases), and that this growth was retarded significantly during the 1970s. Of the individual products, heavy fuel oil experienced the greatest demand decrease by far in all the countries

Table 2.2: Average Annual Percentage Changes in Final Consumption of Petroleum Products: OECD Europe and Individual Countries. Selected Periods, 1960–87.

		Gasoline	Light Fuel Oil	Heavy Fuel Oil[a]	LPG	Jet Fuel	Naphtha	Kerosine	Total
Austria	1960–70	10.5	10.7	11.5	10.8	16.9	n.a.	−2.2	11.2
	1970–80	4.4	6.3	1.3	12.6	3.4	−9.5	3.5	3.1
	1980–87	0.4	0.7	−7.4	−1.9	49.7	29.9	−1.8	−0.7
Belgium	1960–70	7.4	14.3	13.7	7.7	11.0	24.8	−9.4	13.1
	1970–80	2.9	0.5	−3.3	1.3	2.2	−1.5	0.4	−0.7
	1980–87	−0.6	−0.6	−12.5	−0.4	2.6	3.4	24.4	−2.7
Denmark	1960–70	6.2	15.7	15.4	7.6	16.2	n.a.	2.9	13.8
	1970–80	0.2	−1.0	−5.8	0.8	2.6	n.a.	−8.6	−2.8
	1980–87	−0.1	−1.5	−14.5	−6.1	−0.9	n.a.	−3.8	−3.8
Finland	1960–70	11.6	16.1	17.0	16.9	20.6	50.6	−4.1	15.9
	1970–80	2.8	1.4	0.2	5.9	11.4	17.1	−8.5	1.5
	1980–87	3.8	−1.9	−6.0	8.8	3.0	−11.5	−2.6	−0.6
France	1960–70	8.5	15.2	13.4	8.8	16.7	n.a.	−4.6	13.5
	1970–80	3.8	0.7	1.9	5.6	8.4	3.8	1.7	2.0
	1980–87	0.6	−2.0	−16.0	0.8	−1.7	2.2	−2.4	−3.3
Germany	1960–70	10.8	16.3	14.6	14.4	16.4	n.a.	3.7	15.1
	1970–80	4.3	0.2	−2.3	0.4	4.0	8.9	−4.5	0.9
	1980–87	0.8	−0.2	−11.1	3.5	5.0	−6.0	0.5	−1.9
Greece	1960–70	15.8	10.4	11.5	26.0	17.7	n.a.	−5.4	11.9
	1970–80	7.8	5.9	7.8	4.6	6.5	−1.7	−6.7	6.8
	1980–87	5.5	4.1	−8.0	1.1	−0.4	−4.5	−4.0	−0.9
Ireland	1960–70	8.3	12.5	19.0	14.7	18.9	n.a.	−1.2	13.7
	1970–80	5.1	5.4	3.5	9.4	−2.4	n.a.	−1.2	3.9
	1980–87	2.9	1.4	−9.6	−2.0	4.5	n.a.	1.7	−3.5
Italy	1960–70	13.6	16.1	14.1	10.0	16.1	26.6	27.5	14.9
	1970–80	2.8	7.0	0.2	2.8	1.6	−2.8	−4.0	1.9
	1980–87	0.2	2.0	−5.7	4.1	0.8	0.9	−3.9	−1.3
Netherlands	1960–70	9.6	11.6	8.5	7.4	10.6	n.a.	9.1	10.9
	1970–80	2.9	−1.1	−1.8	18.4	3.1	3.5	−14.9	0.3
	1980–87	−3.7	−2.9	−20.7	6.7	5.9	−1.7	−5.4	−3.2
Norway	1960–70	8.1	9.6	4.4	32.8	8.2	n.a.	15.5	7.6
	1970–80	4.1	2.1	−5.1	46.0	5.5	−8.8	0.0	0.0
	1980–87	3.4	0.1	−10.6	12.9	4.7	−45.4	−6.0	0.5
Portugal	1960–70	9.0	8.6	9.8	20.6	36.0	33.9	−5.7	10.8
	1970–80	4.7	8.3	12.4	6.7	2.3	0.0	−2.2	8.2
	1980–87	4.9	2.8	−3.2	2.7	−0.6	22.3	−9.6	1.1
Spain	1960–70	14.3	15.5	16.5	36.8	26.7	n.a.	−4.0	16.6
	1970–80	6.9	7.6	6.0	6.1	8.3	11.1	−19.7	6.7
	1980–87	3.3	1.2	−13.4	−0.4	0.8	3.3	−3.3	−3.1

Table 2.2: (cont'd)

		Gasoline	Light Fuel Oil	Heavy Fuel Oil[a]	LPG	Jet Fuel	Naphtha	Kerosine	Total
Sweden	1960–70	5.9	8.2	10.1	14.9	7.7	n.a.	0.3	9.0
	1970–80	2.5	−1.1	−4.1	3.1	0.9	1.0	−18.5	−2.0
	1980–87	2.2	−4.8	−14.9	21.3	3.7	−5.4	−14.9	−4.5
Switzerland	1960–70	8.6	13.3	13.5	17.5	20.5	n.a.	0.0	12.6
	1970–80	2.7	1.0	−6.1	9.5	3.4	−1.3	−4.6	0.4
	1980–87	2.8	−0.3	−9.2	8.7	3.2	−8.6	8.8	−0.7
UK	1960–70	6.3	10.5	8.2	17.7	8.4	18.1	4.7	8.6
	1970–80	3.0	0.6	−6.8	8.3	3.2	−6.0	−1.9	−2.0
	1980–87	2.1	0.1	−8.3	12.2	3.1	−0.3	−0.5	1.2
OECD	1960–70	9.1	14.0	12.0	12.8	13.5	29.8	6.7	12.5
Europe	1970–80	3.6	1.4	−1.0	5.7	4.3	2.0	−4.6	1.1
	1980–87	0.4	0.7	−7.4	4.1	2.2	−0.1	−2.1	−1.9

Note: (a) This includes oil used for electricity generation.

considered. The greatest fall occurred during the early 1980s, with decreases in consumption of well over 10 per cent per annum.

Regarding light fuel oil, again we find that the rate of growth in the 1970s was markedly lower than in the 1960s; and in a few countries – Denmark, the Netherlands and Sweden – light fuel oil consumption was lower in 1980 than it had been ten years previously. This slowdown continued into the 1980s, when an absolute decline took place in many of the countries.

Finally, we see that, although the rate of growth of gasoline demand decreased over the time-interval considered, the decrease was generally much smaller than for the other major products. Further, only a few countries experienced actual demand contractions. This was also the case for LPG and jet fuel, while absolute declines in demand occurred for naphtha and kerosine.

The product composition of European oil consumption consequently changed significantly over the period 1960–87. From the early 1960s up until the mid-1970s, heavy fuel oil accounted for about 40 per cent of total oil consumption. Although the share of heavy fuel oil had been decreasing steadily since the late 1950s, owing to the more rapid growth in the demand for light fuel oil (gas/diesel oils), the absolute decrease in demand following the oil price shocks of the 1970s reduced its share to only 18 per cent by 1987. For light fuel oil, the pattern of development was just the opposite: from a share of 30 per cent in 1960, its demand grew to account for more than 40 per cent of total consumption of petroleum products in the European OECD countries by 1987.

The absolute decline in the consumption of heavy fuel oil also led to an increase in the shares of other petroleum products. The decline in the share of gasoline during the 1960s was reversed in the mid-1970s, and the relative significance of some minor petroleum products – LPG, jet fuel and naphtha – began to increase. By 1987 gasoline accounted for 24 per cent of total oil consumption as compared with 20 per cent in 1960. Over the same period the combined share for LPG, jet fuel and naphtha rose from less than 6 per cent to over 15 per cent. Only kerosine experienced a more-or-less continuing decline, from 2.5 per cent in 1960 to less than 1 per cent in 1987.

This change in the composition of demand for petroleum products was similar for most of the countries. The share of heavy fuel oil decreased between 1960 and 1987 in all countries with the exception of Portugal. In many countries, this share began to decline prior to the first oil crisis, but the most significant change occurred after this time. However, the extent of this decline varied considerably for the individual countries. In the most extreme case, the Netherlands, the share of heavy fuel oil declined from nearly 45 per cent in 1960 to less than 7 per cent in 1987. This was achieved mainly by means of a considerable reduction of oil use in electricity generation which was made possible by a switch to gas-powered plants, and a large increase in LPG consumption – primarily as a feedstock in the chemical industry. The share of LPG increased from 2 per cent in the early 1970s to over 18 per cent in the late 1980s, giving the Netherlands by far the largest share of LPG in total oil consumption of all European countries. The only other countries where LPG made up more than 4 per cent of oil consumption are Norway (15 per cent) and Spain (18 per cent). The use of LPG in Norway is confined mainly to the chemical industry, whereas in Spain nearly 80 per cent is consumed in the residential sector.

Although the majority of countries switched over the period from heavy fuel oil to light fuel oil as the major product consumed, there were some notable exceptions. In France, Germany and Switzerland, light fuel oil made up the greatest share of total oil consumption for the entire period; while in the UK gasoline accounted for 37 per cent of oil consumption in 1987, surpassing both light and heavy fuel oils which accounted for about 29 and 17 per cent respectively.

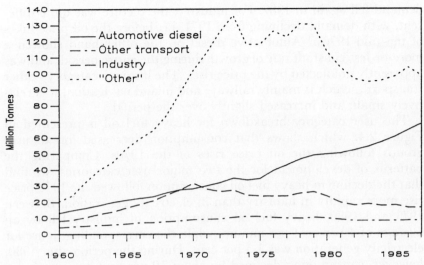

Figure 2.3: Final Consumption of Light Fuel Oil in OECD Europe by Sector. 1960–87.

2.3 Consumption of Oil Products by Sector

As both light and heavy fuel oils are used for a variety of purposes, it is useful to analyse the trends in consumption at a more disaggregated level.[2] In Figure 2.3, light fuel oil onsumption is shown for four main sectors or end-use categories. We see that by far the largest user of light fuel oil is the 'other' sector, a conglomeration of user groups – agriculture, the residential sector and the commercial and public sectors – in which light fuel oil is used chiefly for space heating (although diesel for agricultural vehicles and equipment is also included).

Figure 2.3 clearly shows the enormous increase in demand for light fuel oil in the 'other' sector up until 1973. The first oil price shock clearly led to a sharp fall in demand, but it soon began to pick up again. Following the second oil price shock of 1979, demand declined substantially and continually over the next few years. A slight upturn is evident around 1986, perhaps as a result of the price collapse, but

[2] The other products are each largely consumed within one sector only, and their consumption patterns are discussed in the next section.

demand fell again in 1987. For industry, the picture was quite different, with demand declining from 1971, i.e. before the oil price hikes
of the mid-1970s.[3] Automotive diesel on the other hand showed a
more-or-less constant rate of growth during the entire period, and was
apparently unaffected by the price rises. The last user category, 'other
transport', which is mainly railways and inland navigation, was relatively small, and increased slightly over the period.

The user category breakdown for heavy fuel oil is presented in
Figure 2.4. which shows that consumption decreased for all user
groups following the oil price rises of the 1970s. Comparing the
patterns of development for the two major user categories, we find
that the decline in heavy fuel oil consumption followed the 1974 price
rise more rapidly in industry than in electricity generation. Between
1973 and 1980, heavy fuel oil consumption in industry fell by an
average of 4 per cent per annum, while the corresponding figure for
electricity generation was 1.5 per cent. During the period after 1980,
however, consumption declined by about 10 per cent per annum for
both user categories. The difference in the intertemporal response to
the oil price rises most clearly reflects the relative inflexibility of the
electric power industry in the short term. The existing generating
capacity allowed only a limited degree of inter-fuel substitution, and
the adjustment costs and lead times involved in the conversion of
generators and investment in new plants were greater than those for
the manufacturing industries. Also, much of the new capacity that
became available during the years following the first oil price shock
was based on investment decisions made prior to 1974.

2.4 Final Energy Consumption by Sector

Much of the saving in oil consumption during the past decades has
been accomplished by an increase in the use of other energy forms. As
was noted earlier, the decline in oil consumption was offset by an
increase in the use of coal, gas and nuclear power, so that total energy
consumption continued to increase, albeit a much lower rate than
prior to 1974. In order to understand the nature of this substitution, it
is useful to examine the trends in the consumption of different energy
sources. Because of differences in the substitution possibilities across
both countries and sectors, we discuss the trends in the individual
countries in transport, industry, the 'other' sector and electricity
generation.

---

[3] 'Industry', here and elsewhere in this chapter, refers to manufacturing and extractive industries, and
excludes the energy extraction, production and transformation sectors.

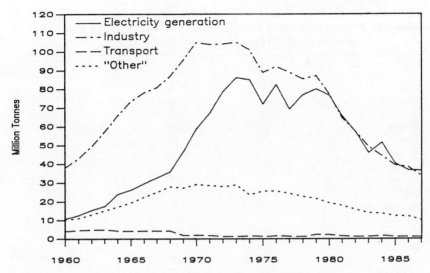

Figure 2.4: Final Consumption of Heavy Fuel Oil in OECD Europe by Sector. 1960–87.

(*a*) *Transport.* Although the transport sector also includes air, rail and sea transport, over 80 per cent of its energy consumption pertains to road transport. The following discussion will therefore be limited to this user category, and therefore only to the consumption of gasoline and diesel.[4]

Generally speaking, oil consumption for road transport is comprised of three different usages: private automobile transport, public transport (buses and taxis) and commercial goods transport. Given the different natures of these, and the varying possibilities for substitution in each particular use, their patterns of development over time might be expected to differ, and it would therefore be preferable to analyse demand in each user group separately.

The available data do not, however, allow this degree of disaggregation. The statistics reported by the OECD on gasoline and diesel consumption pertain to road transport as a whole, and sufficiently detailed time-series data are not available from national sources for all the countries. We are thus limited to the use of aggregate data to illustrate the relative importance of diesel and gasoline in road transport. In Table 2.3 the percentage shares of diesel in total oil consumption for road transport are shown for the individual countries

---

[4] The remaining 1 per cent of oil used for road transport in the European OECD countries is LPG. This is used primarily in Belgium, Italy and the Netherlands.

Table 2.3: Percentage Shares of Diesel in Total Oil Consumption for Road Transport in OECD Europe. 1970 and 1987.

	1970	1987
Austria	26	38
Belgium[a]	31	49
Denmark	23	44
Finland	42	45
France	26	40
Germany	29	34
Greece	40	40
Ireland	21	36
Italy[a]	29	52
Netherlands[a]	24	39
Norway	32	29
Portugal	39	55
Spain	44	45
Sweden	27	28
Switzerland	21	17
UK	26	28
	—	—
OECD Europe	28	40

Note: (a) LPG accounted for percentage shares in oil consumption for road transport in Belgium, Italy and the Netherlands of 1, 3 and 1 per cent respectively in 1970, and 1, 4 and 12 per cent respectively in 1987. (In all other countries its share was less than 1 per cent in both years.)

for 1970 and 1987. In all cases except Belgium, Italy and the Netherlands, the remainder is accounted for by gasoline. In the European OECD countries as a whole, diesel accounted for 28 per cent of oil consumption for road transport in 1970. By 1987 the share of diesel had risen to 40 per cent, indicating a rather substantial shift from gasoline towards diesel. The pattern for the individual countries, however, is far from identical. In 1970, the share of diesel in the individual countries ranged from 21 to 44 per cent.

The differences among countries should primarily be the result of two factors: (a) the relative importance of cars versus commercial vehicles; and (b) the penetration of diesel in each user category. Of the countries with the highest proportions of diesel in 1970 – Finland, Greece, Portugal and Spain – all except Finland had relatively low stocks of cars in relation to commercial vehicles. This is not surprising as these three countries had the lowest per capita incomes, so that private car ownership was not nearly as widespread as in the other countries. Particularly low diesel shares are also noted for Ireland and Switzerland, although the reason for this is not readily apparent. Switzerland did have a high car to commercial vehicle ratio, but Germany and Sweden had higher ratios, and the ratio for Ireland was not above the average. This seems to be indicative of a relatively low use of diesel for commercial transport in these two countries. The diesel shares in the remaining countries are generally quite near the European average.

By 1987 the share of diesel, now ranging from 17 to 55 per cent, had risen significantly in most countries. The most notable exceptions were Greece, Norway, Sweden, Switzerland and the UK, where the diesel share remained more-or-less constant, while the greatest increases are noted for Belgium, Denmark, Ireland, Italy, the Netherlands and Portugal. From the available data, it does not appear that this increase was due to a disproportionate rise in the stock of commercial vehicles as compared with private cars. It seems, therefore, to indicate a substantial substitution of diesel for gasoline, but we do not have sufficient information for all countries to determine whether this took place in the car or the commercial vehicle stock. The increasing use of diesel reduced the share of gasoline for road transport to less than 50 per cent in Italy, the Netherlands and Portugal. In the Netherlands, LPG also played an important role, showing an increase of from 1 per cent in 1970 to 12 per cent in 1987.

(*b*) *The Agricultural, Residential, Public and Commercial Sectors.* As shown in Figure 2.3 above, total European consumption of light fuel oil in the 'other' sector increased steadily up until 1973, decreased in 1974, and then remained more-or-less constant until 1980, when a further decline took place. The development of heavy fuel oil consumption in this sector was rather different. As illustrated in Figure 2.4 above, a slow increase up until 1973 was followed by a slow decline during the remainder of the period. Although this pattern and the extent of the decline differ somewhat for the individual countries, in the majority of cases oil consumption in this sector in 1987 was well below its 1973 level. The only exceptions were Greece, Ireland, Portugal and Spain.

Much of this reduction in oil consumption was achieved by means of increases in the use of other energy sources. To give an indication of the extent of inter-fuel *substitution*, as opposed to actual energy *saving*, in the various countries, the shares of coal, natural gas, electricity, and light and heavy fuel oils in total energy use in this sector are presented in Table 2.4, together with an index of total energy consumption.[5] Of the oil products, light fuel oil accounted for between 80 and 90 per cent for OECD Europe as a whole over the period, but the mix between light and heavy fuel oils varied for the individual countries. We see that total energy consumption in this sector increased in the majority of countries over the entire period. The exceptions were Belgium and the Netherlands, where an absolute decline is noted between 1980 and 1987; and Denmark and Sweden, where total energy consumption in this sector declined over the period as a whole.

Regarding the composition of energy consumption, obvious differences exist among countries. In the early 1970s, oil dominated in all countries except Ireland and the UK, where coal was the major energy source, and the Netherlands and Norway, where the largest shares were held by natural gas and electricity respectively. Of all countries, Ireland and the UK were least dependent on oil for residential heating, with shares of less than 20 per cent. In most countries oil's share increased during the early 1970s and decreased in the latter part of the period. In Germany, the Netherlands and Sweden, however, its share had begun to decline prior to the 1974 price rise. The large increases in the share of natural gas in many countries suggest that there was a high degree of substitution between oil and gas, although this was not the case in Finland, Greece, Ireland, Norway, Portugal, Spain or Sweden, where the availability of gas for space heating was either limited or non-existent. In the Scandinavian countries the decline in oil consumption was achieved instead by a more widespread use of electric heating. In the remaining four countries – Greece, Ireland, Portugal and Spain – there appears to have been little substitution away from oil in this sector.

Common to all countries was the decline in the share of coal, particularly in the early 1970s. This substitution away from coal reflected the continued growth in the use of central heating – and particularly oil-fired heating systems – that began in the 1950s in the majority of European countries. In a few countries, coal's share began to increase again by the mid-1980s, but in general it remained marginal.

By 1987, all the countries except Greece, Spain and Switzerland had reduced the share of oil to under 50 per cent. Oil still held the largest share in most countries, however, the only exceptions being

---

[5] It should be noted that the shares for the given fuels do not add up to 100 per cent since solid fuels other than coal – peat, wood, etc. – and energy produced by combined heat and power plants are also included in total energy consumption. For the OECD European countries these forms of energy accounted for about 5 per cent of consumption.

the Netherlands and the UK where gas was the major energy source, and Norway and Sweden where electricity predominated.

(c) *Industry*. As shown in Figures 2.3 and 2.4 above, consumption of both light and heavy fuel oils in industry in OECD Europe increased steadily up until 1970. The growth rate of consumption of light fuel oil, was higher, however, than that of heavy fuel oil – 14 per cent per annum as opposed to 11 per cent. From 1970 onwards, light fuel oil use began to decrease, with the greatest decline – about 5 per cent per annum – occurring for the period after 1979. For heavy fuel oil the pattern of development was somewhat different. Demand was more-or-less constant between 1970 and 1974. After a sharp fall in 1975, consumption stabilized once again, only to experience an even more dramatic fall from 1980 onwards. The drastic reduction in industrial heavy fuel oil consumption that took place in the 1980s – at an average rate of 11 per cent per annum between 1980 and 1987 – was not equalled by any other oil product in any sector. These differences in the development of the consumption of light and heavy fuel oils led to a change in the composition of oil consumed by industry: in 1960 heavy fuel oil accounted for 82 per cent of the total industrial consumption of both types of fuel oil; but by the 1970s this share had decreased to 75 per cent, and it remained constant until the early 1980s. By 1987, this share had declined to 68 per cent.

The same general trends are evident in the consumption patterns of the individual countries, particularly those for heavy fuel oil. Only in three countries – Greece, Portugal and Spain – did demand continue to increase after the mid-1970s. For light fuel oil, however, there was far more variation amongst countries, and its demand continued to grow, albeit at a lower rate, in a number of countries.

Some of the reduction in oil consumption can be explained by changes in the level of industrial output. In particular, the recessions following the oil price rises of 1974 and 1979 caused a considerable decline in oil consumption as industrial output levels were far below total production capacity. Although the economic recoveries in the late 1970s and mid-1980s and the renewed growth of output did lead to an increase in oil consumption in some countries, the downward trend was far from reversed.

The greater part of the decline in oil consumption was achieved, however, by an absolute decrease in oil *intensity*, i.e. oil *consumption per unit of output*. This trend is particularly apparent for heavy fuel oil. Common to most countries were a rise in fuel oil intensity in the 1960s and a decline from 1974 onwards, although the magnitude of the changes varied from country to country. The major difference

Table 2.4: Energy Consumption in the Agricultural, Residential, Commercial and
Public Sectors: Percentage Shares of Fuels in Total Energy Use and Total
Energy Consumption Index (1970 = 100). Selected Years, 1970–87.

		Coal	Gas	Electricity	Light Fuel Oil	Heavy Fuel Oil	Index
Austria	1970	30.4	6.7	12.6	14.5	30.3	100
	1980	14.0	13.0	18.4	16.3	23.5	132
	1987	11.2	16.9	20.3	14.8	15.2	150
Belgium	1970	28.0	6.8	5.8	45.7	10.1	100
	1980	6.4	27.7	11.9	45.3	3.8	114
	1987	5.6	30.3	16.1	40.8	2.7	107
Denmark	1970	3.6	1.3	8.7	53.5	25.8	100
	1980	1.1	1.0	16.6	47.3	22.0	92
	1987	4.1	10.6	20.3	36.5	5.7	93
Finland	1970	2.1	0.2	8.1	41.6	16.7	100
	1980	2.4	0.6	17.1	39.5	16.3	113
	1987	2.8	0.8	26.6	28.9	11.8	120
France	1970	22.7	9.4	9.8	50.8	4.2	100
	1980	6.4	19.8	18.4	45.3	4.6	138
	1987	4.4	26.2	27.1	34.2	2.9	143
Germany	1970	25.7	3.8	10.1	57.4	1.1	100
	1980	7.1	18.5	16.3	50.0	2.4	112
	1987	4.3	25.7	19.0	43.8	1.1	117
Greece	1970	2.7	0.0	12.9	47.1	8.5	100
	1980	1.3	0.0	25.2	46.7	4.5	142
	1987	1.0	0.0	29.2	50.1	3.0	187
Ireland	1970	34.5	3.0	13.7	13.7	3.2	100
	1980	29.3	2.8	18.7	17.3	4.6	125
	1987	5.8	4.0	20.7	21.2	3.8	140
Italy	1970	5.5	9.4	10.6	27.5	30.8	100
	1980	1.0	26.3	15.3	40.8	9.1	132
	1987	0.4	35.7	19.2	34.2	3.9	145
Netherlands	1970	6.7	38.8	8.7	28.7	7.7	100
	1980	0.4	74.7	11.3	10.3	1.4	137
	1987	0.4	76.3	13.7	6.1	0.4	135
Norway	1970	9.0	0.3	40.8	30.6	9.1	100
	1980	0.6	0.0	57.5	25.2	1.0	132
	1987	0.3	0.8	63.4	16.1	0.7	168
Portugal	1970	10.0	3.1	13.8	23.2	1.1	100
	1980	0.5	2.7	28.0	19.7	3.8	140
	1987	0.0	2.2	32.8	21.8	4.5	176
Spain	1970	13.4	3.5	19.5	26.1	8.9	100
	1980	2.7	4.6	29.9	37.8	1.9	156
	1987	2.4	5.5	35.6	35.0	2.0	185

Table 2.4: (cont'd)

		Coal	Gas	Electricity	Light Fuel Oil	Heavy Fuel Oil	Index
Sweden	1970	1.7	0.6	12.8	50.4	30.5	100
	1980	0.2	0.5	25.3	41.5	17.4	104
	1987	2.3	0.6	43.3	25.7	8.3	99
Switzerland	1970	4.1	2.0	15.3	70.9	3.4	100
	1980	1.0	5.9	21.2	65.3	1.7	121
	1987	0.4	9.5	23.7	60.7	0.0	138
UK	1970	36.9	19.9	20.4	9.0	9.2	100
	1980	14.7	44.0	22.5	10.9	4.3	111
	1987	11.1	52.6	23.7	7.4	1.8	119
OECD Europe	1970	20.8	9.7	12.6	39.0	10.5	100
	1980	6.7	23.8	18.3	35.3	5.8	124
	1987	5.5	29.0	22.8	29.0	3.0	132

amongst countries relates to the late 1960s and early 1970s. In many countries, oil intensity began to decline well before the price hikes of 1974. This is particularly apparent in the cases of Belgium, Denmark, Germany, Italy, the Netherlands, Norway, Sweden and the UK. The trend towards lower oil intensity began earliest in the Netherlands, where the most substantial decline occurred between 1966 and 1971. In France, Spain and Switzerland, heavy fuel oil intensity began to decline in 1974, while in Greece and Portugal the peaks did not occur until well into the late 1970s.

A similar, albeit less pronounced, pattern is found for light fuel oil intensity, although there appears to have been far more fluctuation within the individual countries. In Belgium and France there were marked declines from the early 1970s onwards, while in Germany, Ireland, Sweden and the UK oil intensities clearly began to decrease in the mid-1970s. In Denmark, the Netherlands, Norway and Spain, there was no obvious long-term decline until the late 1970s.

Much of the reduction in oil intensity in industry was achieved by the substitution of other energy products. This is illustrated in Table 2.5, which shows the shares of the major energy products, together with an index of the total consumption of all energy forms, for selected years from 1970 to 1987. In these data, coal includes all types of coal and coke, while gas includes both natural gas and that produced from gas works. Other oil products include LPG, naphtha, gasoline, refinery gas and kerosine. It should be noted that *all* energy products are included in the totals used to calculate the consumption index, not

Table 2.5: Industrial Energy Consumption: Percentage Shares of Fuels in Total Energy Use and Total Energy Consumption Index (1970 = 100). Selected Years, 1970–87.

		Coal	Gas	Electricity	Light Fuel Oil	Heavy Fuel Oil	Other Oil Products	Index
Austria	1970	29.1	15.2	16.9	0.4	35.8	2.1	100
	1980	25.6	26.2	18.9	0.0	24.8	1.1	121
	1987	24.9	27.9	22.9	0.0	16.7	1.0	111
Belgium	1970	35.5	11.1	9.6	8.9	24.4	10.5	100
	1980	33.1	26.6	13.5	3.2	11.6	9.4	98
	1987	29.1	22.7	18.1	2.8	11.3	14.4	83
Denmark	1970	4.6	0.5	8.9	18.5	63.4	2.7	100
	1980	13.2	0.6	15.7	22.9	39.3	3.8	85
	1987	12.1	12.5	25.7	20.4	18.8	3.8	73
Finland	1970	17.7	0.0	15.7	6.7	31.6	2.0	100
	1980	12.4	4.7	21.8	6.1	21.6	8.6	118
	1987	15.8	8.1	26.4	2.6	12.4	6.5	124
France	1970	26.3	6.7	11.1	25.0	22.9	8.0	100
	1980	17.4	18.1	15.1	12.9	22.2	14.3	97
	1987	19.0	24.9	20.3	7.7	8.8	19.3	79
Germany	1970	32.6	9.5	14.6	10.2	24.8	8.2	100
	1980	24.7	20.4	18.2	6.9	16.4	13.4	109
	1987	24.2	23.2	22.7	7.5	9.2	13.2	95
Greece	1970	17.0	0.0	19.2	5.6	50.2	8.0	100
	1980	11.1	0.0	21.6	6.1	56.8	4.4	186
	1987	27.6	0.0	23.1	7.8	32.5	6.9	178
Ireland	1970	7.1	1.3	9.1	20.0	58.7	3.8	100
	1980	4.6	17.1	12.9	21.6	41.5	2.3	141
	1987	17.6	29.9	13.0	13.2	19.3	5.9	169
Italy	1970	9.6	16.3	14.0	2.2	43.8	13.2	100
	1980	10.5	26.0	18.6	2.7	30.2	11.3	105
	1987	13.6	31.0	21.4	2.5	13.0	17.8	96
Netherlands	1970	11.4	33.5	10.7	1.7	23.7	18.9	100
	1980	7.5	41.6	11.7	5.9	4.3	29.1	142
	1987	9.9	41.4	12.1	1.6	2.7	32.4	147
Norway	1970	11.8	0.0	47.9	4.1	32.5	3.5	100
	1980	12.1	0.0	45.7	10.5	16.5	12.3	129
	1987	11.2	0.0	49.0	9.8	7.3	17.5	132
Portugal	1970	14.2	0.0	15.6	3.3	38.4	12.5	100
	1980	6.7	0.0	18.9	3.6	49.3	10.0	172
	1987	13.2	0.0	19.2	3.5	29.0	24.8	215
Spain	1970	28.8	0.6	15.3	0.9	48.6	5.7	100
	1980	14.4	2.8	20.8	2.6	45.6	13.8	141
	1987	20.5	9.2	24.6	2.3	19.4	23.8	128

Table 2.5: (cont'd)

		Coal	Gas	Electricity	Light Fuel Oil	Heavy Fuel Oil	Other Oil Products	Index
Sweden	1970	8.6	0.1	21.2	6.5	39.6	5.5	100
	1980	9.3	0.1	26.5	6.3	28.2	6.7	95
	1987	10.2	1.2	34.2	4.2	12.4	9.0	93
Switzerland	1970	4.3	1.0	22.5	25.1	43.4	3.6	100
	1980	5.4	10.0	24.9	28.3	22.6	5.3	105
	1987	9.8	15.5	33.2	15.5	14.5	4.1	94
UK	1970	33.3	5.1	11.2	8.1	29.9	11.7	100
	1980	14.8	30.5	16.6	8.1	18.4	11.3	71
	1987	20.2	31.4	18.6	7.2	6.7	15.9	66
OECD	1970	25.4	8.5	13.8	10.0	31.2	9.3	100
Europe	1980	17.5	19.6	18.1	7.2	23.0	12.5	103
	1987	19.7	22.3	21.9	5.5	11.5	16.3	95

only those listed in the table. These include solid fuels other than coal and heat from combined heat and power plants, which together accounted for between 2 and 3 per cent of industrial energy consumption during the period. From the last column of Table 2.5 we find that total industrial energy consumption actually decreased during the 1970s in Belgium, Denmark, France, Sweden and the UK. By 1987, three additional countries – Germany, Italy and Switzerland – also used less energy in their industrial sectors than they had done in 1970. Although this clearly represents an increase in energy efficiency, it should be noted that these eight countries experienced a lower-than-average growth in industrial output over the period. Of the remaining countries, those where energy consumption increased the most were also those with the most rapid growth of industrial production – Greece, Ireland, Norway and Portugal. The only country with a large increase in energy consumption that was not accompanied by above-average growth in ouput was the Netherlands, where a change in industrial structure due to the rapid expansion of the chemical industry led to an increase in energy use.

In nearly all the countries, oil held the largest share of all energy sources in 1970, accounting for between 38 and 85 per cent of total industrial energy consumption. The only exception was Norway, where the major energy source was electricity, with a share of 48 per cent as compared with a 40 per cent share for oil. Of the other countries where oil comprised less than 50 per cent of energy use, the major competitor was coal (in Austria, Belgium, Germany and the UK) or gas (in the Netherlands). Relatively high gas shares are also to be noted for Austria, Belgium, Germany and Italy at this time, while the shares of electricity were comparatively large in Sweden and Switzerland, reflecting the availability of cheap sources of these two energy products in these countries.

Generally, we find that the share of oil diminished over the entire period. In many countries, the decline had begun even before the oil price rise of 1974. By 1980 the share of oil had fallen in all the countries except Greece, Portugal and Spain. The reduction in oil use during the 1970s was achieved primarily by means of an increase in the use of natural gas in Austria, Belgium, France, Germany, Ireland, Italy, the Netherlands, Switzerland and the UK, and by an increase in electricity consumption in Denmark and Sweden. In Denmark there was also a significant increase in coal consumption.

During the 1980s oil's shares continued to fall considerably in most countries, so that by 1987 they had fallen to between 18 and 57 per cent of total energy consumption. Clearly, some countries managed to reduce their dependence on oil better than others, but only in Portugal did oil still hold a majority share. It is apparent that the decline in the oil share was accelerated by the oil price rise of 1979 in virtually all countries. The decline in the oil share was met predominantly by an increase in the share of gas or electricity. The substitution patterns for the individual countries were the same as those noted for the previous period. To be added to this are increases in the shares of· electricity in Finland, of natural gas in Denmark and Spain, and of coal in Greece and Ireland.

The decline in oil consumption and the increases in natural gas and electricity use during this period clearly led to a considerable change in the composition of industrial energy consumption, and also resulted in a marked diversification, so that their degrees of dependence on any one product were less pronounced than previously. We also see that the mix of oil products consumed in industry changed substantially. In Europe as a whole, light and heavy fuel oils accounted for about 80 per cent of oil use. By 1987, their combined share had fallen to only 50 per cent, increasing the significance of the other oil products, and particularily of naphtha and LPG. The importance of these other products varied considerably from country to country; for 1987 their shares ranged from 1 per cent of total industrial energy consumption in Austria to 32 per cent in the Netherlands. As the consumption of naphtha and LPG is largely limited to the chemical industry, where these products primarily serve as feedstocks, their use in the various countries is directly related to the significance of this industry. For the same reason, the increase in the consumption of these products over the past decades is a result of the expansion of the chemical industry in some countries.

As is apparent from Table 2.5 and the discussion above, the characteristic feature of the development of industrial energy consumption during the post-1970 period was the shift from oil to natural gas. Prior to 1960, natural gas was produced and consumed in only Austria, Belgium, France, Germany, Italy, the Netherlands and the UK. In 1960 Italy accounted for slightly more than half of European natural gas production, while Austria and France together accounted for 37 per cent. Total production more than quadrupled during the 1960s as a result of discoveries in the UK sector of the North Sea in the mid-1960s, the increased exploitation of the Dutch fields and the new discoveries made in France, Germany and the Netherlands. By 1973, gas consumption had increased considerably in these countries and had begun making inroads in Spain and Switzerland.

By 1980, the gas market had extended to Ireland and Finland as a result of discoveries in the Irish Sea and the importation of Soviet gas respectively. Production in Greece began in 1982, but on a comparatively small scale, so that gas still provided only a marginal share of energy consumption. Finally, the spread of gas to Denmark and Sweden followed the Danish discoveries in 1984.

The increased availability of cheap gas and the building of pipelines and gas networks created a momentum for the growth of gas demand in much of Europe. The oil price rises of the mid-1970s improved the competitive position of gas, leading to further fuel-switching and a curtailment of oil consumption. After 1979 gas prices on the whole kept closely aligned with those of oil. However, in many countries, particularly those with large supplies of gas, government subsidies were introduced in order to encourage gas consumption. The use of domestically produced gas was also well in keeping with various countries' national energy policies of reducing their dependence on imported oil through the development of indigenous energy sources. The existence of long-term contracts assuring an uninterrupted supply at reasonably stable prices provides an added incentive for consumers, particularly as there is so much uncertainty with regard to oil.

(d) Electricity Generation. It is apparent that the oil price rises of the 1970s had a considerable effect on oil demand in the electric power industry in Europe. As shown in Figure 2.4, heavy fuel oil consumption in this sector rose steadily up until 1973, with the most rapid growth occurring during the period 1968–73. This increase in demand can be attributed mainly to the rapid growth of electric power

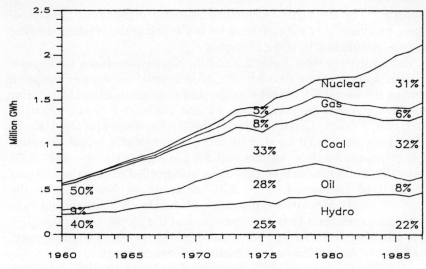

Figure 2.5: Electricity Production in OECD Europe by Primary Energy Source. 1960–87.

generation, which rose at an average annual rate of 7 per cent during the period as a whole. This is clearly illustrated in Figure 2.5, which shows the development of electricity production by primary energy source for the period 1960–87. We see that the greater part of the growth in production up until 1973 was met by thermal power plants, as the contribution of hydroelectric sources to new capacity declined over the period. Because of this, the share of thermal generation in total production increased from 59 per cent in 1960 to 69 per cent in 1973, while the share of hydroelectric generation fell from 40 to 25 per cent during the same period. This, in combination with a shift from coal to oil in thermal electricity generation, led to an increase in oil's share from about 9 per cent in 1960 to 28 per cent in 1973.

The oil price rise of 1974 and the economic recession that followed changed this picture considerably. As shown in Figure 2.4, the growth trend of fuel oil consumption in electricity generation was immediately broken. A slow decline began in the late 1970s, while a substantial reduction is to be noted for the post-1980 period. This development can be explained by three main factors: (a) a retarded growth of electricity production in general; (b) the continuing expansion of the nuclear power industry; and (c) the substitution away from oil towards solid fuels in the production of thermal electricity.

Returning to Figure 2.5, we see that electricity consumption (and production) growth slowed down substantially after 1973. The average annual rate of growth declined to around 3 per cent, as compared with the 7 per cent of the previous decade. Moreover, most of this growth in electric power production was met by nuclear power plants and very little by thermal generation. This is most apparent for the period after 1979, where we find an actual fall in thermal electricity generation. Between 1973 and 1980, the share of thermal generation decreased from 69 to 64 per cent, and by 1987 had declined to 46 per cent. At the same time, oil began to be replaced by coal in thermal generation, so that the share of oil in thermal generation fell from 40 per cent in 1973 to 17 per cent in 1987. Taken together, these two factors led to a decline in the share of oil in total electricity generation from 28 per cent in 1973 to only 8 per cent in 1987.

Clearly the composition of fuel inputs in electricity generation has changed considerably over the period 1960–87. In the early 1960s, 90 per cent of electricity was generated by coal-fired power plants and hydroelectric sources. By 1973 their combined share had declined to less than 60 per cent and that of oil had risen to 28 per cent as a result of the increasing use of oil during the 1960s and early 1970s. Finally, the oil price rises and the expansion of the nuclear power industry led to a decrease in oil use in both relative and absolute terms. By 1987, the share of oil had declined to 8 per cent, while the share of nuclear power had increased to 31 per cent of total electricity generation. Over the same period oil consumption had decreased to less than half its 1973 level.

Of course, the development of oil consumption varied considerably in the individual European countries because of differences in the pattern of growth of electricity production and the choice of primary fuels used for its generation. The responses to the oil price rises also varied according to the different countries' degrees of dependence on oil for electricity generation, the availability of alternative sources and differences in their energy policies.

The general pattern in most countries, however, was one of an increase in oil consumption during the early 1970s, a slight fall or marginal increase after 1973, and a significant decrease in the 1980s. Two countries – the Netherlands and Sweden – showed declines before 1973, as a result of an increase in the supply and use of natural gas and an increased exploitation of hydroelectric sources respectively. For the post-1973 period, only Portugal does not show an absolute decrease in oil consumption.

Some relevant information about electricity generation in the individual countries is presented in Table 2.6. Their dependence on oil prior to the price hikes can be measured by the share of electricity generated by oil-fired plants in 1973. We see that this varied from

Table 2.6: Percentage Shares of Primary Energy Sources in Total Electricity Generation, and Indices for Total and Thermal Production (1970 = 100). Selected Years, 1970–87.

		Total Index	% of Total			Thermal Index	% of Total			
			Hydropower	Nuclear	Thermal		Coal	Other	Oil	Gas
Austria	1970	100	71	0	29	100	10	1	7	12
	1973	104	61	0	39	138	10	1	14	14
	1980	140	69	0	31	146	7	1	14	9
	1987	168	73	0	27	157	10	2	5	11
Belgium	1970	100	1	0	99	100	34	0	52	13
	1973	135	2	0	98	133	22	0	53	23
	1980	176	2	23	75	133	30	1	34	11
	1987	208	2	66	31	66	24	1	4	3
Denmark	1970	100	0	0	100	100	31	0	69	0
	1973	95	0	0	100	95	36	0	64	0
	1980	134	0	0	100	134	82	0	18	0
	1987	147	0	0	99	146	95	0	4	0
Finland	1970	100	42	0	58	100	20	10	28	0
	1973	119	40	0	60	122	19	9	32	0
	1980	185	25	17	58	185	31	12	11	4
	1987	243	26	37	37	157	17	12	4	4
France	1970	100	39	4	57	100	30	0	22	4
	1973	124	26	8	65	142	19	0	40	6
	1980	176	27	24	49	150	27	0	19	3
	1987	258	19	70	11	47	8	0	2	1
Germany	1970	100	7	2	90	100	69	1	15	6
	1973	123	5	4	91	124	64	1	14	12
	1980	152	5	12	83	140	58	1	7	17
	1987	172	5	31	64	122	53	1	3	7
Greece	1970	100	27	0	73	100	38	0	35	0
	1973	151	15	0	85	175	35	0	50	0
	1980	231	15	0	85	268	45	0	40	0
	1987	308	10	0	90	380	68	0	22	0
Ireland	1970	100	14	0	86	100	1	31	54	0
	1973	127	9	0	91	134	1	24	66	0
	1980	188	11	0	89	195	1	15	59	15
	1987	226	9	0	91	239	39	21	14	18
Italy	1970	100	37	3	60	100	5	1	49	5
	1973	124	29	2	69	144	4	1	62	3
	1980	158	27	1	72	190	10	1	56	5
	1987	171	21	0	77	222	16	0	45	16
Netherlands	1970	100	0	1	99	100	20	0	33	47
	1973	129	0	2	98	127	6	0	12	80
	1980	159	0	6	94	150	14	2	38	40
	1987	167	0	5	95	160	28	1	5	60

Table 2.6: (cont'd)

		Total Index	% of Total Hydropower	Nuclear	Thermal	Thermal Index	Coal	Other	Oil	Gas
Norway	1970	100	99	0	1	100	0	0	1	0
	1973	116	100	0	0	47	0	0	0	0
	1980	144	100	0	0	37	0	0	0	0
	1987	179	100	0	0	139	0	0	0	0
Portugal	1970	100	78	0	22	100	5	2	14	0
	1973	131	75	0	25	151	4	2	19	0
	1980	204	53	0	47	440	2	2	43	0
	1987	269	46	0	54	670	26	3	26	0
Spain	1970	100	49	2	49	100	22	0	27	0
	1973	135	39	9	53	146	19	0	33	1
	1980	196	28	5	67	270	30	0	35	3
	1987	236	21	31	48	231	42	0	5	1
Sweden	1970	100	68	0	31	100	0	0	31	0
	1973	129	77	3	21	84	1	1	19	0
	1980	159	61	27	11	58	0	1	10	0
	1987	243	49	46	5	36	2	1	2	0
Switzerland	1970	100	89	5	6	100	0	0	6	0
	1973	107	77	17	7	124	0	0	7	0
	1980	166	58	24	1	27	0	0	0	0
	1987	169	60	38	2	53	0	1	1	0
UK	1970	100	2	10	87	100	68	0	18	0
	1973	113	2	10	88	115	62	0	26	1
	1980	114	2	13	85	112	73	0	12	1
	1987	121	2	18	80	111	70	0	9	1
OECD Europe	1970	100	29	4	67	100	38	0	24	5
	1973	122	25	5	70	125	33	1	28	8
	1980	152	24	12	64	143	36	1	20	7
	1987	185	22	31	47	129	32	1	8	6

almost zero in Norway to over 60 per cent in Denmark, Ireland and Italy. The average for all countries was 32 per cent. The countries with the lowest dependences on oil were generally those with well-developed hydroelectric systems – Austria, Norway, Portugal, Sweden and Switzerland – or an abundant domestic supply of coal – Germany or the UK. Although nuclear power programmes were well under way in many countries, the actual amounts of electricity generated by nuclear plants were still marginal in all but France, Spain, Switzerland and the UK.

The oil price shocks of 1974 and 1979 led to a shift away from oil in most countries, so that by 1980 oil's share was reduced to around 20 per cent in OECD Europe as a whole and in all countries except Belgium, Greece, Ireland, Italy, Portugal and Spain. By 1987, the share had declined to well under 10 per cent in all countries with the exceptions of Greece, Ireland, Italy and Portugal. Of all the countries, Italy remained the most highly dependent on oil for electricity generation, with a share of 45 per cent in 1987. The reduction of oil consumption was achieved primarily by the expansion of nuclear capacity in Belgium, Finland, France, Germany, Spain, Sweden, Switzerland and the UK. Coal was the most important substitute for oil in Denmark and Ireland, and also played a significant role in Greece, the Netherlands and Spain. Only in Ireland and the Netherlands was there any noticeable substitution towards natural gas.

All of the countries that still relied most heavily on oil for electricity generation in 1987 – Greece, Ireland, Italy and Portugal – have plans to reduce this dependence, mainly by the construction of new coal-fired capacity or through the conversion of oil-fired generating units. Of these countries, only Italy had a nuclear power programme.

In general, the tendency in the European countries has been to reduce their reliance on oil by the expansion of nuclear and coal-based plants. Because of the uncertainties concerning oil supply and price, most countries have taken decisions to limit the construction of new oil-fired power stations, and in many cases existing generating units have been converted from oil to coal. This policy will be reflected in a further decrease in the role of oil in electricity production in the future.

It is clear that the demand for oil in electricity generation in the medium term will largely be determined by policy decisions and that the role of oil prices will be marginal. Of course, the energy policies of the last decade were the result of the situation in the oil market – the oil price increases, the uncertainty over future prices and supply and the desire to ensure a secure fuel supply for electricity generation. Lower oil prices may increase oil demand in the short run by allowing a greater utilization of the existing oil-fired generating capacity, particularly in countries with over-capacity where coal predominates and where multi-fuel capacity exists. In those countries where oil has mainly been replaced by nuclear power, or where the expansion of nuclear programmes is planned, the demand for oil will most probably continue to fall, regardless of oil prices. Of course, if political attitudes towards nuclear power change, and nuclear programmes are curtailed or abolished, as is planned in Sweden for example, oil demand may well rise again in the long run.

3   An Econometric Analysis of the Demand for Oil Products

Joyce Dargay

3.1 Introduction

Although a few energy demand studies were carried out prior to 1974, the first oil crisis created a new interest in, and a greater impetus to study, the factors determining energy demand. Producers were concerned primarily with consumers' reaction to the higher oil prices, i.e. with the effects these higher prices would have on the demand for their products. Governments of consuming countries, on the other hand, were interested in the effects that higher energy prices would have on their economies and the possibility of reducing energy or oil demand and encouraging substitution towards alternative (possibly domestic) energy sources. The ability to forecast energy demand took on a new significance for producers and policy-makers alike, so that the question of the price sensitivity of energy demand became one of the utmost importance. As a result, enormous efforts went into the analysis of energy demand. Theoretical and empirical models were developed and numerous applied studies were carried out.

The overwhelming majority of these studies were based on econometric models, using statistical methods to estimate demand elasticities on the basis of historical data. There are obviously drawbacks to this approach: there are many reasons why future demand relationships need not conform to patterns observed in the past. This is particularly so in cases where the events to be explained differ drastically from those of past experience. Energy demand, and especially oil demand, provide good examples. The spectacular oil price rises of the 1970s were in marked contradistinction to the general pattern of slowly falling real oil prices of the previous decades. In general, the variation in energy prices prior to 1974 was minimal. As a result, energy price elasticities estimated solely on the basis of pre-1974 data were generally very low and often not significantly different from zero. As post-1974 data became available and were included in the estimations, the picture began to change.

The empirical evidence obtained in the more recent studies strongly supports the view that energy prices are of far greater importance in determining energy demand than was previously believed. However, the estimates of energy price elasticities fall in a rather wide range, and a great deal of uncertainty still exists concerning the effect of energy prices on demand. This is true not only for total energy demand, but also for the demand for individual energy forms such as oil and electricity, and even for particular energy sources – such as a given oil product – in a specific end use in an individual country.

Despite the abundance of econometric studies of oil demand for individual countries or groups of countries, the empirical evidence on the demand for individual petroleum products in Europe *as a whole* is rather limited. There are, for example, numerous studies of total oil demand and gasoline demand, but very few on diesel or heavy fuel oil. There are many studies published for the USA, but relatively few for Europe. Of those available, few include post-1980 data in the analysis. Perhaps more comprehensive and up-to-date investigations exist for individual countries, but these results are not easily accessible, and in any case it would be difficult to draw general conclusions from them as the underlying data and model specifications would not necessarily be comparable.

The aim of this chapter is to provide a set of estimates of the demand elasticities for specific petroleum products in OECD European countries, using a common model and estimation technique and comparable data. Because of the probable structural differences between countries, which may have a bearing upon the demand relationships, each country is treated individually. There appear to be few studies involving many countries that do this, so the results of applying a common methodology to a large group of countries should be of interest in themselves.

The coverage is therefore rather extensive – sixteen countries and five categories of end-use product are considered. In contrast with the approach adopted in many other studies, we estimate demand in each country separately, instead of using a combination of time-series and cross-sectional data, since empirical results based on the aggregation of data on countries with such vast differences in production structures, access to competing energy forms and energy policies may give misleading information about their adjustment to oil price changes, particularly in the short and medium term. Similarly, disaggregation in terms of the end uses of particular oil products is equally important. For example, the uses of light fuel oil – for industrial purposes, in residential heating and as automotive fuel – are vastly different, with correspondingly different possibilities for substitution, and one would hardly expect the demand relationships to be identical. The five

categories of end-use product that we consider are: gasoline; automotive diesel; light fuel oil in the agricultural, residential, commercial
and public sectors; light fuel oil in industry; and heavy fuel oil in
industry.

The main questions addressed are:

(a) How do the price elasticities of the various products compare?
    Which are most/least price sensitive?
(b) What is the time-structure of the price response? What are the
    effects on demand after one year, five years, etc.? Does the speed
    of adjustment vary for the different products and end uses?
(c) Do price and income/output elasticities vary amongst countries?

However, we cannot hope to answer these questions conclusively.
Given the large number of countries, oil products and end uses
considered, the models used, of necessity, must be simple ones. It is,
for example, beyond the scope of this study comprehensively to model
and analyse the interdependence between oil demand and the consumption of alternative energy products. Moreover, given that the
data sample only extends up until 1985, we are unable either to
analyse the effects of the 1986 price collapse or to ascertain the extent
to which the demand relationships estimated will hold for a further
downward trend in prices.

3.2 The Model

The analysis of the demand for oil products should ideally treat oil
demand in the context of total energy demand and in conjunction
with the substitution among alternative energy forms. At the same
time, the model should allow for the dynamic nature of the demand
responses, so that both short- and long-term elasticities may be estimated. Although it is possible to formulate models that capture
inter-fuel substitution and dynamic adjustment separately, it is not a
simple matter to capture both of these in a single model. A few studies
have attempted to do so, particularly in the area of industrial energy
demand, but rarely with totally satisfactory results. The theoretical
and econometric problems involved, in combination with the stringent data requirements, make such an approach too ambitious for the
present study. We must therefore restrict ourselves to fairly simple
model specifications.

The results presented below are therefore based on simple, single-
equation, reduced-form models, in which the demand for each product is treated separately and in isolation from the demand for other

forms of energy. The relationship between energy and the capital
stock is accounted for implicitly by allowing the response to changes
in the exogenous variables to be distributed over time, so that both
short- and long-run demand relationships can be estimated. The
partial nature of our approach makes it difficult, however, to gain any
firm understanding of the mechanism behind the adjustment to oil
price changes, and in particular of the possibilities of inter-fuel substitution.

The model employed is based on the partial-adjustment hypothesis
which assumes that actual demand diverges from the desired or
long-run equilibrium level because of constraints imposed by the
technical characteristics of the present capital stock and the rate at
which it could be replaced. In this approach, one begins by specifying
the long-run demand function. The model estimated assumes a logarithmic functional form which relates the desired, or long-run demand
$Q*_t$ for a particular oil product to its price P_t^o, the prices of substitute
energy forms P_t^s and some measure of income Y_t:

$$\ln Q*_t = \alpha + \beta_1 \ln P_t^o + \beta_2 \ln P_t^s + \beta_3 \ln Y_t \tag{1}$$

Because of the inflexibility of the capital stock or the costs involved in
changing the stock rapidly, the actual change in demand between
period $t - 1$ and period t will diverge from the desired change. The
adjustment mechanism in the logarithmic case is:

$$\ln Q_t - \ln Q_{t-1} = \phi(\ln Q*_t - \ln Q_{t-1}) \tag{2}$$

where ϕ represents the adjustment coefficient, i.e. the proportion of
the desired adjustment that occurs within one time-period. The closer
ϕ is to unity, the greater is the adjustment made in the current period.
Combining (1) and (2) gives:

$$\ln Q_t = \alpha\phi + \beta_1\phi \ln P_t^o + \beta_2\phi \ln P_t^s + \beta_3\phi \ln Y_t + (1 - \phi)\ln Q_{t-1} \tag{3}$$

The short-run price and income elasticities are given simply by the
coefficients of these variables, while the long-run elasticities are calculated as the short-run elasticities divided by the adjustment coefficient
ϕ which is obtained from the coefficient of the lagged consumption
term. In a similar fashion, the response after various time-intervals
can be calculated. Finally, an indication of the speed of adjustment
can be given by the median lag, which is defined as the time required
for half of the total adjustment (or long-run response) to changes in

the independent variables to take place. The median lags are calculated as:

$$T = \ln 0.5/\ln (1-\phi) \tag{4}$$

3.3 The Empirical Results: Introductory Remarks

The countries covered in the study are all the OECD European countries with the exceptions of Iceland, Luxembourg and Turkey, while the data sample covers the period 1960–85. Some countries are excluded totally from the analysis of certain products, or in some cases included with shorter observation periods, either owing to the lack of adequate price data or because of changes in the classification of the consumption data.

The particular products investigated are: gasoline, light fuel oil (gas/diesel oils) and heavy fuel oil (residual fuel oil). The minor products – LPG, jet fuel, naphtha and kerosine – are excluded because of the lack of price data. The products considered accounted, however, for nearly 85 per cent of total oil consumption in 1985, so the exclusion of the minor products is not too serious.

Light and heavy fuel oils are further disaggregated by end-use category. Because of the differences in user groups and the varying possibilities for substitution in different uses, one would expect considerable variations in price responses. This is also the consensus of most energy demand studies that attempt to disaggregate the various products by end use.

For light fuel oil, consumption of automotive diesel, consumption by industry and consumption in the 'other' sector (agricultural, residential, public and commercial) are estimated separately. It can be noted that in 1985, automotive diesel accounted for approximately one-third of all light fuel oil consumption, about 12 per cent was used in industry, and slightly more than half in the 'other' sector, predominantly for space heating. The remaining 4 per cent of consumption, which is used for non-road transport such as railways and navigation, is excluded from the analysis.

The analysis of the demand for heavy fuel oil pertains solely to industrial consumption. Industry refers to manufacturing and extractive industries, with the exclusion of the energy extraction, production and transformation sectors. The industrial sector so defined accounted for around 41 per cent of the total consumption of heavy fuel oil in 1985. Heavy fuel oil use in public electricity generation, which makes up about one-third of the total, is excluded from the analysis. It is very difficult – if not impossible – to study this segment of demand econometrically. Any attempt to do so would require models quite different from those used here. The long time-lags involved in the planning process and in the construction of power plants, and thus the importance of price expectations as well as the availability of other means of electricity generation, for example the existence of hydroelectric sources, would have to be taken into consideration. Most problematic, however, is the development of nuclear power, which is in part a political, rather than a purely economic, decision in many countries. Also excluded from the analysis are heavy fuel oil consumption in the 'other' sector, co-generation of electricity in industry, district heating and the transport sector, which together accounted for less than 25 per cent of heavy fuel oil use in 1985.

3.4 Results on Demand for Gasoline and Automotive Diesel in Road Transport

Because of the possibility of substitution between gasoline and diesel for road transport, the demand for these two products will be discussed together. Generally speaking, oil consumption for road transport is comprised of three different usages: private automobile transport, public transport (buses and taxis) and commercial goods transport. Given the different natures of these, the probable differences in their development over time and the different possibilities for substitution in each particular use, one might also expect the demand relationships to differ. For this reason, it would be preferable to be able to model demand in each user group separately. The available data, however, do not allow this distinction, so that the analysis of gasoline and diesel consumption pertain to road transport as a whole.

It is generally assumed in demand studies that total gasoline consumption for road transport can be equated with consumption by private cars, while diesel consumption relates mainly to consumption by commercial vehicles. Although this is largely the case, the extent to which this is true varies from country to country. For example, according to EEC sources, over 70 per cent of light commercial vehicles (below 3,500 kg) in Germany were diesel driven in the late 1970s. The figures for France and Belgium (vehicles below 4,000 kg) were less than 20 per cent. Clearly, a larger percentage of gasoline demand in the latter two countries relates to commercial vehicles. In the UK, one of the countries with the lowest diesel penetration, estimates for 1980 indicate that gasoline accounted for more than one-third of oil use for goods transport, and that about 15 per cent of gasoline consumption could be attributed to commercial vehicles.

Unfortunately, we have no comparable information on the other European countries. Since the breakdown in use of the individual fuels differs across countries, if the demand relationships for the two user groups are not identical, then the estimated elasticities for the individual countries will reflect this.

Another problem resulting from the lack of more specific information on the use of the individual products is the inability to estimate the impact of the substitution of diesel- for gasoline-driven cars that has taken place in many European countries during the past ten years. This has also varied considerably among countries. For example the EEC estimates that in 1986 diesel cars represented about 18 per cent of new car registrations in the EEC as a whole. The highest diesel shares – over 25 per cent – were found in Germany, Belgium and Italy. The corresponding figure for these countries in the late 1970s was less than 5 per cent. The countries with the lowest proportions of diesel-driven cars, Greece, the UK and Denmark, had shares in the number of new registrations of 0, 4 and 6 per cent respectively in 1986. In the remaining countries – Austria, France, Ireland, the Netherlands and Spain – the share of diesel cars in new registrations was somewhere between 13 and 17 per cent. In all of these countries the market share of diesel cars increased markedly from the late 1970s onwards.

All of this suggests that the breakdown in the use of the individual fuels for private as opposed to commercial transport varies amongst the different countries. Keeping this in mind, we will proceed to a presentation and discussion of the results of the econometric analysis for gasoline and automotive diesel.

(*a*) *Gasoline.* The estimates for the partial-adjustment model for gasoline are shown in Table 3.1. The dependent variable Q_G is total gasoline consumption, and $Q_{G(-1)}$ is consumption in the previous year. Real private household consumption, C, is taken as a measure of disposable income. This is a usual assumption, and although it does not account for changes in wealth, past experience shows this omission to have negligible effects. P_G is the price of gasoline deflated by the consumer price index. A dummy variable D_R, set equal to 1 for the year 1974 and 0 for all other years, is included to account for the effects of the gasoline rationing that was imposed during the oil crisis in many of the countries. Since 1974 was also a year of high price increases, omitting the dummy variable could cause the price effect to be over-estimated, since the decrease in consumption achieved by rationing might be falsely attributed to the price rise. The constant term is denoted by k.

Table 3.1: Estimated Parameters for Gasoline Demand. 1960–85.

	P_G	C	$Q_{G(-1)}$	D_R	k	R^2	DWS
Austria	−0.31	0.24	0.81	−0.08	−0.97	0.99	1.96
	(4.39)	(1.53)	(9.36)	(2.69)	(0.76)		
Belgium	−0.42	0.42	0.65	−0.06	−2.05	0.99	1.77
	(5.33)	(2.40)	(5.31)	(2.08)	(1.50)		
Denmark	−0.37	0.39	0.43	−0.06	−0.05	0.99	2.02
	(11.53)	(7.45)	(8.10)	(2.26)	(0.19)		
Finland	−0.22	0.19	0.82	−0.09	−0.63	0.99	1.78
	(3.42)	(1.78)	(14.5)	(2.86)	(0.81)		
France	−0.34	0.31	0.68	−0.02	−0.95	0.99	2.00
	(9.49)	(4.19)	(11.9)	(2.01)	(2.04)		
Germany	−0.29	0.49	0.60	−0.03	−2.55	0.99	2.18
	(6.16)	(4.12)	(8.59)	(1.17)	(2.83)		
Greece	−0.25	1.91	n.a.	−0.03	−18.44	0.99	1.45
	(3.25)	(43.9)	(0.54)	(45.2)			
Ireland	−0.12	0.68	0.60	−0.05	−3.19	0.99	1.99
	(5.74)	(1.51)	(5.74)	(2.50)	(3.32)		
Italy	−0.23	0.23	0.77	0.14	−0.82	0.99	1.99
	(3.07)	(1.60)	(7.60)	(6.22)	(0.45)		
Netherlands	−0.19	0.19	0.52	−0.12	1.71	0.90	1.84
	(4.33)	(0.69)	(2.42)	(2.21)	(0.93)		
Norway	−0.28	0.22	0.81	−0.09	−0.85	0.99	2.18
	(5.61)	(2.63)	(14.6)	(4.14)	(1.57)		
Portugal	−0.33	0.44	0.71	−0.10	−2.93	0.99	1.79
	(6.21)	(3.03)	(7.34)	(3.01)	(2.24)		
Spain	−0.12	0.51	0.71	−0.08	−5.19	0.99	2.16
	(0.94)	(0.88)	(2.94)	(2.35)	(0.69)		
Sweden	−0.21	0.86	0.38	−0.13	−5.48	0.99	1.63
	(4.23)	(5.42)	(3.86)	(9.64)	(4.48)		
Switzerland	−0.13	1.02	0.35	−0.04	−6.64	0.99	1.77
	(0.94)	(2.96)	(1.82)	(1.14)	(2.63)		
UK	−0.16	0.20	0.88	−0.04	−1.35	0.99	1.99
	(5.95)	(2.69)	(25.2)	(2.84)	(2.43)		

Note: The figures given in parentheses for this and all subsequent tables are *t*-values.

In addition to the specification shown, models including the *current* diesel price as well as various past diesel prices were also estimated. The reason for including past diesel prices is that the substitution between diesel and gasoline requires changes in the car stock, and it may be that there is some delay before the effects become apparent. However, no significant indication of cross-price effects was noted for any of the countries other than for Belgium and Portugal, where the diesel price appears to have had a small but positive effect. For this reason the results presented here are based on the model excluding the diesel price.

The lack of significance of the diesel price seems surprising for a number of reasons. First, the share of diesel in total consumption for road transport increased from 26 per cent in 1970 to 37 per cent in 1985 in the OECD European countries. We would expect this change to reflect a substitution away from gasoline- towards diesel-powered vehicles. Secondly, the use of diesel-engined vehicles for private and commercial transport appears to have grown in at least some of the countries, as have the numbers of makes and models of diesel cars available.

The explanation for our results may be found in the development of relative prices. In the majority of the countries, the rate of increase of diesel prices was slightly higher than that of gasoline prices over most of the observation period, mainly as a result of the lower level of taxation levied on diesel. It is thus not surprising that relative price changes were not found to have a significant effect on gasoline consumption. However, the incentives to use diesel fuel may have increased. In some countries, for example Germany and Austria, tax incentives were introduced which favour diesel cars. The price of diesel is still appreciably lower than that of gasoline, and the diesel engine is much more fuel efficient than the gasoline engine so that fuel costs per kilometre are significantly lower for diesel vehicles. On the other hand, diesel cars are more expensive and generally more highly taxed than their equivalent gasoline models. As fuel prices increase, fuel costs become a larger proportion of total running costs (i.e. fuel costs plus capital costs plus road tax etc.). For this reason, diesel cars will become more competitive as oil prices rise, given that all other costs remain constant. This, combined with the fact that higher prices tend to make consumers more price conscious, probably accounts for the increase in diesel consumption.

Returning to Table 3.1, we see that all the estimated parameters are of the expected sign, and that they are statistically significant in the overwhelming majority of cases. The gasoline price is seen to have had a negative effect on gasoline consumption, and income a positive effect. The estimated coefficients of the lagged consumption variable are greater than zero and less than one, indicating that adjustment is not instantaneous and that the lag structure is therefore of an acceptable form. The only exception was in the case of Greece, for which the coefficient of the lagged demand variable was not significantly different from zero, indicating that the full adjustment occurs within one year. For this reason, the results presented in this case are based on a static model, i.e. one in which the lagged demand variable is not included. Finally, we see that the dummy variable for rationing in 1974 was significantly negative in all instances, suggesting that rationing *did* serve to decrease demand as one would expect.

The explanatory power of the model is very good, as witnessed by the high R^2 values; and the Durbin–Watson statistics suggest that the errors are not serially correlated. The Durbin–Watson statistic is of course not strictly applicable in models with lagged dependent variables, but the existence of autocorrelation was investigated by other methods and corrected for by appropriate estimation techniques where it was deemed appropriate.[1]

The implied price and income elasticities in the short run, after five years, and in the long run (which indicates full adjustment), are presented in Table 3.2. We see that the response of demand to price and income changes varies considerably for the different countries. The short-run own-price elasticity is generally quite small, lying in the region of -0.1 to -0.4. The spread in the long run is considerably greater, with the estimated elasticities falling in a range from -0.2 in Switzerland to -1.6 in Austria. In eight of the sixteen countries, demand is inelastic (the absolute value of the price elasticity is less than 1), even in the long run.

The differences in the reaction to gasoline price changes amongst countries can depend on many factors: the availability and convenience of alternative means of transport, the practicality and expense of switching to other fuels, the degree of the price rise, the income level and consumers' preferences. All of these can vary among countries and some are clearly difficult, if not impossible, to measure. Unfortunately, there seems to be no obvious way of explaining the wide differences among countries.

The income elasticities also vary somewhat, although these are greater than unity in the long run in twelve of the countries. Again, there seems to be no clear-cut explanation for the differences noted. The income elasticities appear to be highest for the countries with the lowest incomes – Greece, Ireland, Portugal and Spain. However, some high-income countries, most notably Switzerland and the UK, have equally high elasticities.

The adjustment coefficient, ϕ, and the median lag are also shown in

[1] The Cochrane–Orcutt procedure was used for all estimations. In those cases where the estimated autocorrelation coefficient was statistically different from zero, the resulting estimates were used in place of the OLS estimates.

Table 3.2: Estimated Elasticities for Gasoline Demand. 1960–85.

	Price			Income			φ	Median Lag
	Short-run	Five-year	Long-run	Short-run	Five-year	Long-run		
Austria	−0.31	−1.06	−1.60	0.24	0.82	1.23	0.19	3.2
Belgium	−0.42	−1.07	−1.21	0.42	1.06	1.21	0.35	1.6
Denmark	−0.37	−0.64	−0.65	0.39	0.67	0.68	0.57	0.8
Finland	−0.22	−0.77	−1.22	0.19	0.66	1.06	0.18	3.5
France	−0.34	−0.91	−1.06	0.31	0.83	0.97	0.32	1.8
Germany	−0.29	−0.67	−0.73	0.49	1.13	1.23	0.40	1.3
Greece	−0.25	−0.25	−0.25	1.91	1.91	1.91	1.00	0.0
Ireland	−0.12	−0.28	−0.30	0.68	1.57	1.70	0.40	1.3
Italy	−0.23	−0.73	−1.00	0.23	0.73	1.00	0.23	2.6
Netherlands	−0.19	−0.38	−0.40	0.19	0.38	0.40	0.48	1.0
Norway	−0.28	−0.95	−1.47	0.22	0.75	1.16	0.19	3.3
Portugal	−0.33	−0.94	−1.16	0.44	1.26	1.55	0.29	2.0
Spain[a]	(−0.12)	(−0.34)	(−0.41)	0.51	1.44	1.76	0.29	2.0
Sweden	−0.21	−0.34	−0.34	0.86	1.38	1.39	0.62	0.7
Switzerland[a]	(−0.13)	(−0.19)	(−0.19)	1.02	1.56	1.56	0.65	0.6
UK	−0.16	−0.63	−1.33	0.20	0.79	1.67	0.12	5.4
Average[b]	−0.25	−0.67	−0.91	0.40	0.97	1.26		

Notes: (a) Elasticities in parentheses are based on parameters that are not
significantly different from zero.
(b) Average of the elasticities of all countries weighted by their shares in
consumption in 1985.

the last two columns. Between 12 and 65 per cent of the total adjustment occurs within one year of the price/income change (except in the
case of Greece for which adjustment within the year is indicated). It is
also seen that 50 per cent of the total response is achieved after
between one and five years, with an average of somewhere in the
region of two years.

At the bottom of Table 3.2 the weighted averages of these elasticities for OECD Europe as a whole are given. The elasticities for the
individual countries are weighted by their respective shares of total
European gasoline consumption in 1985. The short- and long-run
price elasticities are shown to be −0.25 and −0.91 respectively and
the corresponding income elasticities are 0.40 and 1.26 respectively.

The estimates presented above are based on the assumption that
the demand relationships remained unchanged over the entire
observation period. Given the vast differences in the development of
prices before and after the first oil 'shock' of 1973–4, and the

differences in estimated elasticities based on different sample periods
noted in other studies, this assumption may not be justified. In order
to investigate the structural stability of the demand relationships, the
sample was divided into two sub-periods, 1960–73 and 1974–85, and
the elasticities for each sub-period were estimated separately. By
contrasting the sum of the residual sums of squares for the two
sub-periods with that of the restricted model, we can test for the
equivalence of the estimated parameters. If the errors are significantly
reduced by allowing for differential parameters, the hypothesis of a
common structure must be rejected.

The results of these tests indicated that the hypothesis of a common
structure can not be rejected for the majority of countries. Even for the
two countries for which the test statistics indicate a structural difference in the overall demand relationship between the two periods,
there is no evidence of different price or income elasticities. The fact
that we are unable to reject the hypothesis of a common structure for
the two sub-periods does not mean, however, that estimates based on
pre-1974 data are identical to those based on data from the later
period. For ten of the sixteen countries, the own-price elasticities
estimated on the basis of pre-1974 data alone are not significantly
different from zero, and in most cases they are quite different from
those based on data from the later period. Generally speaking, the
coefficients based on the individual sub-samples are poorly determined, so that any difference between them could not be supported on
statistical grounds.

(b) *Automotive Diesel.* The analysis of diesel consumption for road
transport is based on a model similar to that used for gasoline. Since
we can safely assume that the larger part of diesel consumption relates
to commercial vehicles, GDP rather than private consumption is used
as the income variable and prices are deflated using the GDP deflator.
Besides the price of diesel, the gasoline price is also included in an
attempt to measure any cross-price response. Models with lags of up
to three years for the gasoline price were estimated.

In most instances, the majority of the estimated own-price elasticities were not statistically significantly different from zero. Attempts to
lag the price of diesel – to allow for any delayed price response – did
not lead to any substantial change in the results, and the results
presented below are those based on estimations with only the diesel
price in the current year.

From Table 3.3 we see that the coefficient of the price of diesel is
generally negative, but significantly so in only five of the countries –
Austria, Ireland, Norway, Sweden and Switzerland. On the other

hand, the gasoline price has a significantly positive influence on diesel demand in eight of the countries. The coefficients of the income variable are all positive, as would be expected, and in all cases highly significant. In three cases – Austria, France and Norway – the coefficient of the lagged consumption variable is not significantly different

Table 3.3: Estimated Parameters for Automotive Diesel Demand. 1960–85.

	P_D	GDP	$Q_{D(-1)}$	P_G	k	R^2	DWS
Austria[a]	−0.48	1.60	−0.13	–	−13.63	0.97	2.46
	(3.10)	(4.09)	(0.50)		(3.87)		
Belgium	−0.07	0.83	0.57	0.41	−10.31	0.97	2.16
	(0.44)	(2.19)	(2.54)	(2.16)	(2.20)		
Denmark	−0.11	0.97	0.62	0.37	−10.38	0.95	2.08
	(0.83)	(1.86)	(3.65)	(1.81)	(1.80)		
Finland	0.02	0.49	0.57	–	−2.95	0.99	1.87
	(0.34)	(3.16)	(5.45)		(2.44)		
France	−0.06	1.73	0.11	–	−17.59	0.99	1.60
	(0.85)	(4.07)	(0.54)		(3.97)		
Germany	−0.08	0.79	0.51	0.28	−6.79	0.99	2.10
	(0.82)	(3.41)	(3.51)	(3.53)	(3.40)		
Greece[b]	−0.19	1.47	0.53	–	−17.40	0.84	1.55
	(0.71)	(2.20)	(2.35)		(2.11)		
Ireland	−0.59	0.74	0.60	0.69	−4.39	0.96	1.94
	(2.79)	(2.07)	(3.37)	(3.08)	(1.99)		
Italy	0.01	0.31	0.79	0.37	−6.57	0.99	1.68
	(0.10)	(1.77)	(9.08)	(4.20)	(1.98)		
Netherlands	0.06	0.57	0.73	0.55	−5.28	0.99	1.98
	(1.02)	(3.03)	(8.18)	(2.92)	(2.86)		
Norway[c]	−0.32	1.69	0.21	–	−15.78	0.97	2.03
	(2.49)	(2.43)	(0.72)		(2.35)		
Portugal[b]	−0.14	0.77	0.68	0.38	−9.57	0.99	1.93
	(1.40)	(2.26)	(3.87)	(2.32)	(2.33)		
Spain	0.25	0.83	0.54	–	−10.65	0.95	1.53
	(1.95)	(2.78)	(3.43)		(2.63)		
Sweden[d]	−0.20	0.87	0.28	–	−6.21	0.70	2.44
	(3.50)	(2.05)	(2.01)		(1.08)		
Switzerland	−0.44	0.67	0.56	0.53	−5.31	0.74	1.65
	(1.86)	(2.56)	(3.52)	(1.85)	(2.05)		
UK	−0.11	0.53	0.60	–	−3.15	0.98	0.81
	(0.77)	(2.80)	(5.04)		(2.14)		

Notes: (a) Sample period 1960–78.
   (b) Sample period 1970–85.
   (c) Sample period 1960–76.
   (d) Sample period 1975–85.

from zero, indicating instantaneous adjustment. Generally, the results are quite acceptable from an economic point of view, and judging from the high R^2 the fit of the model is rather good.

The elasticity estimates are shown in Table 3.4. The results indicate that the short-run own-price elasticity is very small – if not zero – for most countries, as is the long-run own-price effect. The relationship between the short- and long-run elasticities, of course, follows from the lag structure assumed. The speed of adjustment appears to be quite rapid, with a median lag of less than two years in most cases. Diesel demand seems to have been most price sensitive in Ireland, with an estimated own-price elasticity of -1.48, and a cross-price elasticity of 1.73, indicating substantial substitution of diesel for gasoline. This is well in accordance with the large increase in the share of diesel in total consumption for road transport in this country and the growth of the diesel-engined car stock. As Ireland is one of the few countries where the price of diesel actually decreased in comparison with the price of gasoline over much of the period, this substitution appears to be directly price related. The other country displaying high own- and cross-price elasticities is Switzerland. However, despite these high elasticities, there seems to have been little substitution between 1970 and 1985. The reason for this is that the prices of diesel and gasoline followed each other closely during this period, so that the own-price and cross-price effects will have cancelled out.

The other countries with significant own-price elasticities – Austria, Norway and Sweden – show no cross-price effects. Of these, only Austria experienced an increase in the share of diesel in oil consumption for road transport in the past fifteen years, and the corresponding shares for Norway and Sweden are among the lowest in Europe. In itself, this seems to suggest that there was little inter-fuel substitution in these latter two countries. Furthermore, in all of these countries, adjustment appears to have been more-or-less instantaneous. None of these results, is based on the full observation period, however, because of breaks in the data on either consumption or prices.

When they are significantly different from zero, the cross-price elasticities fall in the intervals 0.3–0.7 and 0.6–2.0, in the short and long run respectively. In some cases, these appear to be unacceptably large. Interestingly, with the exceptions of Germany and Switzerland, the countries displaying significant cross-price effects are those where the share of diesel in oil consumption for road transport increased most during the period from 1970 to 1985. Finally, the average elasticities for Europe are given at the foot of Table 3.4. We find that the own-price effect is minimal, even in the long run, while the gasoline price has a considerable effect on diesel demand. The

Table 3.4: Estimated Elasticities for Automotive Diesel Demand. 1960–85.

	Own Price			Income			Gasoline Price			φ	Median Lag
	Short-run	Five-year	Long-run	Short-run	Five-year	Long-run	Short-run	Five-year	Long-run		
Austria[a]	-0.48	-0.48	-0.48	1.60	1.60	1.60	0.00	0.00	0.00	1.00	0.0
Belgium[b]	(-0.07)	(-0.16)	(-0.17)	0.83	1.81	1.93	0.42	0.79	0.96	0.43	1.2
Denmark[b]	(-0.11)	(-0.27)	(-0.29)	0.97	2.33	2.58	0.37	0.75	0.99	0.38	1.5
Finland[b]	(0.02)	(0.04)	(0.05)	0.49	1.07	1.14	0.00	0.00	0.00	0.43	1.2
France[b]	(-0.06)	(-0.06)	(-0.06)	1.73	1.73	1.73	0.00	0.00	0.00	1.00	0.0
Germany[b]	(-0.08)	(-0.15)	(-0.16)	0.79	1.57	1.63	0.28	0.49	0.57	0.49	1.0
Greece[bc]	(-0.19)	(-0.39)	(-0.40)	1.47	3.00	3.13	0.00	0.00	0.00	0.47	1.1
Ireland	-0.59	-1.36	-1.48	0.74	1.71	1.85	0.69	1.35	1.73	0.40	1.4
Italy	(0.01)	(0.03)	(0.04)	0.31	1.02	1.46	0.37	0.88	1.72	0.21	2.9
Netherlands	(0.06)	(0.19)	(0.23)	0.57	1.68	2.13	0.55	1.24	2.06	0.27	2.2
Norway[d]	-0.32	-0.32	-0.32	1.69	1.69	1.69	0.00	0.00	0.00	1.00	0.0
Portugal[bc]	(-0.14)	(-0.37)	(-0.44)	0.77	2.06	2.41	0.38	0.81	1.19	0.32	1.8
Spain	0.25	0.52	0.54	0.83	1.72	1.80	0.00	0.00	0.00	0.46	1.1
Sweden[e]	-0.20	-0.28	-0.28	0.87	1.21	1.21	0.00	0.00	0.00	0.72	0.6
Switzerland	-0.44	-0.94	-1.00	0.67	1.45	1.53	0.53	0.99	1.20	0.44	1.2
UK	(-0.11)	(-0.25)	(-0.28)	0.53	1.22	1.33	0.00	0.00	0.00	0.40	1.4
Average[f]	-0.08	-0.13	-0.14	0.88	1.53	1.68	0.19	0.41	0.64		

Notes: (a) Sample period 1960–78.
(b) Elasticities in parentheses are based on parameters that are not significantly different from zero.
(c) Sample period 1970–85.
(d) Sample period 1960–76.
(e) Sample period 1975–85.
(f) Average of the elasticities of all countries weighted by 1985 consumption shares, with positive own-price elasticities set equal to zero.

inelasticity of diesel demand is perhaps not surprising, since the majority of this consumption is for commercial transport for which there is no obvious alternative. Also, the evidence strongly suggests that a switch from gasoline- to diesel-driven vehicles served to increase the demand for diesel, but that this occurred chiefly as a result of rises in gasoline prices.

As in the case of gasoline, no indication of structural change in the demand relationships was found for the pre- and post-1974 periods.

To summarize our results for automotive fuels, the evidence strongly suggests that the demand for gasoline has been far more price sensitive than the demand for diesel. There appears to have been a certain degree of substitution away from gasoline towards diesel, but little of this can be explained in terms of changes in their relative prices. The gasoline price seems to have been the moving force, affecting both the demand for gasoline itself and the demand for diesel through substitution. The negligible effect of the diesel price can be explained by the close similarity in the development of the prices of diesel and gasoline in the majority of countries during the period. If relative prices develop differently in the future, substitution relationships may be quite different.

3.5 Oil Demand in the Agricultural, Residential, Commercial and Public Sectors

The demand for oil in this 'other' sector can basically be regarded as the demand for space heating. Since there are a number of alternative heating sources, oil consumption will partially be determined by the availability of substitutes and their relative prices.

Given the obvious importance of inter-fuel substitution, the demand for oil in this sector should ideally be modelled in the context of total energy demand, in which the consumption levels of alternative energy products are determined simultaneously. As discussed earlier, however, time and data limitations do not allow this sort of approach, so that again we must resort to simple, single-equation model formulations. This, of course, limits the information that can be gained from our results. More particularly, we will be unable to distinguish between energy or oil conservation and inter-fuel substitution.

The model chosen is again that presented earlier, with only income and prices as explanatory variables. Since the larger part of oil consumption in this sector is for residential heating, real private consumption is used as the income variable and prices are deflated with the consumer price index. Further, as oil consumption in this sector is largely for heating, demand will clearly be affected by temperature variations. As our data are annual, some variation in demand may be explained by the fact that winters in some years were colder or warmer than in others. It would thus be desirable to include some measure of temperature variation in the demand equation. Unfortunately, we do not have the necessary information on degree days for all the countries over the entire sample period. Omitting this variable from the demand equation will most probably reduce the explanatory power of the estimated model. The effects on the estimated elasticities will depend, however, on the degree of correlation between annual temperature variations and the price and income variables. If there is little or no correlation between these – which one can probably safely assume – the effects will be minimal. Since we are primarily interested in the elasticity estimates, rather than in forecasting oil demand, the omission of the temperature variable should not be serious.

In an attempt to estimate price-related inter-fuel substitution, models were estimated including substitute prices – of natural gas, electricity and coal – in combination and individually and with lags of up to five years. In very few instances, however, was the substitute price found to have a positive and statistically significant effect. In general, the results are extremely difficult to interpret in any meaningful way. This is perhaps not surprising given the partiality of our approach. In effect, we are attempting to measure inter-fuel substitution on the basis of only one of a system of simultaneously-determined demand equations. The demand elasticities for the various energy forms are obviously interrelated, and by basing estimates of these solely on the demand equation for oil, we have no assurance that they are consistent with the actual consumption of other energy products.

Since the models that include the prices of alternative energy forms were unable to capture the effects of cross-price substitution, the results presented in Tables 3.5 and 3.6 are based on the model that includes only the oil price.

The estimated parameters, R^2 values and Durbin–Watson statistics are presented in Table 3.5. We see that the estimated parameters are generally of the correct sign and significantly so. Judging from the high R^2 values and Durbin–Watson statistics, the model performs rather well. The most obvious exception is in the case of Portugal, where both the price and income coefficients are of the incorrect sign and the fit of the model is quite poor. It should be noted, however, that the estimates for Portugal are based on a shorter sample period than the other countries (1970–85).

The resulting price and income elasticities are displayed in Table 3.6. Excluding Spain, where the elasticities are not significantly different from zero, the own-price elasticities fall in the interval from −0.2

Table 3.5: Estimated Parameters for Light Fuel Oil Demand in the Agricultural, Residential, Commercial and Public Sectors. 1960–85.

	P_{LFO}	C	$Q_{LFO(-1)}$	k	R^2	DWS
Austria	−0.76	0.64	0.68	0.27	0.98	1.95
	(5.67)	(2.83)	(8.13)	(0.14)		
Belgium	−0.44	1.00	0.51	−6.43	0.97	2.00
	(3.63)	(2.69)	(3.58)	(2.00)		
Denmark	−0.27	0.85	0.63	−5.37	0.96	1.91
	(3.88)	(2.49)	(7.05)	(1.75)		
Finland	−0.41	0.56	0.75	−1.63	0.98	1.99
	(3.66)	(2.30)	(12.2)	(0.96)		
France	−0.41	0.89	0.63	−6.08	0.98	1.90
	(3.87)	(2.77)	(5.78)	(2.14)		
Germany	−0.22	0.50	0.67	−2.03	0.98	2.01
	(2.87)	(1.86)	(7.23)	(0.88)		
Greece[a]	−0.61	0.99	0.63	−5.30	0.96	1.72
	(2.62)	(2.32)	(5.16)	(0.94)		
Ireland	−0.25	1.00	0.73	−5.72	0.98	2.26
	(4.46)	(2.47)	(6.77)	(2.07)		
Italy	−0.28	0.95	0.79	−12.79	0.99	1.55
	(4.81)	(3.20)	(10.2)	(2.57)		
Netherlands	−0.31	−0.05	0.81	3.89	0.95	2.12
	(2.80)	(0.31)	(11.1)	(3.95)		
Norway	−0.45	0.77	0.58	−2.83	0.97	1.93
	(5.72)	(4.35)	(6.91)	(2.64)		
Portugal[a]	0.23	−1.05	0.55	14.96	0.44	2.22
	(2.51)	(3.01)	(2.79)	(3.66)		
Spain	0.02	0.62	0.70	−7.75	0.96	1.77
	(0.18)	(1.40)	(4.56)	(1.21)		
Sweden	−0.40	1.21	0.32	−6.46	0.94	1.71
	(6.11)	(4.49)	(2.48)	(2.82)		
Switzerland	−0.20	0.63	0.61	−2.77	0.97	1.98
	(2.52)	(1.95)	(5.56)	(1.12)		
UK	−0.18	0.12	0.93	−0.04	0.99	1.96
	(3.44)	(0.54)	(16.3)	(0.01)		

Note: (a) Sample period 1970–85.

to −0.8 in the short run, and from −0.6 to −2.6 in the long run. Some of these, particularly those for Austria and the UK, seem unreasonably high. The income elasticities are also generally much higher than one would expect. Finally, from the calculated median lag we find that adjustment is rather rapid in the majority of countries, generally with half of the total response occurring within two years of the initial price rise.

Table 3.6: Estimated Elasticities for Light Fuel Oil Demand in the Agricultural, Residential, Commercial and Public Sectors. 1960–85.

	Price			Income			φ	Median Lag
	Short-run	Five-year	Long-run	Short-run	Five-year	Long-run		
Austria	−0.76	−2.03	−2.37	0.64	1.70	1.99	0.32	1.78
Belgium	−0.44	−0.87	−0.90	1.00	1.98	2.05	0.49	1.03
Denmark	−0.27	−0.66	−0.74	0.85	2.07	2.30	0.37	1.50
Finland	−0.41	−1.25	−1.64	0.56	1.74	2.24	0.25	2.41
France	−0.41	−1.00	−1.11	0.89	2.17	2.41	0.37	1.50
Germany	−0.22	−0.57	−0.66	0.50	1.32	1.53	0.33	1.74
Greece[a]	−0.62	−1.51	−1.68	0.99	2.41	2.68	0.37	1.50
Ireland	−0.25	−0.74	−0.94	1.00	2.94	3.71	0.27	2.20
Italy	−0.28	−0.92	−1.33	0.95	3.13	4.52	0.21	2.94
Netherlands[b]	−0.31	−1.05	−1.61	(−0.05)	(−0.17)	(−0.26)	0.19	3.29
Norway	−0.45	−1.00	−1.06	0.77	1.71	1.83	0.42	1.26
Portugal[a]	0.23	0.48	0.51	−1.05	−2.22	−2.33	0.45	1.16
Spain[b]	(0.02)	(0.05)	(0.06)	(0.62)	(1.72)	(2.07)	0.30	1.94
Sweden	−0.40	−0.59	−0.59	1.21	1.77	1.78	0.68	0.61
Switzerland	−0.20	−0.47	−0.52	0.63	1.48	1.62	0.39	1.39
UK[b]	−0.18	−0.78	−2.57	(0.12)	(0.52)	(1.71)	0.07	9.55
Average[c]	−0.29	−0.74	−0.96	0.70	1.79	2.20		

Notes: (a) Sample period 1970–85.
  (b) Elasticities in parentheses are based on parameters that are not significantly different from zero.
  (c) Average of the elasticities of all countries, excluding Portugal, weighted by 1985 consumption shares with those not significantly different from zero set equal to zero.

Again we find a good deal of variation in price sensitivity amongst countries, in both the short and the long term. Unfortunately, there seems to be no simple way of explaining these variations in terms of either the differences in consumption patterns and substitution possibilities discussed earlier or the development of prices. To do so in any convincing manner would require the estimation of a complete energy demand system. With the partial approach employed here, we can only assume these differences to reflect a myriad of factors: differences in the development of relative prices, the availability of alternative heating sources, energy policy decisions and so forth.

Finally, the average elasticities for Europe are presented at the foot of Table 3.6. We find that the average price elasticity is −0.3 in the short run and −1.0 in the long run, which are nearly identical to those obtained for gasoline. The income elasticities, however, are considerably higher than those for gasoline, and rather higher than one might expect.

Tests were performed to investigate the stability of the demand relationships over the pre- and post-1974 periods. Only in the case of France could we reject the hypothesis of a common structure for the two sub-periods at the 5 per cent level. The results for France indicate an increase in the price elasticity and a decrease in the income elasticity for the post-1974 period. The estimates for the majority of the other countries suggest that this may have occurred in other countries as well. Specifically, the estimated price elasticities for the pre-1974 period are generally insignificant, while those based on the post-1974 sample are significantly negative. Similarly, there is an indication that the income elasticities have decreased. However, the parameters based on the individual sub-periods are poorly determined, so that the statistical evidence is too weak for any meaningful conclusions to be drawn.

3.6 Oil Demand in Industry

Oil consumption in the industrial sector is primarily composed of light and heavy fuel oils. The demand for these two products will basically be determined by the same factors, so the same model can be applied to both. However, their demand relationships, i.e. their price and output elasticities, need not be identical, as the uses of the two products are not the same and the possibilities for substitution may differ.

Because of the importance of the effects of energy price rises in the industrial sector on the economy in general, a great deal of effort has been given to the development and empirical implementation of industrial energy demand models. It was recognized early on that the demand for energy must be seen in terms of its role in the production process. Energy is only one of many inputs in production and the demand for it is determined by the same variables as the demands for other factors of production – the level and composition of output, the technical possibilities of substitution among inputs, and relative factor prices. For this reason, and because of the difficulties encountered in attempting to estimate energy demand in this sector on the basis of simpler models, the majority of industrial energy demand studies have been based on a production (or cost) function approach. Generally, energy demand is analysed along with other production factors – labour, capital and intermediate goods – the demands for which are derived from the technical constraints of the production function and the assumption of cost-minimizing behaviour on the part of firms. By making various assumptions with regard to substitution relationships, either two-stage models that consider total energy demand and inter-fuel substitution simultaneously or partial inter-fuel substitution models can be estimated.

The majority of studies based on the production function approach rely on static model formulations. Although some information is gained about substitution relationships, virtually nothing can be said about the intertemporal response to price or output changes. Most problematic, however, is the interpretation of the results obtained from such models. The models are derived under the assumption of long-run optimizing behaviour, and should be estimated on the basis of data that represent long-run equilibria. The time-series data that are generally used to estimate the models can hardly be considered to satisfy this criterion. Numerous attempts have been made to introduce a dynamic element into the modelling of factor demand, but the empirical performance of these models has not been wholly satisfactory.

The difficulties involved in formulating and estimating dynamic production models, together with the stringent data requirements, make such an approach infeasible in the present study. We therefore restrict ourselves once again to rather simple, partial models. Clearly, the information that may be gained on the basis of such models will be limited.

Initially, the partial-adjustment model described earlier was estimated for both light and heavy fuel oil. Manufacturing production, Y, was used as a measure of output and prices were deflated using the GDP deflator. The results of this specification were, however, unacceptable. In particular, the effects of output volume on oil demand were rarely found to be significant and in many cases were negative, which is of course hardly realistic. The reason for this may be that the partial-adjustment model requires that the effects of all explanatory variables have the same distribution over time, and that long-run elasticities are greater in absolute value than short-run elasticities. This does not seem too restrictive an assumption for the demand for automotive fuels or heating oil, where one would be justified in assuming that the long-run effects of price and income are greater than the short-run effects, but the position for industrial oil demand is rather different. Clearly, the level of industrial output must be considered as a determinant of oil demand, but we have no justification for restricting the short-run output elasticity to be smaller than the long-run output elasticity. Neither does it seem reasonable to assume that the adjustment to changes in the level of output and the input price would have the same distribution over time.

An alternative model was therefore estimated in which it is assumed that oil demand reacts immediately to changes in the output level, so that the short- and long-run oil-output elasticities are constrained to be identical.

The effects of prices on demand are still assumed to follow a geometrically declining lag structure, so that both short- and long-run price elasticities can be calculated. The various specifications included the prices of alternative energy sources – coal, natural gas and electricity – with lags of up to five years. Although some indications of significant cross-price effects were noted in a few of the countries in the heavy fuel oil demand equations, no set of consistent results could be found. In most cases cross-price elasticities were not significant and in many instances they were of the wrong sign. Our doubts about the possibility of estimating inter-fuel substitution on the basis of the oil demand equation alone are unfortunately confirmed.

There are, however, other factors that may have influenced our results. Much of the decline in oil demand was met by an increasing use of gas. In many countries, the switch from oil to gas was not entirely price induced, but was more a result of institutional factors and political decisions. The availability of gas certainly also played a decisive role, and this was limited over some of the years of the observation period in many countries. Coal poses another, though rather different, problem: although its *price* was relatively low over much of the period in many countries, the actual *costs* of using coal – including handling costs, inconvenience, environmental considerations – are not reflected in the quoted price. Finally, in the two countries where electricity provided the major alternative to oil – Norway and Sweden – cheap hydroelectric power allowed the price to remain more-or-less constant in real terms, particularly from the 1970s onwards. Because of this development, including the real price of electricity in the demand equation along with the real price of oil provided no additional explanatory power.

Given these problems, it is perhaps not surprising that our model has not been able to capture the influence of inter-fuel substitution. Since the specification including only the oil price provides the most convincing set of estimates for the largest number of countries, the results presented in the following sections are based on this model.

(a) *Light Fuel Oil in Industry.* The parameter estimates are presented in Table 3.7. Judging from the R^2 and Durbin–Watson statistics and the significance levels of the estimated parameters, we find that the model does not explain the data particularly well. The R^2 are very low for some countries, the income variable is significant for only five countries and the price coefficient for only six. In five of the countries, only the lagged consumption term is significant, which suggests that a

Table 3.7: Estimated Parameters for Light Fuel Oil Demand in Industry. 1960–85.

	P_{LFO}	Y	$Q_{LFO(-1)}$	k	R^2	DWS
Belgium	−0.62	0.17	0.54	8.03	0.94	2.39
	(3.68)	(0.52)	(4.05)	(4.74)		
Denmark	−0.11	0.86	0.64	1.57	0.49	1.98
	(0.90)	(1.20)	(2.86)	(1.38)		
France	−0.26	0.53	0.68	3.77	0.82	1.29
	(2.11)	(1.12)	(4.83)	(3.00)		
Germany	−0.17	0.49	0.70	2.84	0.93	2.31
	(3.39)	(1.13)	(8.62)	(6.42)		
Greece	0.01	1.08	0.60	−0.36	0.97	1.66
	(0.00)	(9.86)	(3.01)	(0.29)		
Ireland	−0.09	0.68	0.87	0.72	0.96	2.43
	(1.69)	(1.28)	(10.82)	(2.61)		
Italy	−0.25	3.75	0.51	−2.37	0.89	1.90
	(1.13)	(5.89)	(2.70)	(1.04)		
Netherlands	0.13	0.75	0.63	0.21	0.66	1.97
	(0.57)	(0.99)	(3.03)	(0.18)		
Norway	0.29	3.17	0.57	−5.12	0.99	2.50
	(1.81)	(5.67)	(3.05)	(2.08)		
Portugal[a]	0.03	0.27	0.70	0.77	0.85	2.37
	(0.31)	(0.81)	(3.72)	(1.51)		
Spain[a]	−0.30	0.40	1.07	2.67	0.81	1.18
	(1.38)	(0.37)	(4.87)	(1.59)		
Sweden	−0.26	1.03	0.27	3.08	0.79	1.79
	(4.58)	(6.36)	(1.71)	(3.90)		
Switzerland	−0.08	1.08	0.26	1.85	0.65	1.88
	(0.76)	(4.42)	(1.22)	(2.23)		
UK	−0.15	0.63	0.90	1.21	0.96	2.53
	(3.35)	(1.52)	(21.05)	(3.42)		

Note: (a) Sample period 1970–85.

simple moving average model would perform equally well. The country where the model seems to perform best is Sweden. In general, however, these results do represent an improvement over the unconstrained partial-adjustment model initially estimated.

The resulting price and income elasticities are presented in Table 3.8. We find that the price elasticity is significantly negative only for Belgium, France, Germany, Sweden and the UK. These elasticities also seem quite reasonable, falling between −0.15 and −0.62 in the short run and −0.36 and −1.50 in the long run. Interestingly, these are the only countries in which light fuel oil consumption decreased consistently from the mid-1970s onwards.

Table 3.8: Estimated Elasticities for Light Fuel Oil Demand in Industry. 1960–85.

	Price			Output	ϕ	Median Lag
	Short-run	Five-year	Long-run			
Belgium[a]	−0.62	−1.29	−1.35	(0.17)	0.46	1.1
Denmark[a]	(−0.11)	(−0.27)	(−0.31)	(0.86)	0.36	1.6
France[a]	−0.26	−0.69	−0.81	(0.53)	0.32	1.8
Germany[a]	−0.17	−0.47	−0.57	(0.49)	0.30	1.9
Greece[a]	(0.01)	(0.02)	(0.03)	1.08	0.40	1.4
Ireland[a]	(−0.09)	(−0.35)	(−0.69)	(0.68)	0.13	5.0
Italy[a]	(−0.25)	(−0.49)	(−0.51)	3.75	0.49	1.0
Netherlands[a]	(0.13)	(0.30)	(0.35)	(0.75)	0.37	1.5
Norway	0.29	0.60	0.67	3.17	0.43	1.2
Portugal[ab]	(0.03)	(0.08)	(0.10)	(0.27)	0.30	1.9
Spain[ab]	(−0.30)	(−1.73)	(4.29)	(0.40)	−0.07	−10.2
Sweden	−0.26	−0.36	−0.36	1.03	0.73	0.5
Switzerland[a]	(−0.08)	(−0.11)	(−0.11)	1.08	0.74	0.5
UK[a]	−0.15	−0.61	−1.50	(0.63)	0.10	6.6
Average[c]	−0.18	−0.49	−0.72	0.95		

Notes: (a) Elasticities in parentheses are based on parameters that are not
significantly different from zero.
(b) Sample period 1970–85.
(c) Average of the elasticities of all countries, excluding Spain, weighted by
1985 consumption shares, with positive price elasticities set equal to zero.

The output elasticity is significantly different from zero only in
Greece, Sweden and Switzerland, where it is near to unity, and in
Italy and Norway, where it is unreasonably high. Apparently, even
the output elasticity is difficult to estimate on the basis of this model.

The average elasticities for OECD Europe are given at the foot of
Table 3.8. We find the average price elasticities to be around −0.2 in
the short run and −0.7 in the long run, while the output elasticity is
very near to unity. These results seem not at all unreasonable,
although it must be kept in mind that they are largely based on
insignificant parameters. Because of this and the generally poor performance of the model, not much weight can be placed on these
results.

(*b*) *Heavy Fuel Oil in Industry.* The final results presented are for heavy
fuel oil demand. The estimated parameters are shown in Table 3.9. In
contrast with its application to light fuel oil, we find that the model
performs rather well. The R^2 values are quite good, the Durbin–

Watson statistics acceptable, and the estimated parameters of the right sign and generally statistically significant. The only exception is the output variable, which is significantly positive in only four countries. Both price and output variables are insignificant in the case of Portugal, where a shorter observation period was used because of breaks in the consumption data.

The estimated elasticities are presented in Table 3.10. Again, there is a considerable degree of variation amongst countries. The price

Table 3.9: Estimated Parameters for Heavy Fuel Oil Demand in Industry. 1960–85.

	P_{HFO}	Y	$Q_{HFO(-1)}$	k	R^2	*DWS*
Belgium	−0.49	0.53	0.27	7.86	0.84	1.87
	(3.67)	(2.53)	(1.51)	(4.65)		
Denmark	−0.33	−0.21	0.46	6.59	0.86	1.76
	(3.67)	(0.89)	(3.28)	(4.46)		
Finland[a]	−0.27	0.50	0.69	3.31	0.88	1.68
	(3.50)	(1.22)	(5.90)	(2.76)		
France	−0.17	0.40	0.95	1.42	0.95	2.43
	(4.70)	(1.04)	(17.07)	(2.85)		
Germany	−0.24	0.22	0.79	3.06	0.97	2.33
	(8.98)	(1.03)	(8.98)	(8.01)		
Greece	−0.27	0.43	0.91	2.76	0.98	2.34
	(3.83)	(1.07)	(17.09)	(4.56)		
Ireland	−0.16	0.08	0.80	1.98	0.87	2.52
	(1.76)	(0.16)	(11.07)	(4.19)		
Italy	−0.20	0.41	0.81	3.68	0.96	1.77
	(5.48)	(1.61)	(13.37)	(5.03)		
Netherlands	−0.48	−1.26	0.46	9.80	0.93	2.40
	(3.14)	(3.69)	(3.13)	(4.21)		
Norway	−0.16	0.95	0.91	1.21	0.92	2.47
	(2.42)	(0.95)	(8.87)	(1.42)		
Portugal[a]	−0.06	0.22	0.87	1.33	0.93	2.70
	(1.12)	(0.86)	(7.54)	(3.29)		
Spain	−0.38	1.70	0.43	3.03	0.93	2.12
	(2.34)	(8.57)	(1.95)	(2.56)		
Sweden	−0.21	0.74	0.75	2.50	0.93	1.99
	(2.32)	(1.95)	(5.87)	(2.32)		
Switzerland	−0.47	1.47	0.72	2.59	0.90	2.82
	(3.25)	(3.10)	(6.27)	(3.17)		
UK	−0.25	0.27	0.95	1.36	0.97	1.38
	(4.20)	(0.60)	(16.01)	(1.88)		

Note: (a) Sample period 1970–85.

elasticities for the individual countries are in most instances higher than those for the product-user groups presented earlier. Excluding Portugal, for which the price effect is not significantly different from zero, the short-run price elasticities vary from about −0.2 to −0.5. After five years, the elasticities range from −0.5 to −1.4, and in the long run from −0.6 to −5.0. Some of these do seem unreasonably high, particularly those for France, Greece and the UK. It should be noted that the short-run elasticities for these countries are not unusually high, but that the adjustment to the long run is exceedingly slow, so that the difference between the short- and long-run responses is exceptionally large. In these three countries, after ten years the effects would be −1.4, −1.8 and −2.0 respectively, still rather far from the long-run responses. For all other countries, with the exceptions of Norway and Portugal, over 90 per cent of the long-run adjustment is realized in well under ten years.

Table 3.10: Estimated Elasticities for Heavy Fuel Oil Demand in Industry. 1960–85.

	Price			Output	φ	Median Lag
	Short-run	Five-year	Long-run			
Belgium	−0.49	−0.67	−0.67	0.53	0.73	0.5
Denmark[a]	−0.33	−0.60	−0.61	(−0.21)	0.54	0.9
Finland[ab]	−0.27	−0.73	−0.87	(0.50)	0.31	1.9
France[a]	−0.17	−0.77	−3.40	(0.40)	0.05	13.5
Germany[a]	−0.24	−0.79	−1.14	(0.22)	0.21	2.9
Greece[a]	−0.27	−1.13	−3.00	(0.43)	0.09	7.4
Ireland[a]	−0.16	−0.54	−0.80	(0.08)	0.20	3.1
Italy[a]	−0.20	−0.69	−1.05	(0.41)	0.19	3.3
Netherlands	−0.48	−0.87	−0.89	−1.26	0.54	0.9
Norway	−0.16	−0.67	−1.78	0.95	0.09	7.4
Portugal[ab]	(−0.06)	(−0.23)	(−0.46)	(0.22)	0.13	5.0
Spain	−0.38	−0.66	−0.67	1.70	0.57	0.8
Sweden	−0.21	−0.64	−0.84	0.74	0.25	2.4
Switzerland	−0.47	−1.35	−1.68	1.47	0.28	2.1
UK[a]	−0.25	−1.13	−5.00	(0.27)	0.05	13.5
Average[c]	−0.25	−0.75	−1.66	0.54		

Notes: (a) Elasticities in parentheses are based on parameters that are not significantly different from zero.

(b) Sample period 1970–85.

(c) Average of the elasticities of all countries weighted by 1985 consumption shares.

We find that the five-year elasticities, on the other hand, fall generally within a rather narrow range, between −0.6 and −0.8 for ten of the countries. Only the estimates for Greece, Switzerland and the UK are appreciably above this range, with elasticities above unity. There seems to be no obvious way of explaining the high elasticities for these countries.

Regarding the output elasticities, we find these are generally rather low, and in the majority of countries not significantly different from zero. It is rather difficult to interpret these results, as we would expect to find a clear relation between oil consumption and the industrial production level, given that all else remains constant. There were many factors at work during the period under study, however, which affected oil demand and which have not been included in the model. As was pointed out earlier, the increased availability of natural gas led to considerable inter-fuel substitution, which has not been determined solely by relative prices. Another important factor was technical change, which served to increase the productivity of all inputs – including energy – in production. The changing structure of production from heavy process industries to lighter high-technology industries over the period also led to a reduction in energy use in many countries. The extent to which these factors were correlated with the production level – which is highly likely – will be reflected in the estimated parameters. Specifically, the coefficients will be biased and the standard errors large.

Obviously, a far more detailed model than that employed here would be needed to give an adequate formulation of the complex relationships governing oil demand in the industrial sector. As was stressed earlier, industrial oil demand should ideally be studied in conjunction with the demand for other energy products and in the context of its role as an input in the production process. Given the shortcomings of our model, it is perhaps not surprising that the results obtained are not wholly satisfactory.

Finally, we find that the average short-run, five-year and long-run price elasticities for OECD Europe are −0.25, −0.75 and −1.66 respectively. The output elasticity of 0.54 is perhaps lower than one might expect, and as it is based largely on statistically insignificant estimates it must be treated with scepticism.

Tests for the stability of the estimated parameters in the pre- and post-1974 periods were also carried out. The hypothesis that both sub-periods obey the same demand relationship could be not be rejected on statistical grounds in the overwhelming majority of cases. We could reject the hypothesis of structural stability for the pre- and post-1974 time-periods for only five countries – Italy, the

Netherlands, Spain, Sweden and the UK. The estimates based on the individual sub-periods, however, were in many instances either not significant or economically unreasonable. Attempts to test for differences in particular parameters produced little significant evidence of changes in elasticities.

3.7 Conclusions

It is difficult to summarize adequately the large body of results obtained. Readers interested in the estimates for individual countries are referred to the tables above. A few general trends in the demand for petroleum products in OECD Europe are apparent, however, and we shall try to summarize these to see if any evidence is provided relating to the questions posed at the beginning of this chapter.

First, there is a clear indication that the elasticities do vary for the different countries. This suggests that estimates based on aggregate European data may be misleading. The same is true for the elasticities estimated for the various end uses of the individual products. These results clearly support our decision to base our analysis on more disaggregated data, and then to aggregate the resulting elasticities on the basis of the relative consumption levels of the individual countries.

The remaining questions concerning the price sensitivities of the various products and the time-structures of the price responses can be seen for each country individually from the tables presented earlier. Our main interest here, however, is to obtain some indication of the answers to these questions for Europe as a whole.

Most of the discussion will therefore be based on the average elasticities for Europe presented in the tables above. It must be kept in mind that these are in themselves stochastic variables, since they are weighted averages of the estimated elasticities for the individual countries. Unfortunately, we are unable to calculate their variances, so we are unable to test whether the differences in elasticities are statistically well grounded.

The *average* elasticities for the various product end-use categories are summarized in Table 3.11. As far as the relative elasticities of the products are concerned, we do note some differences. Most striking is the insensitivity of automotive diesel demand to changes in its own price, even in the long run. For the majority of countries the estimated elasticity was not significantly different from zero, so neither would be the average for Europe. Comparing the short-run elasticities for the other products, we find that these are very similar, falling in an interval from −0.18 for industrial light fuel oil to −0.29 for light fuel oil in the 'other' sector. The average short-run elasticities for gasoline

Table 3.11: Weighted Average Price and Income Elasticities for Various Products by End-use Category. 1960–85.

	Price			Income Variable		
	Short-run	Five-year	Long-run	Short-run	Five-year	Long-run
Gasoline	−0.25	−0.67	−0.91	0.40	0.97	1.26
Automotive Diesel	−0.08	−0.13	−0.14	0.88	1.53	1.68
Light Fuel Oil ('Other')	−0.29	−0.74	−0.96	0.70	1.79	2.20
Light Fuel Oil (Industry)	−0.18	−0.49	−0.72	0.95	0.95[a]	0.95[a]
Heavy Fuel Oil (Industry)	−0.25	−0.75	−1.66	0.54	0.54[a]	0.54[a]

Note: (a) These elasticities are constrained to be equal to the estimated short-run elasticities.

and industrial heavy fuel oil are identical, at −0.25. However, as stated earlier, without the standard errors of the average elasticities we have no basis for determining whether or not these differences are statistically significant. It seems that the only safe conclusion that can be drawn concerning short-run behaviour is that the elasticities are rather low and that automotive diesel is much less price sensitive than other oil products.

After five years, we find that the price elasticities begin to diverge somewhat. Disregarding automotive diesel, for which the elasticity is near zero, we find that industrial light fuel oil is still the least responsive to price changes. Light fuel oil use in the 'other' sector and heavy fuel oil consumption in industry both have elasticities of around −0.75, while the elasticity for gasoline is only marginally smaller. Again, nothing can be said about the statistical significance of these differences.

The greatest discrepancies in price elasticities are found in the long run. We see that the long-run price elasticity of industrial heavy fuel oil, −1.66, is nearly twice as great as those for either gasoline or light fuel oil in the 'other' sector. After automotive diesel, industrial light fuel oil is still the least price responsive, with an elasticity of −0.72 in the long run. Although the ranking of the elasticities is not identical for the individual countries, of the twelve countries with generally reasonable results, we found that the heavy fuel oil demand was most price sensitive in five and 'other' light fuel oil in six.

Table 3.12: Average Aggregate Price Elasticities for Petroleum Products.

	Short-run	Five-year	Long-run
Gasoline	−0.25	−0.67	−0.91
Light Fuel Oil	−0.20	−0.49	−0.63
Heavy Fuel Oil	−0.25	−0.72	−1.53

As was noted earlier, the speed of adjustment to the long run varied in the individual countries for each product user group, so it is difficult to draw any general conclusion concerning this speed on the basis of the results obtained. However, for the majority of countries, the time required for full adjustment was longer for heavy fuel oil than for the other products, as was the average median lag. This seems quite reasonable, considering the longevity of industrial capital equipment as compared with vehicles or home heating devices.

In order to answer our first question concerning the relative elasticities of the individual petroleum products, the elasticities for the various end uses of each product must be aggregated. This can be done by weighting the elasticities for each user group by its share in the total European consumption of the relevant oil product in 1985, the last year of the data sample. These aggregate elasticities are presented in Table 3.12.

In 1985, 53 per cent of light fuel oil was used in the 'other' sector, 33 per cent for road transport (automotive diesel), 10 per cent in industry and 4 per cent for non-road transport.[2]

Regarding heavy fuel oil, in 1985, 45 per cent was used for electricity generation, 41 per cent in industry, 13 per cent in the 'other' sector and 1 per cent for transport. For transport, we again assume a zero elasticity. Since we have no estimates of elasticities for the 'other' sector, we will assume these to be the same as those for light fuel oil in this sector. The shares of these two user groups, however, are relatively small, so that the aggregate elasticities should not be very sensitive to the assumptions made. More problematic is the lack of estimated elasticities for heavy fuel oil demand for electricity generation. As was pointed out earlier, this user category is very difficult to model econometrically, and would require rather more data than are available. Some assumptions will therefore have to be made, and, given the large share of this user category, our conclusions will be highly dependent

---

[2] We assume the price elasticity for non–road transport to be zero, which seems reasonable considering the development of consumption over time (see Figure 2.1 above).

on these assumptions. In Table 3.12, we assume that the elasticities for electricity generation are the same as those for industry.

Comparing the short-run elasticities for the different products, we find very little difference between them. Gasoline and heavy fuel oil both have elasticities of −0.25 and that for light fuel oil is only marginally lower. Judging from these results, we would have to conclude that the response to price changes after one year is identical for the three products. There is somewhat more variation in price effects after five years, although those for heavy fuel oil and gasoline are still very similar. Compared with these products, light fuel oil is considerably less price sensitive. The differences in price elasticities are most apparent in the long run. Clearly, heavy fuel oil is most responsive to price changes, light fuel oil least so, and gasoline somewhere in between.

These conclusions are of course based on elasticities estimated from historical data, so that they pertain to demand relationships of the past. It is obvious that the events of 1974 and 1979 have had a considerable impact on energy demand in Europe, and it seems unlikely that this change will be totally reversed by falling oil prices – at least in the foreseeable future. It has become the policy of most European countries to diversify their sources of energy, so as to avoid undue dependency, and to rely more heavily on domestic energy sources. Many investments have been undertaken to reduce oil consumption and to utilize other energy products. The increased availability of natural gas and the long-term contracts involved also play important roles in determining future oil demand. Given these factors, it seems highly unlikely that the estimated elasticities will hold for a future characterized by falling oil prices. This is of course particularly the case for heavy fuel oil, and probably somewhat less so for light fuel oil, given the high proportion of the latter fuel that is used for transport. For gasoline, on the other hand, for which there is presently no viable non-oil substitute, there is less reason to question the reversibility of demand behaviour to future price falls.

Appendix to Chapter 3

Data Sources

(*a*) *Consumption*. Annual data on the quantities of various oil products consumed in the European OECD countries are obtained from the OECD *Energy Statistics*. The OECD data cover the period 1960–85 and include information on the following oil products and categories:

Gasoline consumption;
Diesel consumption for road transport;
Diesel consumption for non-road transport (i.e. railways and navigation);
Gas/diesel oil consumption in industry;
Gas/diesel oil use in other sectors (i.e. commercial and public, agricultural and residential);
Residual fuel oil use in industry;
Residual fuel oil use in public electricity generation;
Residual fuel oil use in other sectors (i.e. commercial and public, agricultural and residential).

It should be noted that there are some inconsistencies in a number of these series for certain countries due to changes in classification over the time-period, as well as other changes in the national statistics on which they are based. This was taken into account in determining the time-period used for the econometric analysis of the individual countries and products.

(*b*) *Prices*. Data on oil product prices are taken from a number of different statistical sources and the entire 1960–85 time-period cannot be covered using an individual source. The primary sources are the EIA, the OECD and the EEC.

The OECD prices are the most comprehensive. They are taken from the publication *Energy Prices and Taxes* and cover the years 1978–85 for most of the principal products and countries. The data are defined as average annual end-use prices net of rebates, and include transport costs to the consumer as well as non-refundable taxes paid by the consumer. The following series were used:

Gasoline;
Automotive diesel;
Light fuel oil (gas/diesel oil) – for industrial and household consumers
separately;
Heavy fuel oil – for industry;
Coal – for industry;
Natural gas – for industrial and household consumers separately;
Electricity – for industrial and household consumers separately.

The EIA prices (for 1960–83) come from a publication on OECD prices. These are published in US dollars and converted into local currencies.

The EEC data (1960–80) are taken from *Energy Price Indices* (1982). These are preferable to the EIA data as they are given as average annual prices. These data exist for Belgium, France, Germany, Italy, the Netherlands and the UK. Where the series overlap, these data agree quite well with the OECD data.

Since data for a sufficiently long time-period are not available from a single source, different series need to be chained. EEC prices chained with OECD average annual prices are used for the six countries for which EEC data exist. For the other countries, the EIA prices are used for the period prior to 1978, and prices for Finland were provided by Neste Oy.

(c) Economic Variables. Data on private consumption, GDP, industrial output and exchange rates are taken from IMF and OECD sources.

4 The European Refining Industry: Structure and Changes, 1976–86

David Long

4.1 Introduction

The changes in the growth and pattern of demand for petroleum products as described in Chapter 2 above called for a major transformation of the refining system in Europe. Much capacity built in the 1960s and early 1970s in anticipation of continued growth became redundant. Refinery owners were therefore faced with difficult decisions on the scale and timing of closures. Changes in the composition of the demand barrel of products called for the upgrading of refining capacity in order to reduce the supply of fuel oil relative to the supply of middle and light distillates.

Thus the response to changes in the behaviour of demand and more generally to related changes in the 'economics' of refining involved both disinvestment in the form of closures and investment in upgrading capacity, specialized plants and new technology.

Adjustments to refining capacity – in terms of both quantity and quality – are typically slow. This is not simply because the very action of closing a plant or building a new one takes time. There are reasons to believe that the 'decision time-lag' (i.e. the interval of time which elapses from the moment significant changes in demand or the economic conditions begin to take place to the moment when the decision to close capacity is taken) is fairly long. Delays are due to a wide variety of causes. There are perception lags and evaluation lags because disinvestment often involves high costs and in some countries involves political constraints. Furthermore, decision-makers may delay their responses until they are persuaded that the changes that require such adjustments are of a truly long-term nature. They may be inhibited for a while by strategic considerations, e.g. by the view that it is important to retain a refinery in a given market or to retain refining capacity as a central feature of vertically integrated operations. Because of these various factors, adjustments to capacity may be slow, and the responses to the 'demand shock' of the late 1970s and early 1980s may still be short of the full adjustments required by the changes that have occurred in demand and in the broader economic conditions of the product market. A frequent complaint of oil companies in the late 1980s is that there is still too much refining capacity in Europe. It is also possible that further investments to increase the flexibility of the European refinery system are still required, although this point is not usually made with the same emphasis as that concerning excess capacity.

The importance of analysing the changes in European refining in recent years is therefore clear. We are interested in the actual pattern of changes, the lags involved and the factors that may explain the observed patterns. In order to undertake this analysis we collected comprehensive, very detailed, data on all refineries that were in operation in Europe *at any time* during the period 1976–86. This enables us to describe and analyse the features of the European refining industry in 1976 and 1986 as well as the changes that have taken place between these two years in terms of three sets of criteria: (a) a broad set of locational characteristics describing the refinery sites; (b) a set of technical characteristics of the plants available at each site – their number, dates of commission, capacities, and the technologies that define them; and (c) a set of ownership criteria. We seek both to establish the extent of the changes that took place and the time-pattern of these changes, and also to form a preliminary view on which particular refinery characteristics are associated with closures.[1]

4.2 Changes in Refinery Sites

The total number of refinery sites in Europe fell from 174 at end-1976 to 123 at end-1986; and this change was due to fifty-four sites being closed and three being opened. The vast majority of the closures occurred from 1982 onwards (forty-four of the fifty-four sites that closed were closed in this period and seventeen sites, almost one-third, were closed in 1982 alone).

The crude distillation capacity of about 20,527 thousand bpcd that was available at end-1976 was reduced to some 14,496 thousand bpcd by end-1986 (a reduction of 29 per cent). There was a similar decline in catalytic reforming, from 2,535 thousand to 1,790 thousand bpcd between these two years (also a 29 per cent reduction). The capacity of other types of plant, from continuous catalytic reforming to flexi-coking, increased, however, from 1,704 thousand to 4,098 thousand bpcd (i.e. by 140 per cent) during the same period (see Table 4.1).

---

[1] A fuller analysis of the factors determining refineries' propensity to close or survive is undertaken in Chapter 5 below.

Table 4.1: Changes in Refinery Plant Capacity by Type of Plant. 1976–86.
Thousand Barrels per Calendar Day.

Plant Type	1976	1986	Change in 1976–86	% Change
Crude Distillation	20,527	14,496	−6,031	−29
Catalytic Reforming[a]	2,535	1,790	−745	−29
Continuous Catalytic Reforming	0	389	+389	n.a.
Thermal Cracking[b]	500	1,528	+1,028	+206
Thermal Coking[c]	61	80	+19	+31
Delayed Coking	97	177	+80	+83
Catalytic Cracking	986	1,647	+662	+67
Hydrocracking	60	247	+186	+309
Flexicoking	0	30	+30	n.a.
Lubricants[d]	144	145	+1	+1
Bitumen[d]	479	398	−81	−17

Notes: (a) Semi-regenerative and fully regenerative only
(b) Both long- and short-residue feed
(c) Premium coke process (thermal cracking and delayed coking)
(d) Production capacity

Site-specific locational characteristics may have influenced the decision to shut or keep open a refinery. The important characteristics include the country in which the refinery is situated, the relevant spot market served by the refinery (Rotterdam or the Mediterranean), its access to supply facilities, structural links such as associated petrochemicals plants or local crude oil production, and distances from the relevant market's basing-point and to the next refinery.

Table 4.2 shows how the distribution of these various locational characteristics amongst the operating refineries and the geographical distribution of refinery sites among the different countries changed between end-1976 and end-1986, and compares the proportions of sites with each of the locational characteristics considered that closed with the average proportion for Europe as a whole. It reveals that some characteristics appear to favour sites' survival while others favour their closure. The characteristics that favour survival include being on the coast, having access to a major product pipeline, being either a long way away from the next refinery or further than average from Rotterdam or Genoa, and being associated with an adjacent petrochemicals plant. The only significant characteristic favouring closure, apart from not having one of the survival characteristics mentioned above, is being on an inland waterway (but this is probably equivalent to not being on the coast anyway). The percentages of

Table 4.2: Numbers of Refinery Sites Closing and Opening, by Locational Characteristics of Sites and by Country. 1976–86.

	Open at end-1976	Closed in 1976–86	Opened in 1976–86	Open at end-1986	% Closed in 1976–86	Difference from Average % Closed
All Sites	174	54	3	123	31	0
Locational Characteristics						
Market – Rotterdam	95	29	2	68	31	0
– Mediterranean	79	25	1	55	32	+1
Supply – Coastal	110	25	2	87	23	–8
– Inland Waterway	50	21	–	29	42	+11
– Crude Pipeline	69	25	1	45	36	+5
– Product Pipeline	58	14	2	46	24	–7
– Next Refinery: Close	135	48	1	88	36	+5
: Far	39	6	2	35	15	–16
– Distance from Basing-Point: < Average	135	48	1	88	36	+5
> Average	39	6	2	35	15	–16
– Local Crude Supply	18	5	–	13	28	–3
Special Products						
– Petrochemicals	63	9	1	55	14	–17
– Lubricants	37	7	–	30	19	–12
– Bitumen	87	17	1	71	20	–11

The European Refining Industry: Structure and Changes, 1976–86

Country						
Austria	1	–	–	1	–	–
Belgium	7	3	–	4	+12	43
Cyprus	1	–	–	1	–	–
Denmark	3	–	–	3	–	–
Finland	2	10	–	2	+10	41
France	24	14	–	14	+8	39
Germany	36	–	–	22	–	–
Greece	4	–	–	4	–	–
Ireland	1	–	–	1	–	–
Italy	38	18	–	20	+16	47
Netherlands	8	1	1	7	–18	13
Norway	4	–	–	4	–	–
Portugal	2	–	–	3	–	–
Spain	10	–	–	10	–	–
Sweden	6	–	–	6	–	–
Switzerland	2	–	–	2	–	–
Turkey	4	1	1	5	–	–
UK	21	8	1	14	+7	38

sites that closed with the remaining characteristics (i.e. being supplied by a crude oil pipeline, being very close to another refinery site or close to Rotterdam or Genoa, or having local crude oil production associated with the refinery) do not appear to be sufficiently different from the average to suggest that these had any significant effect on the propensity to close.

Table 4.2 also shows the percentages of sites that closed in each country. These numbers are more difficult to interpret, since many countries have only a few refineries. In fact sites were closed in only six of the eighteen countries, all of which had seven or more refineries in operation in 1976. One possible interpretation of this result is that only the larger countries (France, Germany, Italy and the UK) and those with major concentrations of refining activity (Belgium and the Netherlands) had sufficiently diverse refinery industries to allow closures to take place, despite the presence of over-capacity in Europe as a whole. To close Ireland's only refinery, for example, would leave it wholly dependent upon imports, which perhaps explains why ownership was transferred from a consortium of BP, Esso, Shell and Texaco to the Irish National Petroleum Corporation (INPC) in 1982.

Of course, this type of single-factor analysis is merely suggestive. It is only by combining all the characteristics of refineries in a statistical multi-factor analysis of the type undertaken in Chapter 5 below that a more robust conclusion can be reached. Nevertheless the results presented above provide preliminary indications of the types of locational characteristics that may be important in deciding which refineries will close, and on how significant these characteristics are likely to be.

4.3 Changes in Refinery Plant

As can be seen from Table 4.1 above, which presents data on capacity by type of plant, there were two forces at work in the European refinery industry over the ten-year period considered. We mentioned before that there were significant reductions in crude distillation, catalytic reforming and bitumen manufacturing capacities, which were achieved partly through the closure of entire refinery sites and partly through the closure of redundant units at surviving sites. There were also large increases in upgrading capacity of various types, in particular thermal cracking and catalytic cracking plant. This was partly the result of investment in new plant types at sites that had previously had none, and partly the result of expanding the capacity of existing plants.

Table 4.3 summarizes our information on the numbers of refinery sites at which facilities of each major plant type were installed at end-1976 and end-1986, and on the average capacities of each type of plant in these two years. Changes in the numbers of sites and in the average capacities for each type of plant are also measured. The same broad distinction can be drawn between those processes that became less common (crude distillation, catalytic reforming, and bitumen and lubricants production) and those that became more common (continuous catalytic reforming and all types of cracking and coking plant except thermal coking).

It is interesting to observe, however, that despite the very large percentage reductions in the *total* crude distillation and catalytic reforming capacities experienced by the industry, the *average* capacities of plants of these types hardly changed at all. The average crude distillation capacity at each site only increased from 118 thousand bpcd in 1976 to 122 thousand bpcd in 1986, an insignificant change, while the average catalytic reforming capacity remained between 18 and 19 thousand bpcd. This suggests that capacity reductions were not concentrated at one end of the spectrum of sizes of refineries, as one might have expected if scale were a significant factor in determining the closure or survival of a refinery site.

The actual distributions of crude distillation capacity across refinery sites at end-1976 and end-1986 are shown in Figure 4.1. The two graphs plot the plant capacities in thousand bpcd in descending rank order from left to right.

Figure 4.1 shows very clearly the wide range of sizes of refinery in Europe. In 1976, for example, there was a continuum of sizes from the largest, with over 550 thousand bpcd of distillation capacity, to the smallest, with only 1 thousand bpcd. By 1986, however, the capacity of largest refinery had fallen to 428 thousand bpcd, while that of the smallest had risen to 3 thousand bpcd, indicating that closures occurred at both ends of the spectrum of refinery sizes.

A more precise description of the changes in the distribution of plant capacity can be obtained from measurement of the standard deviation of the distribution. These are also given in Table 4.3 for the eleven types of plant identified. The standard deviation is a measure of the spread of the capacity data, and will increase if the distribution becomes wider and decrease if it becomes narrower.

In the case of crude distillation capacity installed at refinery sites, the standard deviation fell from 103 thousand bpcd in 1976 to 81 thousand bpcd by 1986, indicating a narrowing of the spread of distillation capacities in the period 1976–86. This suggests that capacity reductions were not evenly distributed across the size spectrum, but more concentrated at the two ends. In other words it was the biggest and smallest refiners that contributed most to the cuts in

Table 4.3: Changes in Numbers and Average Capacities of Plants. Range and Standard Deviation of the Distribution of Plant Capacities. 1976–86. Thousand Barrels per Calendar Day.

Plant Type	Number of Sites			Average Plant Capacity		Capacity Range (Max/Min Size)		Standard Deviation	
	1976	1986	Change in 1976–86	1976	1986	1976	1986	1976	1986
Crude Distillation	174	119	−55	118.0	121.8	564.3/0.9	427.5/3.0	102.8	81.2
Catalytic Reforming	138	96	−42	18.4	18.7	71.2/1.3	53.9/1.3	11.7	10.4
Continuous Catalytic Reforming	–	19	+19	–	20.5	–	38.4/6.2	–	9.4
Thermal Cracking	27	56	+29	18.5	27.3	43.0/1.7	92.0/7.5	9.1	14.0
Thermal Coking	2	2	–	30.5	40.0	40.0/20.0	59.0/21.0	n.a.	n.a.
Delayed Coking	4	7	+3	24.3	25.3	46.0/11.0	60.0/13.5	13.4	15.4
Catalytic Cracking	47	56	+9	21.0	29.0	81.5/4.0	86.5/4.0	16.9	19.0
Hydrocracking	4	12	+8	15.0	20.6	28.5/8.0	30.4/10.2	8.1	7.0
Flexicoking	–	1	+1	–	30.4	–	30.4	–	n.a.
Lubricants	37	30	−7	3.9	4.8	13.3/0.5	13.3/1.2	2.5	2.7
Bitumen	87	67	−20	5.5	5.9	20.2/0.3	20.2/0.6	3.9	4.2

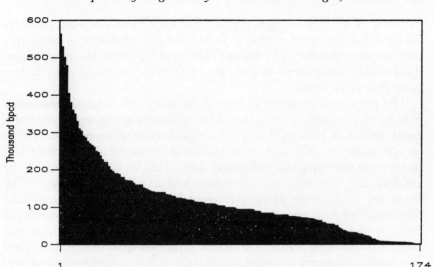

Figure 4.1a: Distribution of Crude Distillation Capacity in Rank Order of Capacity at each Site. End-1976.

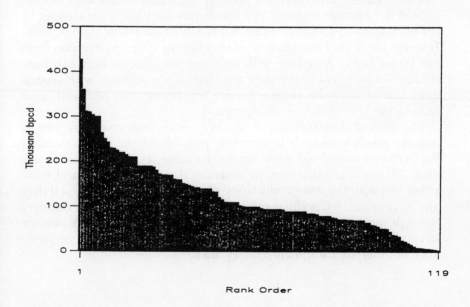

Figure 4.1b: Distribution of Crude Distillation Capacity in Rank Order of Capacity at each Site. End-1986.

capacity. The standard deviations of the distribution of plant capacity for the ten other types of plants (from catalytic reforming to lubricants and bitumen production) did not change in a systematic manner (see Table 4.3); and except in the case of thermal cracking the changes were relatively small.

The pattern of closure of crude distillation and catalytic reforming *capacity* also relates to the structure of refineries at the *unit* level. For a combination of historical and operational reasons many refinery sites in operation in 1976 had more than one crude distillation unit and more than one catalytic reforming unit. This was either because the refinery site was old, and therefore had expanded its capacity by investing in a series of progressively larger units in order to take advantage of scale economies as market demand grew, or because the refinery needed more than one distiller in order to maximize the benefit of running a mix of different crude oil qualities.[2] Thus, once the market stopped growing in the late 1970s a number of refiners were able to adjust their capacity by closing surplus units at a site rather than closing the entire site.

It is also interesting to observe that the proportion of crude distillation units that closed (39 per cent) was much greater than the proportion of distillation capacity lost (29 per cent), which suggests that it was the smaller (and therefore possibly older) units that were closed. Indeed the average capacity of a distillation unit also increased by 15 per cent, from 63 thousand bpcd in 1976 to 72 thousand bpcd in 1986. It seems likely that the smaller refiners faced a different decision from the larger ones. A refiner with only one distillation unit can only reduce capacity by closing the entire site, while a refiner with several units can achieve the same objective by closing only one unit, thus leaving the rest of the site in operation.

The date of construction, or 'vintage', is an important attribute of refinery plant, because it is not really possible for the refiner to bring the performance of old plant up to the same level as that of newer plant. Refiners are therefore prisoners of their own history and must either live with the low-productivity plant they have or reinvest if they are to improve its performance. Thus changes in refinery capacity through investment and disinvestment imply changes in the vintage structure of refinery plant, and hence changes in the relative performance of different European refinery sites.

---

[2] Given the need to boost the levels of octane occurring naturally in crude oil in order to meet gasoline quality specifications, investment in new distillers usually required corresponding investment in new catalytic reforming capacity.

Table 4.4: Average Age of Refinery Units in Years. 1976–86.

Plant Type	Average Age		
	1976	*1986*	*Change in 1976–86*
Crude Distillation	9	18	+9
Catalytic Reforming	9	18	+9
Continuous Catalytic Reforming	–	3	–
Thermal Cracking	12	8	–4
Delayed Coking	10	14	+4
Catalytic Cracking	12	14	+2
Hydrocracking	6	7	+1
Flexicoking	–	0	–

Table 4.4 shows the change in the average age of process units by plant type between 1976 and 1986. It can be seen that in 1976 the average age of crude distillation units and catalytic reformers was nine years. By 1986 this had increased to eighteen years for both plant types, indicating that there was very little investment in crude distillation and catalytic reforming plants between 1976 and 1986.[3]

At the same time as refiners were reducing their distillation and conventional catalytic reforming capacities, the same or other refiners were expanding or renewing their thermal and catalytic cracking capacities and installing the new continuous catalytic reforming process. As Table 4.3 shows, there were net increases between 1976 and 1986 in the numbers of sites at which these types of upgrading capacity were installed, and in the average plant capacities available at each refinery. The largest increase in the number of sites was for thermal cracking, which also experienced the greatest rise in average plant capacity (almost 50 per cent between 1976 and 1986); but catalytic cracking and hydrocracking were not far behind, with increases in average capacity of close to 40 per cent in each case. There was only a small rise (4 per cent) in the average plant capacity for delayed coking.

The expansion in thermal cracking capacity was achieved primarily through investment in new units at sites that previously had none. Thirty-eight of the forty-five new thermal cracking units, which accounted for 85 per cent of gross additional capacity, were built at

---

[3] Since we did not record start-up dates for units that were already in operation by 1960, the average age of plants is understated in both 1976 and 1986. In fact just under a quarter of all distillation and reforming capacity operating in 1976 was commissioned in or before 1960. However, this had fallen to around 15 per cent by 1986, indicating a net loss of older (pre-1960) plant.

sites where no capacity of this type had existed before. The expansion of hydrocracking capacity also followed the same pattern, but on a much smaller scale.

Catalytic cracking, however, followed a different course. A large part of the increase in catalytic cracking capacity was achieved through investment at sites that already had some capacity installed. This was the result of either expanding existing units (16 per cent) or of replacing older smaller units with newer bigger ones (13 per cent). Twenty-three new catalytic cracking units were commissioned between 1976 and 1986 (including four replacements of existing units), but thirteen were shut down, giving a net gain of only ten units, nine of which were at sites that had previously had none.

The impact of this explosion of investment activity on the vintage structure of upgrading plant can be seen from Table 4.4 for thermal cracking, hydrocracking and catalytic cracking. In 1986 the average age of all types of upgrading plant was slightly higher than in 1976 (except for thermal cracking).

4.4 The Pattern of Refinery Ownership and Industrial Concentration

Two aspects of ownership are worth noting. First, a substantial number of refinery sites experienced a change in ownership between 1976 and 1986, either through the outright sale of the entire site, or by a take-over, merger or sale of a part interest in the site to a third party. Table 4.5 shows that, in 1976, 133 out of 174 existing sites were wholly owned by single entities (76 per cent), while in 1986, 90 out of 123 sites were wholly owned, a slightly lower proportion than in 1976 (73 per cent). Between 1976 and 1986, sixty-two of the 174 sites operating in 1976, or more than one-third, experienced some change of ownership: thirty of the single-owner sites were wholly or partly sold to a third party, and stakes in thirty-two of the jointly owned sites were sold by their owners. It is interesting to note that the survival rate of sites that changed hands (76 per cent) was higher than the survival rate of the total stock of refinery sites in operation in 1976 (69 per cent). Finally, forty-three out of the fifty-four sites (or 80 per cent) that closed between 1976 and 1986 were single-owner sites, a marginally higher proportion than the share of these sites in the initial stock at end-1976 (76 per cent). This difference is not significant enough to support the view that a company finds it much easier to close a wholly owned site than a jointly owned site where the decision has to be agreed with a number of partners.

Secondly, the patterns of investment and disinvestment of the

Table 4.5: Changes in Ownership of Refinery Sites in Relation to Closure. 1976–86.

	Open at end-1976	100% Sold to Third Party	Part Sold to Third Party	Changed Hands	Then Closed	Survivors that Changed Hands	Closed Without Change of Ownership
		Sold to Existing Owner	Sold to New Company				
Wholly owned	133	18	12	30	7[a]	23	36
Jointly owned	41	19	13	32	8	24	3
	—	—	—	—	—	—	—
Total	174	37	25	62	15	47	39

Note: (a) These refineries were all still wholly owned at the time of their closure.

various companies involved in the European refinery industry were different, and this led to substantial changes in the distribution of capacity among the companies. In almost all cases the net effect was to spread the distribution of the various types of refinery capacity more evenly among the companies, thus decreasing the concentration of the industry. The most pronounced changes in the distribution of refinery capacity among owners were seen in the case of upgrading plant, where a large number of companies that had previously had no upgrading facilities acquired them between 1976 and 1986. It is interesting to note, however, that there was also a decrease in the concentration of ownership of crude distillation and catalytic reforming plant, which suggests that there was an increase in the number of companies involved in these activities or that the capacity reductions were concentrated amongst the larger companies.

In the case of crude distillation, the number of companies involved increased only slightly, from sixty-six in 1976 to sixty-eight in 1986. However, the largest crude distillation capacity held by any one owner fell from 2,817 thousand to 1,839 thousand bpcd (35 per cent), i.e. by a greater proportion than the overall reduction in crude distillation capacity (29 per cent), suggesting that the reduction was concentrated amongst the larger owners. A similar picture also emerges for conventional catalytic reforming capacity, where the largest capacity also fell, from 403 thousand to 252 thousand bpcd (37 per cent), again by more than the overall reduction in capacity (29 per cent); but in this case the number of companies involved increased substantially, from forty-eight in 1976 to sixty in 1986.

That the largest owners reduced their capacities by higher proportions than others is confirmed by Table 4.6, which shows the changes in the shares of crude distillation and catalytic reforming capacities belonging to the ten and twenty largest companies.

A more formal method of summarizing the distribution of plant capacity among owners is to calculate a Herfindahl index. This is often used by economists in studies of industrial structure and provides a convenient method of measuring the concentration of ownership. The index takes into account the number of companies in the industry and their shares of plant capacity. Its inverse is equivalent to the number of *equal-sized* companies that would yield the same degree of market concentration as the *actual* distribution of companies with unequal shares.

Table 4.7 shows the results of this calculation for each of the major plant types in 1976 and 1986. It can be seen that they indicate a substantial reduction in the concentration of ownership of crude distillation and conventional catalytic reforming capacities.

Table 4.6: Changes in Crude Distillation and Catalytic Reforming Capacities by Owner. 1976–86. Thousand Barrels per Calendar Day and Percentage Shares.

	1976		1986		Change in 1976–86	
	Volume	%	Volume	%	Volume	%
Crude Distillation						
Top Ten Owners	13,684	67	9,111	63	−4,573	−33
Next Ten	3,665	18	2,640	18	−1,025	−28
Remainder	3,178	15	2,745	19	−433	−14
Total	20,527	100	14,496	100	−6,031	−29
Catalytic Reforming						
Top Ten Owners	1,812	71	1,170	65	−642	−35
Next Ten	445	18	328	18	−117	−26
Remainder	278	11	292	16	+14	+5
Total	2,535	100	1,790	100	−745	−29

Table 4.7: Inverse Herfindahl Indices (1/H) for Ten Major Plant Types. 1976 and 1986.

Plant Type	1976	1986	Change in 1976–86
Crude Distillation	14.98	18.38	+3.40
Catalytic Reforming	13.67	16.89	+3.22
Continuous Catalytic Reforming	–	5.97	n.a.
Thermal Cracking	4.39	17.04	+12.65
Thermal Coking	2.03	1.76	−0.27
Delayed Coking	3.07	5.52	+2.45
Catalytic Cracking	9.20	14.98	+5.78
Hydrocracking	1.86	9.47	+7.61
Lubricants	9.07	9.17	+0.10
Bitumen	12.91	16.04	+3.13

In the case of upgrading capacity, much larger changes can be observed. The number of companies owning upgrading capacity increased substantially. For example, the number owning thermal cracking capacity increased from sixteen to forty-seven, and the number owning catalytic cracking capacity increased from twenty to thirty-five. In both cases, however, the increase in the largest capacity

Table 4.8: Changes in Thermal Cracking and Catalytic Cracking Capacities by
Owner. 1976–86. Thousand Barrels per Calendar Day and Percentage
Shares.

	1976		1986		Change in 1976–86	
	Volume	%	Volume	%	Volume	%
Thermal Cracking						
Top Five Owners	359	72	680	45	+321	+89
Next Five	103	21	298	19	+195	+189
Remainder	38	8	550	36	+512	+1,348
Total	500	100	1,528	100	1,028	+206
Catalytic Cracking						
Top Five Owners	606	61	787	48	+181	+30
Next Five	211	21	386	23	+175	+83
Remainder	169	17	474	29	+305	+180
Total	986	100	1,647	100	+661	+67

held by any single owner was much less than the average increase for
the industry as a whole, suggesting that investment was concentrated
either amongst the smaller firms or amongst those that had previously
had no capacity of this type.[4]

This observation is supported by Table 4.8, which shows the
changes in the shares of thermal cracking and catalytic capacity
owned by the five and ten largest companies. In the case of thermal
cracking, for example, it can be seen that the share of capacity owned
by the five largest companies fell from 72 per cent of the total in 1976
to 45 per cent in 1986. It is clear that the smaller refining companies
as a group invested relatively more in upgrading capacity than the
larger companies.

As might be expected, this bias in the pattern of investment led to a
substantial decrease in the concentration of ownership of upgrading
capacity. It can be seen from Table 4.7 that the index 1/H for the
concentration of thermal cracking capacity rose dramatically, from
4.34 in 1976 to 17.04 in 1986, while the corresponding indices for
catalytic cracking and hydrocracking rose from 9.20 to 14.98 and from
1.86 to 9.47 respectively.

[4] For thermal cracking the capacity of the largest owner increased from 222 thousand to 231 thousand bpcd
(i.e. by only 4 per cent, compared with a 206 per cent increase in total capacity), and for catalytic cracking it
increased from 195 thousand to 231 thousand bpcd (i.e. by 18 per cent, compared with a 67 per cent increase
in total capacity).

4.5 The Refinery Owners

It is useful to classify refinery owners into groups. We distinguish first between companies with shareholdings in *more than one* refinery site in Europe (Group A), companies with a *majority* shareholding in *one* site (Group B), and companies with a *minority* interest in *one* site (Group C). Group A is further divided into three sub-groups: A.1, the traditional majors; A.2, private non-major oil companies; and A.3, oil companies wholly or largely owned by a state or a public-sector entity.

Group A.1. In 1976, this group consisted of eight companies: BP, Chevron, Esso, Gulf, Mobil, Shell, Texaco and CFP-Total. In 1986, it consisted of only six companies: BP, Esso, Mobil, Shell, Texaco and CFP-Total. Thus the only changes between 1976 and 1986 were the transfer of Chevron to Group B and the disappearance of Gulf, which merged with Chevron.

The companies in Group A.1 owned, wholly or jointly, sites in a large number of European countries both in 1976 and in 1986. In all cases the geographical spreads of their shareholdings were narrower in 1986 than in 1976, as is shown in Table 4.9.

Group A.2. In 1976, this group included four US independents (Amoco, Conoco, Marathon and Phillips) and ten European oil companies (Antar, Cepsa, Garrone, Montedison, Monti, Moratti, Nynas, Petrofina, Rio Tinto and Wintershall). By 1986, the size of this group had been considerably reduced by closures of sites or transfers of ownership. In particular, three of the US independents (Amoco, Marathon and Phillips) ceased to be multi-site owners and therefore moved to Group B. There were also mergers between 1976 and 1986, which affected the composition of the group. In 1986, Group A.2 consisted of Cameli, Cepsa, Conoco, Garrone, Moratti, Norsk Hydro, Nynas and Wintershall.

Group A.3. There were only seven national oil companies owning more than one refinery site in Europe in 1976. These were: Agip, Campsa/EMP, Elf, Neste, Petrogal, Turkish Petroleum and Veba. In 1986 their number increased to twelve, through the addition of Hellenic/DEP, KPC, Statoil, Svenska Petroleum and PDVSA. The new interesting features of these changes were: (a) that no national oil company with refinery ownership in 1976 withdrew from the downstream sector in 1976–86; and (b) that other national oil companies entered the scene during this period by acquiring or investing in more than one refinery in Europe.

Table 4.9: Geographical Distribution of Refineries Owned by Group A.1 Companies. 1976 and 1986.

	BP 1976	BP 1986	Esso 1976	Esso 1986	Mobil 1976	Mobil 1986	Shell 1976	Shell 1986	Texaco 1976	Texaco 1986	CFP-Total 1976	CFP-Total 1986
Belgium	X	X	X	X			X	X	X			
Cyprus	X	X			X	X	X					
Denmark	X		X				X	X				
France	X	X	X	X	X	X	X	X	X		X	X
Germany	X	X	X	X	X	X	X	X	X	X	X	
Greece	X		X									
Ireland	X		X				X		X			
Italy			X	X	X	X	X	X	X	X	X	X
Netherlands		X	X	X			X	X	X	X	X	X
Norway			X				X					
Spain			X									
Sweden	X	X			X		X	X	X	X		
Switzerland	X	X			X	X	X	X	X			
Turkey		X		X			X		X			
UK	X	X	X	X	X	X	X	X	X	X	X	X
Total Number of Countries	10	9	11	7	7	6	13	9	10	5	5	4

Group B. Companies with a controlling interest in only one refinery numbered twenty-seven in 1976 and twenty in 1986. Only eight companies are common to the two lists, however. These are: ICI, Motor Oil, ÖMV, Peretti, Petrola, Smid and Hollander, Tarmac and URBK.

Fourteen companies that belonged to this group in 1976 had disappeared from the refining scene altogether by 1986 or were taken over by others (Alma, Berry Wiggins, Burmah, Ilsea, Iplom, Lombarda, Maura, Occidental, Omar, RDP, ROL, Sardoil, Sengwald and Volpato). These are mainly Italian, but include some UK and US companies. Two companies (Norsk Hydro and Hellenic/DEP) moved to Group A by expanding into other sites, and by 1986 three small companies had become minority shareholders.

In 1986, the twenty companies in Group B consisted of:

(a) the eight survivors from 1976 listed above;
(b) six new entrants to European refining (INPC, Libyan Banks, Petromed, Pontoil, Profumo and Sofimi);
(c) six companies that fell from Group A.1 (Chevron) or Group A.2 (Amoco, Marathon, Montedison, Phillips and Rio Tinto – appearing in 1986 as Union Explosivos).

Group C. The number of companies owning a minority interest in a single European refinery increased significantly from eight in 1976 to seventeen in 1986. The more interesting feature of this change is that nine companies belonging to this group in 1986 were new investors in European refining. These included producing-country interests (Pemex), Middle Eastern private interests (Gatoil, Iranian Sea Oil and Tamraz) and US companies (Dow and Murphy Oil). It is slightly surprising to observe this increase in the number of small investors in a declining and reputedly unprofitable industry.

4.6 Distribution of Capacity by Groups of Companies

The distributions of capacity among these four groups in 1976 and 1986 by plant type are shown in Tables 4.10 and 4.11 and the changes in the volumes of capacity they owned are presented in Table 4.12.

Group A.1. In 1976 the companies in this group dominated the European scene, and owned 58 per cent of the extant crude distillation capacity and between 59 and 84 per cent of the other types of capacity in which they held shares, namely catalytic reforming, thermal cracking, catalytic cracking, hydrocracking, and bitumen and lubricants

Table 4.10: Refinery Capacity by Plant Type and Group of Company. 1976. Thousand Barrels per Calendar Day and Percentage Shares.

Plant Type	Group A.1		Group A.2		Group A.3		Group B		Group C		Total
	Volume	%	Volume	%	Volume	%	Volume	%	Volume	%	Volume
Crude Distillation	12,009	58	3,668	18	3,054	15	1,445	7	351	2	20,527
Catalytic Reforming	1,570	62	376	15	443	17	95	4	51	2	2,535
Thermal Cracking	313	62	33	7	90	18	66	13	–	–	502
Thermal Coking	–	–	40	66	–	–	–	–	21	34	61
Delayed Coking	–	–	86	89	11	11	–	–	–	–	97
Catalytic Cracking	634	64	178	18	159	16	14	1	–	–	985
Hydrocracking	51	84	–	–	10	16	–	–	–	–	61
Lubricants	102	71	21	15	6	4	15	10	–	–	144
Bitumen	282	59	89	19	74	15	34	7	–	–	479
Number of Companies	8		14		7		26		10		65
Number of Site Shares	119		44		39		27		9		238

Table 4.11: Refinery Capacity by Plant Type and Group of Company. 1986. Thousand Barrels per Calendar Day and Percentage Shares.

Plant Type	Group A.1		Group A.2		Group A.3		Group B		Group C		Total
	Volume	*%*	*Volume*	*%*	*Volume*	*%*	*Volume*	*%*	*Volume*	*%*	*Volume*
Crude Distillation	6,529	45	1,737	12	4,099	28	1,607	11	524	4	14,496
Catalytic Reforming	839	47	277	15	470	26	135	8	69	4	1,790
Continuous Catalytic Reforming	189	49	49	13	119	31	30	8	2	0	389
Thermal Cracking	613	40	211	14	425	28	197	13	82	5	1,528
Thermal Coking	–	–	65	81	15	19	–	–	–	–	80
Delayed Coking	14	8	76	43	61	34	27	15	–	–	177
Catalytic Cracking	861	52	205	12	388	24	146	9	48	3	1,648
Hydrocracking	102	41	20	8	84	34	28	11	14	6	248
Lubricants	94	65	8	5	29	20	14	10	–	–	145
Bitumen	181	45	62	16	116	29	37	9	2	1	398
Number of Companies	6		10		12		19		17		64
Number of Site Shares	62		29		53		21		17		182

Table 4.12: Changes in Refinery Capacity (Volumes and Percentages) by Plant Type and Group of Company. 1976–86. Volumes in Thousand Barrels per Calendar Day.

Plant Type	Group A.1		Group A.2		Group A.3		Group B		Group C		Total
	Volume	*%*	*Volume*	*%*	*Volume*	*%*	*Volume*	*%*	*Volume*	*%*	*Volume*
Crude Distillation	−5,480	−13	−1,931	−6	+1,045	+13	+162	+4	+173	+2	−6,031
Catalytic Reforming	−731	−15	−99	0	+27	+9	+40	+4	+18	+2	−745
Continuous Catalytic Reforming	+189	n.a.	+49	n.a.	+119	n.a.	+30	n.a.	+2	n.a.	+389
Thermal Cracking	+300	−22	+178	+7	+335	+10	+131	0	+82	n.a.	+1,026
Thermal Coking	–	–	+25	+15	+15	+19	–	–	−21	−34	+19
Delayed Coking	+14	+8	−10	−46	+50	+13	+27	+15	–	–	+81
Catalytic Cracking	+227	−12	+27	+5	+229	+8	+132	+8	+48	+3	+663
Hydrocracking	+51	−43	+20	+11	+74	+18	+28	+11	+14	+6	+187
Lubricants	−8	−6	−13	−10	+23	+16	−1	0	–	–	+1
Bitumen	−101	−14	−27	−3	+42	+14	+3	+2	+2	+1	−81
Number of Companies	−2		−4		+5		−7		+7		−1
Number of Site Shares	−57		−15		+14		−7		+8		−57

production. Curiously, however, they owned no coking capacity at all. The companies in this group had 119 separate interests in ninety-seven refinery sites. Between 1976 and 1986 their shares of all these types of capacity, though remaining the highest in the majority of cases, declined very considerably. In 1986, these shares ranged between 40 and 65 per cent, and this group still had only a very minor share of European coking capacity. The number of separate refining interests declined dramatically to only sixty-two, at fifty-six sites, and the average crude distillation capacity of the companies in this group fell from 1,501 thousand to 1,088 thousand bpcd.

Group A.2. In 1976 the companies in this group held shares of between 7 and 19 per cent of most types of capacity, with the notable exceptions of thermal and delayed coking, in which they held dominant shares, and hydrocracking, of which they had none. Their shares of the various types of capacity remained broadly similar in 1986, although they lost their dominant role in delayed coking and acquired hydrocracking capacity. As with Group A.1, however, the total number of site shares declined significantly, from forty-four (at forty-three sites) in 1976 to twenty-nine (at twenty-four sites) in 1986.

Group A.3. In 1976 the companies in this group held shares of between 4 and 18 per cent of all types of capacity (except thermal coking). These shares all rose over the period, and ranged between 19 and 34 per cent in 1986. In contrast with Groups A.1 and A.2, the number of site shares held by the companies in this group increased over the period, from thirty-nine (at thirty-five sites) in 1976 to fifty-three (at forty-eight sites) in 1986.

Groups B and C. These groups, which held small ownership shares in 1976,[5] increased the volumes of almost all types of capacity they owned during 1976–86, *including* crude distillation and catalytic reforming.

Thus, it may be seen that the changes in capacity between 1976 and 1986 by different groups of owners were not all of the same relative magnitude, and in many instances not of the same sign. While crude distillation capacity was reduced by Group A, it was increased, albeit by small amounts, by the minor groups. Furthermore, the latter

---

[5] 9 per cent of crude distillation, 6 per cent of catalytic reforming and 13 per cent of thermal cracking capacities.

groups accounted for large proportions of the increases in catalytic and thermal cracking capacities that were made during this period, relative to their shares of refinery ownership. Table 4.13 shows that the minor groups contributed some 21–27 per cent of the increase in cracking capacity, although their share of cracking capacity in Europe in 1976 was of a much smaller order of magnitude.

Our analysis in Section 4.4 above, which revealed that the absolute size of a company's total refining assets (in terms of its crude distillation capacity) played an important part in determining the response of refiners to their market environment, is confirmed by Table 4.13. The overall disinvestment from crude distillation and conventional catalytic reforming capacity was almost entirely the work of the eight big companies in Group A.1, but the larger part of investment in upgrading capacity was undertaken by companies in the other groups. As a result, the European refining industry, which went through considerable retrenchment and restructuring during the period under study, became *less* concentrated – not more, as one would have expected in such circumstances – in all respects.

Our interpretation of these results is that the major companies in Group A.1, which were so dominant until the mid-1970s, had over-invested in refining during the twenty years preceding the 'oil price shock', first to cater for the growth in oil demand, and secondly in anticipation of continued growth. They had too much crude distillation and conventional reforming capacity, but they also had an equivalent share (about two-thirds) of European upgrading capacity. The adjustments they had to make thus involved a considerable reduction in distillation capacity (of which they had too much) and *relatively less* investment in upgrading capacity than their competitors in the other groups (because they already owned such a large share of this type of capacity, which was much needed now that the composition of the demand product barrel had so radically changed).

Companies in Groups A.2, A.3, B and C owned much smaller shares of total capacity. Furthermore, the companies belonging to these groups operated at most two or three sites; and almost all of them operated in only one country. Survival involved different choices for companies in Group A.1 than for companies in the other groups. The former had the option of retrenchment: they could close a few sites, thus reducing both the number of refineries they owned and the number of countries in which they operated, and still retain a significant presence in the refinery business. Companies belonging to the other groups, particularly those owning only one site, faced a different choice. For them closure was not an option when survival was the objective. All those that were able to finance new investments (and

Table 4.13: Percentage Contributions of Each Group to Changes in Capacity by Plant Type. 1976–86. Volumes in Thousand Barrels per Calendar Day.

	Total Change in Capacity Volume	% Share of Decrease/Increase				
		Group A.1	Group A.2	Group A.3	Group B	Group C
Crude Distillation	−6,031	+90	+32	−17	−3	−3
Catalytic Reforming	−745	+98	+13	−4	−5	−2
Continuous Catalytic Reforming	+389	+48	+13	+31	+8	+0.5
Thermal Cracking	+1,026	+29	+17	+33	+13	+8
Thermal Coking	+19	n.a.	+132	+79	n.a.	−110
Delayed Coking	+81	+1	−13	+62	+33	n.a.
Catalytic Cracking	+663	+34	+4	+35	+20	+7
Hydrocracking	+187	+27	+11	+40	+15	+7
Lubricants	+1	−800	−1,300	+2,300	−100	n.a.
Bitumen	−81	+125	+33	−52	−4	−2

many were in this situation, either because they were state owned or because they had special ties with exporting countries or some local market advantage) took the option of adjusting the *quality* of their refinery capacity by modifying their plant or adding new cracking and coking facilities.

Of course, some companies were unable to follow this route and disappeared from the scene, as a comparison of the lists of owners for 1976 and 1986 shows; but the remarkable facts are that many did survive, that some expanded, and that a number of new entrants, not all of them state owned, appeared on the European refining scene. Finally, considering that adjustment through capacity reductions was slow and far from complete by end-1986, and that considerable adjustment also took place through new investment, we conclude that some companies perceived the costs of exit to be high in relation to the benefits of adjustment, and that others found the costs of entry to be justified by the expected returns in terms of either commercial profit or strategic advantage.

4.7 The Ranking of Refinery Owners by Ownership of Distillation Capacity

In the previous section the behaviour of refinery owners was analysed in terms of aggregates or groups. Any analysis based on aggregation, despite the important merits of the method, conceals interesting differences in individual behaviour. We now seek to highlight some of these differences and to qualify the conclusions reached by noting particular exceptions to the behaviour of the groups.

The classification followed here uses a different criterion: the crude distillation capacities owned by each company in 1976 and 1986. Table 4.14 shows the crude distillation capacities owned by each of the companies belonging to Group A in at least one of the chosen years, 1976 and 1986, the percentage changes in these capacities for each company, and the rankings of these companies by capacity in the two years. It immediately appears that the top-ranking companies in terms of distillation capacity were not the traditional majors (members of Group A.1) in all cases, and that geographical spread is not a strict function of size. In 1986, for example, the seven top-ranking companies in terms of crude distillation capacity were Esso, Shell, BP, Agip, CFP-Total, Campsa/EMP (now Repsol) and Texaco (in that order); while the seven companies with interests in three or more countries were Esso, Shell, BP, CFP-Total, Texaco and Mobil (the Group A.1 companies) plus Petrofina (which ranked only thirteenth in terms of capacity).

Table 4.14 also shows that in 1986 only three multinational giants in Europe – Esso, Shell and BP – had more than 1 million bpcd of crude distillation capacity and a presence in seven or more countries (see Table 4.9). The next-largest refiners were Agip (with just less than 1 million bpcd), CFP-Total and the newly-named Repsol. Only these companies and Texaco, Mobil and Turkish Petroleum belonged to the '500,000 bpcd plus' bracket. In 1976, this bracket also contained nine companies (not all the same ones); but the aggregate capacity owned by these top-ranking entities was 13,188 thousand bpcd, compared with 8,785 thousand bpcd in 1986.

Finally, Table 4.14 compares companies in terms of percentage changes in the levels of crude distillation capacity they owned. Those that increased their ownership of distillation capacity included state-owned companies in Spain (Campsa/EMP or Repsol), Portugal (Petrogal), Turkey (Turkish Petroleum) and Greece (Hellenic/DEP); also private sector companies in Italy (Cameli and Garrone), Spain (Rio Tinto/Union Explosivos) and Scandinavia (Nynas and Norsk Hydro). There is a clear geographical pattern in this phenomenon, which we discuss in the next section.

All other entities reduced their levels of crude distillation capacity. Among the majors, we note the virtual disappearance of Chevron/Gulf, and the fact that BP reduced its capacity not only by a larger percentage than the other majors (almost 50 per cent) but also by a larger absolute amount (1,146 thousand bpcd). Taking mergers into account, the percentage reductions effected by such state-owned oil companies as Agip and Elf were of the same order of magnitude (between 40 and 50 per cent) as some of the majors' (BP, Shell, CFP-Total and Mobil). This clearly suggests the existence of a positive relationship between percentage cuts and initial size at the top end of the distribution. At the lower end, small initial size is often associated with additions to holdings. These two factors combined to bring about a decline in the concentration of refinery ownership as discussed above.

4.8 Geographical Patterns

Our analysis so far has concentrated on the changes in the structure of the refining industry at the aggregate European level. It is possible, however, that this aggregate approach is masking important differences in the responses of refiners at the national or regional levels.

(*a*) *National Patterns.* It is interesting to note that all the refinery closures between 1976 and 1986 occurred in countries that had more

Table 4.14: Crude Distillation Capacity by Company. 1976 and 1986. Thousand Barrels per Calendar Day.

Company	Group in 1976	Group in 1986	Rank in 1976	Rank in 1986	Capacity in 1976	Capacity in 1986	% Change in Capacity 1976–86
Esso	A.1	A.1	1	1	2,817	1,839	−34.7
Shell	A.1	A.1	2	2	2,748	1,630	−40.7
BP	A.1	A.1	3	3	2,328	1,182	−49.2
CFP-Total	A.1	A.1	4	6	1,365	765	−44.5
Mobil	A.1	A.1	5	8	999	516	−48.4
Monti	A.2	n.a.	6	n.a.	842	n.a.	n.a.
Agip	A.3	A.2	7	4	806	991	+22.9[a]
Texaco	A.1	A.1	8	7	765	597	−21.9
Chevron	A.1	B	9	29	517	95	−81.6[a]
Elf	A.3	A.3	10	10	497	466	−6.2[a]
Campsa/EMP	A.3	A.3	11	5	497	773	+55.3
Veba	A.3	A.3	12	23	472	126	−73.4
Gulf	A.1	n.a.	13	n.a.	443	n.a.	n.a.
Moratti	A.2	A.2	14	12	370	329	−11.2
Montedison	A.2	B	15	14	360	300	−16.7
Antar	A.2	n.a.	16	n.a.	327	n.a.	n.a.
Neste	A.3	A.3	17	17	326	255	−21.8
Petrofina	A.2	A.2	18	13	320	323	+0.9
Cepsa	A.2	A.2	19	16	281	283	+2.8
Wintershall	A.2	A.2	20	21	275	147	−46.8
Garrone	A.2	A.2	22	15	220	297	+35.0
Amoco	A.2	B	23	45	203	49	−66.0
Petrogal	A.3	A.3	24	11	171	338	+97.1
Turkish Petroleum	A.3	A.3	25	9	163	500	+206.3
Conoco	A.2	A.2	26	20	148	148	0.0
Marathon	A.2	B	33	36	119	70	−41.2

Hellenic/DEP	B	36	25	96	116	+20.8
Phillips	A.2	38	43	74	55	−25.7
Rio Tinto/Union Explosivos	A.2	39	32	66	80	+21.2
Nynas	A.2	40	33	62	79	+27.4
Norsk Hydro	B	42	35	51	71	+39.2
Cameli	C	49	39	27	60	+122.2
PDVSA	n.a.	n.a.	19	n.a.	156	n.a.
KPC	n.a.	n.a.	24	n.a.	123	n.a.
Statoil	n.a.	n.a.	22	n.a.	131	n.a.
Svenska Petroleum	n.a.	n.a.	44	n.a.	50	n.a.

Note: (a) Straight comparisons of 1976 with 1986 cannot be made in the cases of Agip, Chevron and Elf as these companies acquired Monti, Gulf and Antar respectively. Capacity reductions or increases must therefore be estimated for the aggregate of the merged companies in each case. This suggests reductions of 40 per cent for Agip/Monti, 91 per cent for Chevron/Gulf and 43.5 per cent for Elf/Antar.

Table 4.15: Refinery Capacity and Inland Demand^a by Country. 1976 and 1986. Thousand Barrels per Calendar Day.

	Refinery Capacity 1976	Inland Demand 1976	Capacity/Demand Ratio 1976	Refinery Capacity 1986	Inland Demand 1986	Capacity/Demand Ratio 1986
Austria	266	230	1.16	210	210	1.00
Belgium	1,088	560	1.94	713	480	1.49
Cyprus	15	n.a.	n.a.	16	n.a.	n.a.
Denmark	220	335	0.66	182	215	0.85
Finland	326	255	1.28	255	230	1.11
France	3,579	2,430	1.47	2,143	1,820	1.18
Germany	3,016	2,855	1.06	1,647	2,525	0.65
Greece	408	210	1.95	388	250	1.55
Ireland	56	105	0.54	56	90	0.62
Italy	4,239	2,065	2.05	2,762	1,775	1.56
Netherlands	1,886	795	2.37	1,286	690	1.86
Norway	259	180	1.44	258	205	1.26
Portugal	171	145	1.18	338	200	1.69
Spain	1,172	970	1.21	1,363	930	1.47
Sweden	396	590	0.67	446	370	1.21
Switzerland	137	270	0.51	137	280	0.49
Turkey	323	350	1.04	590	390	1.51
UK	2,965	1,860	1.59	1,700	1,640	1.04
Total	20,526	14,205	1.45	14,495	12,300	1.18

Source: (a) *BP Statistical Review of World Energy*, 1987.

Table 4.16: Capacity Changes in the Major European Countries.
1976–86. Thousand Barrels per Calendar Day and Percentages.

	Volume	%
Belgium	−375	−34
France	−1,436	−40
Germany	−1,369	−45
Italy	−1,477	−35
Netherlands	−600	−32
UK	−1,265	−43

than six refineries in 1976. This seems to suggest that the greater the number of refineries in a country, the higher the chance of closures. Such a broad statement, however, does not provide us with much insight. A more interesting approach is to relate refinery capacity to inland demand in each country in order to test the hypothesis that changes in capacity have tended to reduce imbalances between domestic supply and demand for petroleum products.

Table 4.15 shows that in all the countries considered, except Denmark, Ireland, Sweden and Switzerland, refinery capacity exceeded inland demand in 1976. The highest ratios of capacity to inland demand were in the Netherlands, Italy and Belgium, which was to be expected since these countries have important export refineries servicing the Mediterranean and ARA market zones. Nevertheless, in Europe as a whole, capacity exceeded demand by 45 per cent.

Between 1976 and 1986, the ratio of refinery capacity to inland demand declined in all European countries save six,[6] and the changes in crude distillation capacities of the major refining countries are shown in Table 4.16. In all the other countries there were reductions in capacity (or at best no change); and there were decreases in inland demand (except in Greece, Norway and Switzerland). The combined effect of these two factors reduced the ratios of capacity to demand significantly.[7]

Overall, European distillation capacity was reduced by 29 per cent in the face of a fall in inland demand of 13 per cent; but because initial

---

[6] Denmark and Ireland, where the ratio was initially less than one and remained below the balanced level in 1986; Sweden, where the ratio, initially less than one, rose above one in 1986; and Portugal, Spain and Turkey, where the ratio, initially higher than one, rose much further in 1986.

[7] In Germany, where capacity was slashed by 45 per cent, the ratio, which was slightly higher than one in 1976, fell to 0.65; but in Belgium, France, Italy, the Netherlands and the UK, where capacity was reduced by 32–43 per cent, and where the volume reductions in some cases (France and Italy) were larger than in Germany, the capacity/demand ratio remained higher than one in 1986 (see Tables 4.15 and 4.16).

capacity exceeded demand by 45 per cent the average ratio of capacity to demand remained above one (1.18) in 1986. There is no strict relationship between changes in distillation capacity and changes in inland demand by country, partly because their initial positions were different and partly because factors other than domestic demand determined their responses. Nevertheless, capacity was reduced in all European countries but four; and in many countries the capacity/ demand ratio moved closer to one. In 1986 only three European countries – Germany, Ireland and Switzerland – had less distillation capacity than was required to meet their levels of inland demand. This does not mean, however, that these were the only European countries that imported products. All of them do. Trade in products is not a function of these 'sufficiency' ratios.

(*b*) *Regional Patterns.* There are two separate, but related, spot markets operating in Europe. In the north there is a market based on Rotterdam (or more precisely on Antwerp-Rotterdam-Amsterdam or ARA), and in the south there is a market based on Genoa (the Mediterranean market). The northern market trades in both cargoes and barges for delivery to coastal or inland destinations, while the southern market trades only in cargoes. Unlike the north European countries, the countries bordering the Mediterranean have no well-developed network of navigable rivers and canals.

At first sight it appears that there was little difference in the behaviour of refiners in the two regions. As shown in Table 4.2 above, there was no significant difference in the proportions of sites that closed in the north (31 per cent) and in the south (32 per cent). However, important differences begin to emerge if one examines the change in the distribution of refinery plant between the two regions over the period.

Table 4.17 shows the distribution of capacity for each major plant type between the two regions in 1976 and 1986, and the percentage changes in these capacities over the period. It can be seen that the northern region held the majority of the capacity for every type of plant in both years. However, this disparity moved in favour of the south in the cases of crude distillation, conventional catalytic reforming, thermal cracking, and lubricants and bitumen plant, and in favour of the north in the cases of delayed coking, catalytic cracking and hydrocracking.

These changes in the distribution of refinery plant capacity between the two regions are due to the facts that, on the one hand, refineries in the north closed proportionately more crude distillation, catalytic reforming, lubricants, and bitumen production capacity than those in

Table 4.17: Refinery Capacity by Plant Type and Region, 1976 and 1986, and Percentage Changes in Capacity by Plant Type in Each Region. Volumes in Thousand Barrels per Calendar Day.

Plant Type	1976 North		1976 South		1986 North		1986 South		Change in 1976–86 North		Change in 1976–86 South	
	Volume	%	Volume	%	Volume	%	Volume	%	Volume	%	Volume	%
Crude Distillation	11,689	57	8,838	43	7,795	54	6,700	46	−3,894	−33	−2,138	−24
Catalytic Reforming	1,552	61	983	39	1,047	58	743	42	−505	−33	−240	−24
Continuous Catalytic Reforming	–	–	–	–	285	73	105	27	+285	n.a.	+105	n.a.
Thermal Cracking	851	70	149	30	807	53	721	47	+456	+130	+572	+384
Thermal Coking	61	100	–	–	80	100	–	–	+19	+31	–	–
Delayed Coking	62	64	35	36	120	67	58	33	+58	+94	+23	+66
Catalytic Cracking	554	56	432	44	949	58	698	42	+395	+71	+266	+62
Hydrocracking	46	77	14	23	203	82	44	18	+157	+341	+30	+214
Flexicoking	–	–	–	–	30	100	–	–	+30	n.a.	–	–
Lubricants	95	66	49	34	93	64	52	36	−2	−2	+3	+6
Bitumen	284	59	195	41	220	55	178	45	−64	−23	−17	−9

the south, and, on the other hand, they invested proportionately more in continuous catalytic reforming and all types of upgrading capacity (except thermal cracking) than those in the south.

Further differences between the behaviour of refiners in the north and the south are apparent if we examine the change in the distribution of ownership of the various plant types in the two regions. Table 4.18 compares the changes in concentration for the two regions between 1976 and 1986. It can be seen that in 1976, for most plant types (hydrocracking is the only exception), the inverse of the Herfindahl index was much smaller in the north than in the the the south: in other words the refining industry in the north was generally more concentrated than that in the south. In 1986, the picture was less even. Distillation, catalytic cracking, continuous reforming, thermal cracking and bitumen and lubricants production were more concentrated in the north, but catalytic reforming, hydrocracking and delayed coking were less concentrated. It is interesting to observe that in the cases of both crude distillation and conventional catalytic reforming the two regions experienced opposite trends: the south became more concentrated, and the north less concentrated. For all other types of capacity (except bitumen and lubricants production where the changes were small), we observe a similar trend towards less concentration in both north and south.

Taken together, these results suggest that the competitive processes at work in the two regions over the period were different in one respect and similar in another. In the north, the refining industry in 1976 was dominated by a relatively small number of large companies owning more sophisticated refineries. These companies responded to the changes in demand (and prices) by closing distillation capacity and expanding upgrading capacity. However, these were not the only companies in the market, and the combination of fewer reductions in distillation capacity and more new investment in upgrading capacity by the other, smaller, companies led to a reduction in the degree of concentration in the north. In comparison, the industry in the south was already much less concentrated in 1976 and there were more medium-sized and smaller companies. Some of these companies responded to the changing environment by leaving the business altogether (closing or selling their shares in refineries). As a result the ownership of distillation capacity became more concentrated in the south. In this sense there is a difference. In another respect there is similarity of behaviour, as revealed by the reduction in the degree of concentration in the ownership of upgrading capacity in both the north and the south. The force at work here was the need to upgrade for survival.

Table 4.18: Changes in Concentration of Ownership by Plant Type and Region: Inverse Herfindahl Indices (1/H). 1976–86.

Plant Type	1976		1986		Change in 1976–86	
	North	*South*	*North*	*South*	*North*	*South*
Crude Distillation	9.77	18.03	12.91	15.52	+3.14	−2.51
Catalytic Reforming	10.63	13.61	13.31	12.95	+2.68	−0.66
Catalytic Cracking	5.48	9.82	10.72	12.93	+5.24	+3.11
Continuous Catalytic Reforming	–	–	3.66	5.37	n.a.	n.a.
Hydrocracking	2.26	1.00	8.36	3.00	+6.10	+2.00
Thermal Cracking	3.34	5.71	11.11	13.41	+7.77	+7.70
Thermal Coking	2.03	n.a.	1.76	n.a.	−0.27	n.a.
Delayed Coking	1.62	1.76	3.18	2.77	+1.56	+1.01
Bitumen	10.70	12.57	10.70	12.52	0.00	−0.05
Lubricants	6.38	6.90	6.15	6.19	−0.23	−0.70

5 The Propensity of European Refineries to Shut between 1976 and 1986

Robert Bacon

5.1 Introduction

In this chapter we discuss how closure decisions in the European refining sector in the decade 1976–86 can be systematically related to the characteristics of individual refineries.

Some fifty-four of the 174 refineries extant at the beginning of this period had closed by the end. It is clear from the high percentage of total capacity closed, and from the typical sizes of refineries at the beginning and end of the period, that closures were not confined to small (and hence, for the market as a whole, unimportant) refineries. The closure decision was thus both common and important.

The simplest possible account of the closure process would be that it was a purely random process, with no systematic relation to the characteristics or situation of the refineries themselves. All refineries would be equally likely to close and there would be no systematic pattern relating the closures to the observable features of refineries. In this case, for example, the average size of the refineries closing should be similar to the average size of those remaining open. Such an approach implies that the factors leading to closure were so specific to the individual refineries that no overall pattern can be discerned, but that the same factors appear random when looked at in aggregate and from outside.

The alternative approach is to look for regularities in the closure pattern, i.e. for observable variables that are systematically different for those that remained open and those that closed. The statistical material we collected on European refineries enables us to carry out a very detailed investigation into whether or not closure is associated with observable and general features.

The statistical techniques used, involving linear probability and probit models (as described in the Appendix to this chapter below), not only identify the factors that are significantly associated with the decision to close and quantify their relative importance, but also give the individual refineries 'scores' that indicate their propensities to survive. In essence, we use the model to predict whether or not a refinery should have been expected to close on the basis of information available in 1976. This allows us to identify those cases where the model conspicuously fails to predict actual behaviour; and this identification can then be used to highlight 'special' cases.

5.2 Closure of Refineries: Variables Used

We relate the closure decisions that took place some time during 1976–86 to variables that were either invariant (e.g. whether the refinery is on the coast) or measured as of 1976 (e.g. crude distillation capacity). In this way the model attempts to predict closure on the basis of conditions at the *beginning* of the period. This is an important limitation: the model does not, for example, try to explain a refinery's closure by the market situation in the year in which it closed, but solely by the market situation in 1976. This approach loses some sharpness in explanatory power, but is more interesting from the standpoint of forecasting: it shows what can be done to project the future from the present.

In order to explain our results, we first introduce the variables that are used in the analysis, and indicate their expected effects on the closure decision.

The variables used to characterize the individual refineries can be grouped in the following sets:

(a) General;
(b) Location;
(c) Capacity;
(d) Technical characteristics (other than capacity);
(e) Ownership;
(f) Economic (investment, supply and demand).

(a) General

(i) **SHUT**. The dependent variable for our population of 174 refineries is the open/shut dichotomy. If the refinery closed during the period 1976–86 this variable is assigned a value of 0, while if the refinery remained open it is assigned a value of 1.

(ii) **OPEN**. This is the year in which the production of refined products at the site was started (or restarted where complete destruction had taken place). The sign of this variable is ambiguous. A high value for this variable indicates the recent construction of the refinery *in toto*, which implies the use of new plant which is likely to be efficient and hence to increase the likelihood of the refinery's remaining open. On the other hand, the first sites chosen for refineries may have been those in the best locations and therefore most likely to remain open. If we separately identify both the *age* of the plant and the *locational* features that would have been sought by early entrants, then this variable will duplicate other, better measures, and should therefore have no marginal impact of its own.

(b) Location

(iii) **REGION**. If the refinery is in northern Europe, this variable is assigned a value of 1; otherwise it is assigned a value of 0. This is intended to pick up systematic differences in the propensity to close in the two regions, and could have either sign.

(iv) **COAST**, (v) **WATER**, (vi) **CPIPE**, (vii) **PPIPE**, (viii) **PCHEM**, (ix) **CRUDE**. These variables stand for the refinery being (value 1) or not being (value 0) on the coast, on an inland waterway, joined to a crude pipeline, joined to a product pipeline, associated with the production of petrochemicals, and near to a local source of crude respectively. In each case we expect a positive correlation between these variables' taking the value 1 and surviving, on the grounds that being on the coast or on an inland waterway reduces transport costs (and hence increases profits); that pipelines reduce costs and improve access to sources of inputs or markets; and that association with a petrochemicals plant or proximity to a source of crude oil increases competitive strength.

(x) **BASE**. This is an index of the distance of the refinery (in a straight line) from the centre of the northern or southern European market (Rotterdam or Genoa respectively). The refineries are categorized into the two regions as for **REGION** above, and the unit of distance is taken from a map with scale 1 cm = 75 km. The further the refinery is from the local centre of refining, the greater its local market power will be, so we should expect this variable to be positively correlated with survival.

(xi) **NEAR**. This variable measures the distance from the refinery to its nearest competitor (again on a scale of 1 cm = 75 km). The greater the value of this variable, the greater its local domination, so we should expect it also to be positively correlated with survival.

(c) Capacity

(xii) **CDUCAP**. This is the total crude distillation capacity of the refinery as at 1976, giving an absolute measure of the size of the refinery as a topping configuration. If size alone has economies of scale, then this should be positively correlated with survival. Size relative to market size or to the owner's total capacity is measured separately. This variable is measured in barrels per calendar day (bpcd) as are all other absolute measures of capacity.

(xiii) **CRFCAP**. This is the total catalytic reforming capacity of the refinery as at 1976. It is an absolute measure of the size of the refinery as a simple configuration. If this capacity is important (relative to topping capacity), then a positive correlation with survival is to be expected.

(xiv) **CRFSH**. This is the ratio of **CRFCAP** to **CDUCAP**: the higher the index the more the 'simple' configuration dominates. A positive correlation with survival is expected if the model is normalized on topping.

(xv) **THTCCAP**. This variable aggregates the capacity of thermal cracking and coking. It is essentially an absolute measure for the capacity of semi-complex refineries. If this is advantageous in product mix terms relative to the configuration on which it is normalized (topping), then the correlation with survival should be positive.

(xvi) **THTCSH**. This is the ratio of **THTCCAP** to **CDUCAP** and measures the proportion of the refinery that is semi-complex. Again it is expected to have a positive correlation with survival.

(xvii) **CHCUCAP**. This is the sum of catalytic cracking and hydro-cracking capacities and measures the refinery's complex capacity in absolute terms. If this is advantageous relative to the normalized configuration (topping), then a positive correlation with survival is expected.

(xviii) **CHCUSH**. This is the ratio of **CHCUCAP** to **CDUCAP** and measures the proportion of the refinery that has a complex configuration. Again a positive correlation with survival is expected.

(d) Technical Characteristics

(xix) **TOPP**. If the refinery was of the topping type in 1976, this variable takes a value of 1, otherwise it is 0. This variable allows us to normalize the propensity to survive by type of refinery. A (relatively) high positive coefficient on this variable would indicate that topping refineries were (all other things equal) more likely to survive than other refinery types.

(xx) **SIMP**, (xxi) **SCOM**, (xxii) **COMP**. These variables take a value of 1 when the refinery is of a simple, semi-complex or complex configuration respectively. Otherwise they take a value of 0. The interpretation in these three cases corresponds to that for **TOPP**.

It must be noted that categories (xix)–(xxii) are mutually exclusive. If a model of closure is to be estimated, we can include *either* all four 'dummies' for refinery type and no constant, *or* any three 'dummies' and the constant. The interpretation is different in the two cases. The first gives the absolute contributions to survival of each type (e.g. the probability that topping refineries survive); and this is the formulation adopted here. The second would give the relative contribution of each type, normalized by the constant that stands for the type of refinery for which the 'dummy' variable was omitted.

(xxiii) **LUB**, (xxiv) **BTN**. These variables take a value of 1 if the refinery was involved in the production of lubricants and bitumen respectively, and 0 if it was not. If lubricants or bitumen production increase a refinery's profitability, then we expect this variable to be positively associated with survival.

(xxv) **LUBCAP**, (xxvi) **BTNCAP**. These variables measure the absolute levels of lubricants or bitumen production capacity on the refinery site respectively. This is a quantification of the qualitative information contained in **LUB** and **BTN**. If the presence of a lubricants or bitumen plant is advantageous, then we should expect that this advantage will increase with the capacity of these units. Thus, a positive correlation with survival is expected.

(xxvii) **LUBSH**, (xxviii) **BTNSH**. These are the ratios of **LUBCAP** to **CDUCAP** and **BTNCAP** to **CDUCAP** respectively. They normalize lubricants and bitumen production capacities relative to the size of the refinery. A positive correlation with survival is expected.

(xxix) **NEWDAT**. For each type of refinery there is a piece of plant
that defines its configuration (e.g. a catalytic reformer is the additional item of plant that indicates that a refinery has a simple rather than
a topping configuration). This variable is the date at which this piece
of plant was installed (or last substantially modified). It therefore
measures the age of the refinery as that of the configuration it had
attained in 1976. If age is associated with poorer technology and
higher running costs, then a later date should increase the probability
of survival, and we would expect the correlation between **NEWDAT**
and survival to be positive. It is important to see that the effect of this
variable is different from the effect of **OPEN**, the age of the site, which
measures the earliest date at which there was production of refined
products under *any* configuration.[1]

(xxx) **NUMCDU**. This is the number of crude distillation units at the
refinery site. Since it is very undesirable to run a CDU at less than a
certain percentage throughput, it follows that a site with (say) two
units is more flexible than a site with the same total capacity with only
one unit. Assuming that a CDU has a 'minimum' throughput of 60
per cent, a site with only one unit must produce at least 60 per cent of
total capacity or not at all while a site with two equal-sized CDUs can
reduce its production to 30 per cent of total capacity (with one unit
shut and the other at 60 per cent of its capacity). Hence the extra
flexibility given by a larger number of CDUs should allow the refinery
to survive in a shrinking market. We therefore expect this variable to
be positively correlated with survival.

(xxxi) **INTEG**. For refiners who have no other business upstream or
downstream of the refinery this takes a value of 1, while for integrated
refiners it takes a value of 0. If the presence of associated business
increases the probability that the owner will keep the refinery open,
then a negative correlation with survival is expected.

(e) Ownership

(xxxii) **NUMOWN**. If the refinery is owned by more than one company this variable is assigned a value of 1, while if it has a single
owner it takes a value of 0. On the assumption that it would be easier
for a single owner to close a refinery than for several owners to agree
to do so (all other factors being the same), we expect a positive
correlation with survival.

---

[1] Other parts of the plant might have that age.

(xxxiii) **MAXSHR**. This is the percentage of the total European refining capacity of the owner represented by the refinery in question. For a single owner who has only one refinery, its value will be 100 per cent. For refineries with more than one owner, we first take as the owners' local capacities the fractions of the refinery's crude distillation capacity corresponding to their ownership shares.[2] These allocated capacities are then expressed as percentages of the individual company's total European crude distillation capacities to give the shares that each refinery represents. The largest such share for each refinery is assigned to **MAXSHR**, on the grounds that it is the company for whom that refinery is most important in total European terms that will determine the closure decision.[3] A high score on this variable suggests that the refinery in question is important for the company's total European refining activity, so that a desire to stay in the market should suggest a positive correlation between this variable and survival.

(xxxiv) **EUROP**. If the refinery owner (or maximum shareholder) has refining interests outside Europe, this variable is assigned a value of 0, while if the owner's activity is entirely based in Europe, then it takes a value of 1. If owners who are internationally diversified are more willing to disinvest from Europe than owners whose activity is confined to that market, then we expect a positive correlation with survival.

(xxxv) **STATOWN**. For refineries where the owner (or largest shareholder) is a national company or government, we assign this variable a value of 1, otherwise it is 0. If considerations of the national interest mean that refineries were being kept open when purely commercial decisions would have led to their closure, then this variable should have a positive correlation with survival.

(xxxvi) **SUMCAP**. This is the sum of all crude distillation capacity that the refinery's owner (or principal shareholder) had in Europe in 1976. If large companies were more willing to shut sites than small ones, then this variable should be negatively correlated with survival. It should be noted that the size of the refinery relative to the company's size (in Europe) is measured separately by the variable (xxxvii) **AVCDUCAP** (see below).

---

[2] Two owners with 40 and 60 per cent shares in an 100,000-unit CDU are given 40,000 and 60,000 units respectively.

[3] Just less than one-quarter of European refineries were jointly owned and had to be treated in this way.

(xxxvii) **AVCDUCAP**. This is the ratio of **CDUCAP** to **SUMCAP**, and can be approximated by their separate presence in a regression. This is distinct from **MAXSHR** above, since it is the ratio for the refinery's largest *shareholder*, whereas **MAXSHR** is the largest *ratio* for any of the shareholders. The more important a given refinery is for a company in the European market as a whole, the less likely it may be to close, so a positive correlation with survival is expected. If there is a technical economy of scale then **CDUCAP** should have a separate effect on the closure decision.

(xxxviii) **NATSHR**. This is the ratio of the crude distillation capacity of the refinery in question to its owner's total crude distillation capacity in the country concerned. For refineries with more than one owner, the highest ratio is taken. This variable, which is analogous to (xlvi) **MSHARE** (see below) and (xxxiii) **MAXSHR**, tries to identify where a given refinery has a large local strategic importance for the owner. The higher its value, the less likely the plant is to be closed, so a positive correlation with survival is expected.

(xxxix) **NATCAP**. This is the total crude distillation capacity of the refinery owner (or major owner as defined for **NATSHR**) in the country in which the refinery is situated. The larger its value (all other things equal), the less likely a given refinery will be to close, so a negative correlation with survival is expected.

(f) Economic Characteristics

(xl) **TOPPDAT**, (xli) **SIMPDAT**, (xlii) **SCOMPDAT**, (xliii) **COMPDAT**. These are the most recent dates at which investment in or improvements to the plant were made in the topping, simple, semi-complex and complex configurations respectively. In all cases a positive correlation with survival is expected.

(xliv) **MARKET**. This is the total consumption of refined products in 1976 (measured in tonnes) for the country in which the refinery is situated, as reported by the IEA.[4] As a measure of the pressure of local demand, it is expected to have a positive correlation with survival.

---

[4] Belgium and Luxembourg are aggregated for this purpose.

(xlv) **CTYCAP**. This is the total crude distillation capacity available in 1976 in the country in which the refinery is situated (in bpcd), and measures the potential supply in the market where the refinery is situated. The larger this was, the more likely the refinery was to close (other things being equal), so a negative correlation with survival is expected.

(xlvi) **MSHARE**. This is the ratio of **CDUCAP** to **CTYCAP**, which is a measure of the importance of the given refinery to the total supply in that country. The larger the value of this variable, the less likely the refinery may have been to close (other things being equal), so a positive correlation with survival might be expected. As before, **CDU-CAP** may enter separately if there are specific economies of scale to plant size.

(xlvii) **EXCESS**. This is the ratio of **CTYCAP** to **MARKET** for the country in which the refinery is located. It is a measure of the potential excess supply (relative to actual demand). This should be negatively correlated with survival. The variable is approximated by the separate presence of **CTYCAP** and **MARKET** in the model.

5.3 The Statistical Model

The methodology used is first to relate the closure decision to all the factors we have identified in order to see which appear to be significant, and then to simplify by progressively removing insignificant factors. Some variables are alternatives for each other, e.g. **BTN** and **BTNCAP**, where the former merely signifies the presence of an associated bitumen plant while the latter measures its size; and such factors are not used simultaneously.

The models used for associating the variables in this way are alternatively the linear probability model and the probit (normal probability) model. The former makes the probability of survival a linear function of the values of the explanatory factors, while the latter is a non-linear function. In practice, the two models yield rather similar results and the best-fitting models are shown in Table 5.1.

We found that only twelve of the forty-seven variables used are significant, and these are listed in Table 5.1. The economic interpretation of these results is given further below. The results of the probit model conform to the actual 'open/shut' decisions for 150 refineries (out of a total of 174), or 78 per cent of the population; whereas the results of the linear probability model correspond to the actual

Table 5.1: Best-fitting Probit and Associated Linear Probability Models for Refineries' Survival. 1976–86.

Variable	Probit[a]		Linear Probability	
	Coefficient[b]	't'-statistic	Coefficient[b]	't'-statistic
CONSTANT	2.24	3.29	−0.11	1.09
REGION	−0.89	2.61	−0.19	2.84
COAST	0.51	1.79	0.13	2.01
PPIPE	0.42	1.37	0.09	1.27
PCHEM	0.44	1.41	0.13	1.97
CRFCAP	0.22 (−4)	1.55	0.42 (−5)	1.45
THTCCAP	0.77 (−4)	2.15	0.79 (−5)	2.54
CHCUCAP	0.45 (−4)	1.99	0.36 (−5)	1.33
LUBCAP	0.23 (−3)	2.35	0.29 (−4)	1.77
BTNCAP	0.84 (−4)	1.50	0.13 (−4)	1.31
INTEG	−1.09	1.91	−0.28	2.39
SUMCAP	−0.48 (−6)	3.08	−0.67 (−7)	2.22
CTYCAP	−0.71 (−3)	4.43	−0.12 (−6)	5.22

Notes: (a) The cut-off point for including a variable in the probit model is that its coefficient should be of the correct (expected) sign and that its 't'-statistic should be greater than 1.28. Such a score, using a one-sided significance test, indicates that a 't'-statistic of that magnitude or greater could have occurred in only 10 per cent of samples if there were no genuine association between the variable and the decision to shut.

(b) The figures in brackets represent multiplication by powers of 10.

decisions for 146 refineries, or 73 per cent of the population. These divide as follows:

Of the fifty-four refineries that shut between 1976 and 1986, the results of the *probit* model indicate that forty-one should have shut and thirteen remained open; and out of the 120 that remained open, its results indicate that 109 should have remained open and eleven should have shut.

Of the fifty-four refineries that shut between 1976 and 1986, the results of the *linear probability* model indicate that thirty-six should have shut and eighteen remained open; and out of the 120 that remained open its results indicate that 110 should have remained open and ten shut.

We discuss these results under three headings: goodness of fit, economic implications and statistical predictions.

(a) *Goodness of Fit.* For both the probit and linear probability models the goodness of fit is very high.[5] In the Appendix to this chapter we explain how the model weights the explanatory factors together to form the probability of observing the given result (open or closed) for the associated levels of the explanatory variables and estimated parameters. If this calculation yields a probability of x that the refinery will remain open, this means that we would expect $100x$ per cent of refineries with the same characteristics to remain open. Our decision rule is that if this probability is greater than 0.5, we predict that the refinery will in fact remain open, while for a probability of less than 0.5 we predict a closure. This rule allows us to calculate how many actual closures and non-closures are correctly predicted by this model.

We can 'normalize' these probabilities by the actual decisions. For example, a refinery that actually remained open and had a probability of 0.6 of doing so is given a 'normalized probability' of 0.6, while a refinery that shut and had a probability of 0.3 of remaining open is given a 'normalized probability' of 0.7.[6] The mean 'normalized probability' is a simple measure of the success of the model in predicting closures in the period 1976–86 from data relating to the market at end-1976.

Using the above ideas, we see that the probit model performs a little better in terms of predicting closures than the linear probability model with the same set of explanatory variables. The probit model predicts 85 per cent of all cases correctly, with a slightly better performance for predicting the refineries that stayed open than for those that closed. Nevertheless, 76 per cent of all closures are predicted from variables that were known at the beginning of the period. The mean 'normalized probability' over all the predictions (correct and incorrect) is 0.78, so that, since incorrect predictions have normalized probabilities of less than 0.5, it is clear that most correct predictions have normalized probabilities substantially higher than the mean.

The linear probability model predicted 84 per cent of all decisions correctly, with 67 per cent of closures correctly predicted. The average normalized probability was 0.73. However, once we compare the distribution of probabilities we see that the non-linear probit model performed better. In the range of normalized probabilities that were

[5] Correlations are not reported because the models are not trying directly to maximize the correlation between variables.
[6] These 'normalized probabilities' are in effect the probabilities that the model predicted the actual outcomes in the individual cases.

Table 5.2: Frequency Distribution of Probabilities of Correct Prediction of Refineries' Survival. 1976–86.

| Probability Range | Frequency of Cases (%) | |
	Probit Model	Linear Probability Model
0.0–0.1	1.1	0.6
0.1–0.2	2.8	0.0
0.2–0.3	1.7	2.3
0.3–0.4	3.4	4.0
0.4–0.5	4.6	9.2
0.5–0.6	6.8	14.9
0.6–0.7	10.3	20.1
0.7–0.8	8.5	14.4
0.8–0.9	16.5	9.8
0.9–1.0	43.2	24.1

only marginal successes (0.5–0.7), the probit model had only 17 per cent of cases while the linear model had 35 per cent (see Table 5.2). Conversely, in the range of very high normalized probabilities (0.8–1.0), the probit model had 60 per cent of all cases, while the linear probability model had 34 per cent.

The extremely skew nature of the distribution makes it clear that for the overwhelming majority of cases the probit model gives a very high probability of being correct.

(*b*) *Economic Interpretation.* The variables that turned out to be significant need individual comment and interpretation.[7] Since the pattern of results is similar for the two models, we concentrate on the parameter values for the linear probability model, since these are capable of a particularly simple and interesting interpretation.

Before we look at the individual variables, it is important to emphasize the difference between a multi-factor model and a series of single-factor models. We might find that survival is correlated individually with crude distillation capacity at the refinery (**CDUCAP**) and also with the total European crude distillation capacity held by the owner (**SUMCAP**). However, when survival is simultaneously related to both factors, only **SUMCAP** appears to make an incremental contribution to the explanation of survival: the two variables (**CDUCAP**

[7] We comment on those that were not significant below.

and **SUMCAP**) are correlated so that on its own **CDUCAP** 'stands in' for **SUMCAP**, but once both are used then **CDUCAP** has no explanatory role of its own. This feature of correlated explanatory variables helps to explain why certain variables, which taken on their own appear to be correlated with survival do not appear in the final probit model.

CONSTANT. This is in essence a variable that takes a value of 1 for all refineries. It stands for a hypothetical refinery that has a value of 0 on all other variables, i.e. which has none of the associated categorical features (e.g. **REGION**, **COAST**, **PPIPE**, **PCHEM**, **INTEG**), and has a value of 0 on the other variables (e.g. **SUMCAP**, **BTNCAP**, **LUBCAP**, **CRFCAP**, **CHCUCAP** and **CTYCAP**).

(iii) **REGION**. Refineries in the northern part of Europe centred on Rotterdam are associated with an incremental probability of 19 per cent of closing.[8] This factor must be related to some variable that we have been unable to measure directly. It cannot be associated with the firm's *size* which is included, nor with the *type* of firm, for example in terms of whether or not it is purely European (since this variable was insignificant).

(iv) **COAST**. If a refinery was situated on the coast, it was 13 per cent more likely to survive than an identical refinery not on the coast. The better transport facilities in terms of access to markets thus improve the margin enough to make a significant difference to survival.

(vii) **PPIPE**. If a refinery was attached to a product pipeline it was 9 per cent more likely to survive. This factor is also thought of as a transport cost/market access advantage. It is worth noting that being attached to a crude pipeline was less important and indeed was insignificant. During this period of excess supply of products and crude, superior access to product markets is likely to have been more important in helping a refinery's survival than superior access to the input of crude. *Refiners* had to compete to sell their *products*, whereas it was the *suppliers* who had to compete to sell *crude*. Security and ease of crude supply were not so crucial in this period, and hence the possession of a crude pipeline was not especially advantageous to refiners. A return to tight supply conditions would reverse this argument.

---

[8] The *negative* coefficient reported in Table 5.1 indicates that the fact that a refinery is in northern Europe makes it 19 per cent less likely to survive than an equivalent refinery in southern Europe.

(viii) **PCHEM**. The association of a refinery with a petrochemicals plant increased the probability of its remaining open by 13 per cent (other factors being equal). The security of having guaranteed outlets to receive some of the higher-value products appeared to be an important competitive advantage during the past decade. To a certain extent, the return of feedstocks from the petrochemicals plant may have the same advantages as other forms of upgrading.

(xiii) **CRFCAP**. The sign of this variable indicates that it was advantageous to own catalytic reforming capacity (as well as topping capacity). The more that was owned, the greater the advantage. Each extra 10,000 bpcd of reforming capacity increased the probability of survival (relative to that of a topping refinery) by 4.2 per cent. Simple refineries thus survived better than topping refineries.

(xv) **THTCCAP**. The presence of thermal treating (thermal cracking or coking) plant was highly significant in aiding survival. Each extra 10,000 bpcd of capacity increased the probability of a refinery's survival by 7.9 per cent. Hence a semi-complex refinery, which has both reforming and thermal treating plant, increases its probability of survival by 12 per cent for every extra 10,000 bpcd on both types of plant.

(xvi) **CHCUCAP**. The possession of catalytic or hydrocracking plant also increased the chance of survival: each extra 10,000 bpcd of this plant increased the chance of survival by 3.6 per cent. Since complex refineries largely had only reforming and catalytic or hydrocracking plant (but not thermal treating plant), the extra advantage of becoming more complex by having an increment of both types of plant was 8 per cent. It is important to note that the competitive gain of having a complex rather than a simple refinery structure appeared less advantageous than that of having a semi-complex rather than a simple configuration.

(xxv) **LUBCAP**. The sign of this coefficient indicates that association with the production of lubricants was a competitive advantage. For every 10,000 bpcd of lubricants production capacity the probability of staying open was increased by 29 per cent. Clearly lubricants production capacity was extremely advantageous – twice as important for staying open as bitumen capacity.

(xxvi) **BTNCAP**. The sign of this coefficient indicates that the association of the refinery with bitumen production was a competitive advantage. For every 10,000 bpcd of bitumen production capacity at the refinery the chance of staying open was increased by 13 per cent. The size of this impact is compared below with the effects of the possession of other types of plant.

(xxxi) **INTEG**. The coefficient on this variable indicates that, for companies that were not integrated either upstream or downstream (**INTEG** = 1), there was a competitive disadvantage of 28 per cent. There were very few such companies, and this variable is most important in explaining closure decisions in Italy.

(xxxvi) **SUMCAP**. The sign on this variable indicates that the larger was the total (European) crude distillation capacity available to the owner (or principal owner), the smaller was the chance that a *given refinery* would remain open. The size of the coefficient indicates that, for every million bpcd of crude distillation capacity available to the refinery owner, the probability of survival of a given refinery decreased by 6.7 per cent.

(xlv) **CTYCAP**. The sign on this variable indicates that the larger the total crude distillation capacity located in the same country as the refinery in question, the greater the chance that the given refinery would close. Each additional million bpcd of crude distillation capacity in the country concerned increased the chance of a given refinery's closing by 12 per cent.

The picture given by these variables and their coefficients must be interpreted carefully. The presence (or absence) of a variable in the final model is not a definitive proof that that variable is or is not important in the closure decision – merely that it was (or was not) associated with closure in Europe during the period 1976–86.

The sizes of the coefficients must be treated merely as a guide to the relative importance of different factors. The results reported above are taken from the linear probability model, whose performance is bettered by the non-linear probit model. This suggests that successive increments of key factors (e.g. bitumen production capacity) will eventually be of decreasing marginal importance. Hence we should not extrapolate too far from refiners' average experience on the basis of the results of the linear probability model, in case we over-emphasize the benefits to be derived from the possession of a large amount of some factor whose incremental effect may vary substantially.

The general pattern of results is clear. Refineries gain from:

(a) better configurations;
(b) association with specialized products;
(c) better access to markets; and
(d) certain features of the owner.

In addition, location in a country with a large total refinery capacity is a disadvantage. Grouping under these factors allows us to relate the results to variables that did not contribute to our final modelling of closure. First, we consider the variables that relate to the plant available at the refinery. The variables that showed no significant association with closure were the *age* variables (age of plant and age of site), the *number* of crude distillation units at the site and the crude distillation *capacity* at the site. This suggests that the age of a given type of plant does not make sufficient difference to the competitive margin to show any association with the decision to close, and that the possession of extra CDUs did not add to flexibility in a way that was not already implicit in the amounts of other types of capacity on site. A semi-complex refinery might for example run one CDU to feed the thermal treating plant, so that the remaining CDU would be no more or less flexible than it would have been at a pure topping refinery. The lack of significance of crude distillation capacity indicates that there is no evidence of economies of scale.

The other plant variables that were insignificant were the simple categorizations of refineries by *type* (as opposed to their *quantitative* versions). This result was expected, since, if having upgrading capacity is important at all, then its importance should be greater for refineries that have more of it. The variables concerned with the shares of different types of capacity appear to have been less significant than the absolute amounts of upgraded or associated capacity.

The locational variables that were insignificant were: **WATER**, **CPIPE**, **CRUDE**, **BASE** and **NEAR**. The transport facilities offered by inland waterways or crude pipelines and access to nearby sources of crude were expected to be important largely from the point of security of supply, and the latter may have been relatively unimportant during the period under study. The two distance variables, which measure the extent to which a given refinery might have a local monopoly, may just not be large enough to be counted as significant. The reduction in transport costs may be small in comparison with other cost advantages, and therefore not observably significant.

The third set of factors that did not show up as being significant were those related to the company owning the refinery. These included **NUMOWN**, **MAXSHR**, **STATOWN**, **EUROP** and **NAT-CAP**. The *absolute* importance of a site for an owner has already been caught by the variable **SUMCAP** (its total European crude distillation capacity). This dominates the *relative* importance of the site, *either* versus all its sites *or* versus its sites in the country in question. *Local* market conditions were caught by the total of all supply in that country (**CTYCAP**). Thus there is no direct evidence of strategy being related to a particular market independent of its size. The behaviour of national companies is not significantly different from that of private companies: nor do purely European companies behave differently from international companies.

(*c*) *Statistical Predictions.* As well as summarizing the *overall* performance of our models by calculating the *mean* probabilities that they predict the actual outcomes correctly, the number of correct predictions they make, and the significance (or insignificance) of the different variables tried, we can also examine the 'normalized probabilities' for each refinery as defined above, in order to highlight those cases for which the probit model failed to make the correct prediction (those with a normalized probability of less than 0.5). Identification of the refineries in question may help to throw light on the failure of the model to predict correctly in these cases.

The probit model can also be used to predict the future behaviour of those refineries that are still open as at end-1986. The model predicted that some of these would close; and others closed that the model predicted would remain open. If we argue that closure is a slow process, and that the pressures of the early 1980s have still not fully worked through the system, then we would expect more refinery closures to occur in the next few years. The model can thus be used to identify the 'weakest' of the survivors using the criteria that explained closure between 1976 and 1986.

We begin with the twenty-four incorrect predictions made by the probit model. These fall into two classes:

(a) those that closed that the model predicted would stay open;
(b) those that remained open that the model predicted would close.

These refineries, their owners and their normalized probabilities are listed in Table 5.3. It can be seen that those that remained open that were predicted to shut include a high proportion with normalized probabilities close to 0.5, i.e. the model predicted their closure by only a narrow margin. Moreover, as we pointed out above, some of these may indeed close post 1986. The conspicuous failures of this model are the refineries owned by Total at Mardyck and Mantova-Frassine, which remained open despite having so few of the factors that the

Table 5.3: Normalized Probabilities for Incorrectly Predicted Cases from Probit Model of Refinery Survivals. 1976–86.

	Actually Open/Predicted Shut			Actually Shut/Predicted Open	
Site	Owner	Normalized Probability	Site	Owner	Normalized Probability
Mardyck	Total	0.09	Isle of Grain	BP	0.01
Mantova-Frassine	Total	0.11	Feluy	Chevron	0.13
Grandpuits	Elf	0.34	Ellesmere Port	Burmah	0.14
Duisburg	Petrofina/Total	0.36	Gaeta	Monti	0.16
Arcola, La Spezia	Phillipps/Moratti	0.39	Amsterdam	Mobil	0.17
Dunkirk	BP	0.40	Frontignan	Mobil	0.21
Cremona	Amoco	0.42	Aquila	Total	0.22
Salzbergen	Wintershall	0.44	Ghent	Texaco	0.26
Hamburg (OJS)	BP	0.48	Dinslaken	BP	0.38
Taranto	Agip	0.49	Raunheim	Texaco/Chevron	0.40
Shell Haven	Shell	0.49	Ingolstadt	Shell	0.41
			Herrlisheim-Drusenheim	Total/Antar/BP	0.43
			Porto Torres	Sardoil	0.47

Table 5.4: Values of Model Variables for Incorrect Predictions of Closure.

Variable	Mardyck	Mantova-Frassine
REGION	1	0
COAST	0	0
PPIPE	0	0
PCHEM	0	0
CRFCAP	22,800	9,900
THTCCAP	0	0
CHCUCAP	0	0
LUBCAP	0	0
BTNCAP	0	0
INTEG	0	0
SUMCAP	1,365,470	1,365,470
CTYCAP	3,579	4,239

model finds to be advantageous. The values of the variables that enter the model for these refineries are listed in Table 5.4.

Both are small simple refineries with no associated production of specialized products. The only locational feature that is of benefit is the location of Mantova-Frassine in southern Europe, where the model predicts fewer closures. Both refineries belong to a large company and are in markets with large total crude distillation capacities. All the variables predispose these refineries to close according to the model. Keeping them open may be as a result of special company policy or a very particular locational advantage that is not caught by the standard variables.

As regards the refineries that in fact shut while the model predicted that they should have remained open, there are eight whose normalized probabilities are sufficiently low for the model to have failed conspicuously. The values of the variables for these cases are given in Table 5.5. These show no particular pattern to explain why those characteristics that normally appear to be competitive advantages, and which should have led to refineries' remaining open, were in fact associated with their closure. Policy in terms of the importance of the given refinery within the total company strategy may be important. If the company assesses that it has excess capacity, the model will measure this by the supply potential of the market (**CTYCAP**) as well as by the total crude distillation capacity available to the company (**SUMCAP**). However, if decisions are taken on a proportional basis, i.e. if companies decide to close 10 per cent of their capacity irrespective of competitors' strengths or weaknesses, and independently of the quality of their refinery capacity (i.e. their ability to compete with

Table 5.5: Values of Model Variables for Incorrect Predictions of Survival.[a]

Variable	Isle of Grain	Feluy	Ellesmere Port	Gaeta	Amsterdam	Frontignan	Aquila	Ghent
REGION	1	1	1	0	0	0	0	1
COAST	1	0	1	1	1	1	1	0
PPIPE	1	1	0	1	1	0	1	0
PCHEM	1	1	1	0	0	0	0	0
CRFCAP	0.040	0.011	0.005	0.012	0.023	0.019	0.017	0.020
THTCCAP	0.019	0	0.002	0	0	0	0	0
CHCUCAP	0.017	0	0	0	0	0.013	0.005	0
LUBCAP	0.004	0	0.003	0.004	0	0	0.001	0
BTNCAP	0.007	0.002	0	0	0	0.001	0.005	0
INTEG	0	0	0	0	0	0	0	0
SUMCAP	2.328	0.517	0.028	0.842	0.999	0.999	1.365	0.765
CTYCAP	2.965	1.088	2.965	4.239	1.886	3.579	4.239	1.088

Note: (a) All capacity figures are in million bpcd.

rivals), then the refinery that is closed will be merely the least desirable of all those available to the company concerned. If all its plants are of a 'strongly competitive' type, then the 'least strong' will be closed, despite its superiority to intra-marginal refineries belonging to other companies who have even weaker plants to close. The Isle of Grain case may well exemplify this, since all of BP's UK refineries are strong by general European standards as calibrated by the model. However, the Isle of Grain site was perhaps seen as the most easily dispensable and hence closed.

The results still leave some unexplained features – notably the reason for the significance of the **REGION** variable. It is important to remember that all the factors used to explain closure during the period 1976–86 were in 1976 terms. If certain important factors changed *differentially* after 1976, this may explain why some refineries closed unexpectedly and other remained open unexpectedly. For example, the total demand for products grew at very different rates in the different countries, as noted in Chapter 2 above, and also the breakdown of the demand barrel shifted. A relatively larger shift towards high-value products (or away from low-value products) would make given capacity more attractive in one region than in others. Similar effects could come from differential taxation policies that could affect the sizes of the margins open to refiners in a given region.

An important way of comparing the performances of the probit and linear probability models is to analyse the failures in the two cases. We do this by identifying cases in which refineries stayed open but were predicted to shut by either of the two models. Table 5.6 lists all these failures and gives the associated normalized probabilities.

The agreement between the two models is very close: of the eleven refineries that were predicted to close by the probit model, nine were also predicted to close by the associated linear model. Moreover, the ranking of refineries in order of their estimated competitive weakness is very similar.

The high level of agreement between the two models allows us to use the preferred probit model to undertake a further analysis of the refining situation as at 1986. Since we can identify 'low-score' types of refineries as at 1976, and since it is generally agreed that even a decade later there was still over-capacity in the European refining industry, we can evaluate the strengths of the surviving refineries in 1986. This will allow us both to identify the 'weaker' refineries at end-1986, and also to see how refineries changed their scores between 1976 and 1986.

In order to determine the 'scores' of the surviving refineries in 1986,

Table 5.6: Comparison of Normalized Probabilities for the Two Models' Incorrect Predictions of Closure.

Refinery	Probit Model	Linear Probability Model
Mardyck	0.09	0.27
Mantova-Frassine	0.11	0.32
Grandpuits	0.34	0.42
Duisburg	0.36	0.43
Arcola, La Spezia	0.39	0.49
Dunkirk	0.40	0.46
Cremona	0.42	0.49
Salzbergen	0.44	0.42
Hamburg (OJS)	0.48	0.49
Taranto	0.49	(0.56)
Shell Haven	0.49	(0.64)
Busalla	(0.51)	0.37

we take the values of the variables in the model in 1986 terms and weight them by the coefficients on these variables as estimated by the probit model from 1976 data. The total score (which is already a standardized normal variate) is then applied to a cumulative normal distribution table to give an 'index of survival' for the refinery in question. Care must be taken in interpreting this index, which is the probability that the refinery *would* have remained open *if* it had possessed its end-1986 characteristics at end-1976.[9] Since the overall market situation changed between these two years, the propensity of a given refinery with unchanged characteristics to close would also have changed, and the model therefore cannot be used to forecast the degree of excess capacity. It does, however, indicate the relative strengths and weaknesses of the various refineries in terms of the pattern of closures already experienced. If we form a view on how much capacity may still have to be closed post 1986, then the model indicates which refineries will be most likely to close following the pattern in the period 1976–86, in the absence of any special local features.

The 120 refineries that survived from 1976 to 1986 can thus each be characterized by two measures of their relative competitive strength: the probability of their staying open estimated from the 1976 values, and the 'index of survival' estimated on the basis of the 1986 values.

---

[9] Some of the variables are unchanged (mainly the categorical values such as **REGION**), some are changed by the actions of the firm in question (e.g. the amount of catalytic reforming capacity (**CRFCAP**), and one is altered by the actions of all the firms in the industry (**CTYCAP**).

Table 5.7: Summary Statistics for Changes in Ranking of Probabilities of Survival for Probit Model. 1976–86.

Number falling by	50+	6
	40–50	7
	30–40	13
	20–30	9
	10–20	6
	0–10	14
Number rising by	0–10	18
	10–20	14
	20–30	11
	30–40	7
	40–50	10
	50+	5
Mean Change in Ranking		0
Standard Deviation of Change		32.3

We found that virtually every refinery had a higher 'probability of survival' by 1986 than in 1976; and many had moved to positions that would have guaranteed their survival had they possessed them in 1976. A more interesting feature is given by the correlation between the rank positions (amongst survivors) in 1976 and 1986. This (squared) correlation is only 35 per cent, which indicates that there was a very great deal of reordering of comparative strengths between 1976 and 1986. This reordering is summarized in Table 5.7, which gives details of the differences in ranking between the two sets of scores. The distribution of the change in ranks is very spread out with an extremely high standard deviation, which confirms that there was a great deal of movement in the relative positions of the refineries as measured by their normalized probabilities as calculated from the probit model.

The second feature to be noted from Table 5.7 is a relation between the size of possible reductions in crude distillation capacity in Europe and the number of refineries that would be required to close to meet this target. For example, if of the 14.2 million bpcd capacity a total of 500,000 bpcd were to be shut, this could be achieved by the closure of the twelve refineries with the lowest indices of survival as calculated from the probit model with 1986 values. If 1.0 million bpcd were to be closed, then this could be achieved by the closure of the nineteen refineries with the lowest indices. Although the model indicates which refinery has the lowest index, this cannot be taken as a prediction that it will be the first to close. Special features, unaccounted for in the model, or management aims different from those that motivated the managers of the refineries that closed, might keep it open when other refineries with higher indices closed.

5.4 Conclusion

This exercise has shown that there is a set of factors known at end-1976 that can be used to predict refinery closures and survivals in Europe between 1976 and 1986 with a high degree of accuracy. The factors that appear to have been important are the refinery's configuration, its association with the production of special products, certain features of its access to markets, the size of the owner in the European refining sector and the total local refinery capacity.

Using the weights on these factors estimated from a non-linear (probit) or linear probability model, it is possible to assign every refinery that remained open a 'probability of survival' based on the 1976 values of these variables and one based on the corresponding 1986 values. These can be taken as telling us how similar a refinery was, in terms of measurable features, to those that closed during the period 1976–86. It does not measure profitability or managerial efficiency. All refineries increased their 'probabilities of survival' during the decade (thereby improving their position as measured in terms of the market situation during the decade). However, not only has the market changed (so that a probability that would have indicated that a refinery was secure in 1976 might well indicate its lack of viability post 1986), but it is also important to note the enormous changes in the ranking of refineries' propensities to stay open. Some refineries clearly improved their characteristics much more than the mean, while others improved much less.

Appendix to Chapter 5

Statistical Techniques for Analysing the 'Open/Shut' Decision

In the text we have pointed to the importance of the closure of refineries as the process whereby not only is excess capacity removed but also the nature of the marginal capacity is altered. In order to understand the forces that have led to closure, we need to model the process. There are a large number of factors that may affect the decision whether a given refinery closes or stays open; and in essence we need to correlate the magnitudes of these factors with whether or not the refineries close.

In statistical terms the decision to close a refinery is a 'categorical' variable: either it shuts or it does not. Such a variable cannot be measured on a continuous scale (at least not directly), and hence cannot be related in a continuous (incremental) fashion to the possible explanatory variables. Hence standard techniques of association, such as regression or correlation, are inappropriate. Instead we use the ideas of the linear probability model and the probit model. Since these are unfamiliar, and indeed have not been used in this context before, it is necessary to develop them rather carefully.

Suppose that for the 'standard' refinery (this is a purely arbitrary notion relative to which other refineries can be measured) there is a variable Z (most likely profitability), for which there is a crucial level $Z*$. If the actual value of Z is greater than $Z*$, the refinery survives, while if it is lower the refinery cannot survive. If we had data on many refineries (all standard) and observed which closed and which stayed open, and we knew their actual Z values, then we could form an estimate of the critical value $Z*$.

This simple idea can be generalized in two important ways:

(i) We can allow for the fact that refineries differ, i.e. that their actual performance is affected by a large number of other factors X_i ($i = 1, 2, \dots, k$), each of which has a relative weight β_i. Hence, for a refinery t, with characteristics $X_{1t}, \dots X_{kt}$, we may define its 'score' as the weighted sum:

$$\beta_1 X_{1t} + \dots + \beta_k X_{kt} \tag{1}$$

If β_i is positive, then as X_{it} increases the performance of the refinery t improves: X_i is 'good' for keeping the refinery open because it makes it more likely that its performance exceeds the critical value. We can now see how to interpret the 'standard' refinery: it is the one (perhaps hypothetical) for which *all* the X_i are zero. The X_{it} thus measure the differences between the characteristics of a given refinery and those of the standard reference case.

(ii) We also allow for the fact that there are many other influences on the performance of each refinery that are unmeasurable, which we encapsulate in a random variable (or error term) u. This allows us to match the actual observations on whether a refinery has closed or not to the weighted sums of X_{it} given in (1) above, and hence to estimate the values of β_i that indicate which variables are of greater or lesser importance in determining a refinery's performance and hence its survival or closure.

For ease of exposition, we first consider the case of a refinery t whose closure or survival is determined by the value of only one explanatory variable X and the error term u. For this refinery:

$$Z_t = \beta X_t + u_t \tag{2}$$

If $Z_t - Z*$ is positive, refinery t remains open, while if $Z_t - Z*$ is negative it closes. We cannot observe u_t but we do observe whether the refinery closes or not. The probability that refinery t closes is therefore the probability that:

$$u_t < Z* - \beta X_t \tag{3}$$

Hence, if we know the value of β and the probability distribution $f(u)$, then the probability that the refinery will close is:

$$P(C|\ X_t,\ \beta) = \int_{-\infty}^{Z*-\beta X_t} f(u)\,du \tag{4}$$

Analogously, the probability that the refinery will remain open is:

$$P(O|\ X_t,\ \beta) = \int_{Z*-\beta X_t}^{+\infty} f(u)\,du = 1 - \int_{-\infty}^{Z*-\beta X_t} f(u)\,du \tag{5}$$

If we use the cumulative frequency function F we have:

$$P(C) = F(Z* - \beta X_t) \tag{6}$$

$$P(O) = 1 - F(Z* - \beta X_t) \tag{7}$$

This formulation, which allows us to attach a probability to the fact that a refinery actually closed or stayed open, needs to be interpreted very carefully. A probability of 0.4 that a refinery remained open, with $X = X_t$, means that our model says that 40 per cent of refineries with $X = X_t$ and the same parameter C that are affected similarly by a random variable u with frequency function $f(u)$ would close. It is clear that a knowledge of the frequency function of the error term is needed before we can use this approach to estimate the parameters.

The general principle of estimation is that of maximum likelihood. Since we know whether or not a refinery closed, we know whether to describe its behaviour by (6) or (7). Hence the probability of the actual set of closures and survivals for *all* the refineries taken together can be expressed (labelling closures 1, ..., s and survivals $s+1$, ..., T) as:

$$\prod_{i=1}^{s} F(Z* - \beta X_i) \prod_{i=s+1}^{T} [1 - F(Z* - \beta X_i)] \tag{8}$$

This is the 'likelihood function', and given a form for F we choose the values of β and $Z*$ that maximize it, i.e. we choose those that give the greatest probability of producing the *actual* pattern of closures.

There are two common forms assumed for the probability distribution:

(a) rectangular distribution (linear probability model);
(b) normal distribution (probit model).

For the rectangular distribution the parameters can be estimated by the linear regression of the X_t on the categorical variable **SHUT** ($Y_t = 1$ if the refinery survived, 0 if it closed). Once we have estimated the parameters B' and β'_i ($i = 1, ... , k$), we can first carry out significance tests on the importance of each factor i in changing the propensity of a refinery to survive. A simple 't' test is equivalent to a likelihood ratio (large sample) test. Measures of goodness of fit can be of three types:

(a) *Multiple Correlation in the OLS Regression.* This is an artificial measure since OLS is purely a computing device. It is known that even very 'successful' models for the prediction of closure can have low R^2 values.

(*b*) *Standard Error of Estimate.* This is the average residual of the regression. It can be interpreted as the one minus the average likelihood or probability per observation of making the correct prediction.

(*c*) *The Percentage of Correct Predictions.* This is the most commonly used measure of goodness of fit. If the model gives a probability greater than 0.5, we take this as predicting that the refinery will survive, while if the predicted probability is less than 0.5 we take this as predicting that the refinery will close. The total number of correct predictions in fact incorporates correct predictions of both survivals and closures. We may attach a greater or lesser weight to one or other category. We calculate the predicted probability of a survival by using the least squares estimator, i.e. $\hat{Y}_t = B' + \beta'X_t$, where Y_t is the predicted probability that refinery t will survive.

We can also see that in the multi-variable case a given factor X_i adds an increment of $\beta_i'X_i$ to the probability of remaining open. Hence, if X_i is itself a categorical variable (e.g. whether or not the refinery is state owned) with values 1 and 0, then the possession of the attribute ($X_i = 1$) increases the probability of survival by β'_i. We also see that the probability of survival is linear in X_i. Each equal increment in X_i (where X_i is a non-categorical variable) increases the probability of survival (assuming $\beta'_i > 0$) by an equal amount.

A final presentational point comes from the property of OLS fits (with models including a constant) that the sum of the fitted errors $\Sigma\hat{u}_t$ is zero. Hence the sum of actual values ΣY_t is equal to the sum of predicted values $\Sigma\hat{Y}_t$. This in turn implies that the *actual* number of survivals ΣY_t is equal to the sum of the *predicted* probabilities of survival over all the refineries. If the underlying distribution is normal (probit model) rather than rectangular, all the same points apply except that:

(a) There is no easy technique for carrying out the estimation and special non-linear methods are used to obtain the probit.
(b) The probabilities of survival that come from (7) are no longer linear in X_t. No single interpretation can be given to the β coefficients, but tests for significance can still be derived. The relationship between survival and X_t is non-linear – as X_t becomes very large or very small the incremental impact on survival decreases rapidly. The score of refinery t, $B' + \Sigma\beta'_{it}X_{it}$, is in fact the normalized standard deviate, i.e. the number of standard deviations the given refinery is from the mean (of zero). Hence cumulative normal distribution tables can be applied to these scores to yield the predicted probabilities of survival.

6 Refinery Yield, Capacity and Output

Margaret Chadwick

The prices of petroleum products are influenced to some extent by the yields of marginal refineries, i.e. those whose levels of utilization change most in response to changes in product supply and demand. One purpose of this chapter is to develop a methodology for identifying the yield of marginal refineries at any particular point in time. This methodology is then applied to the European refining system in the period 1976–86. This enables us to study the way in which the structural changes described in Chapters 4 and 5 affected the yields of the marginal refineries.

6.1 Methodology

Refinery yields are classified into five types:

(a) Topping;
(b) Simple (or hydroskimming);
(c) Semi-complex;
(d) Complex; and
(e) Ultra-complex.

It is usual to group topping and simple together into a single category which we shall refer to from here on as 'simple', and which is sometimes known as 'hydroskimming'. We shall also ignore the ultra-complex yield, because at end-1986 only one such processing train was in operation in Europe. The ultra-complex yield will be a very significant type in the future, however, and the omission will not be legitimate in studies undertaken in a few years' time. In this chapter, therefore, the types of yield considered reduce to three: simple, semi-complex and complex.

The order in which these types of yield are listed also defines a hierarchy. We shall see later that the gross product worth (GPW) of a complex yield is usually higher than the GPW of a semi-complex yield, and the latter higher than the GPW of a simple yield.

Refineries can be characterized or labelled according to the best type of yield they can produce. Thus a refinery that can produce both simple and semi-complex yields, but not a complex yield, is labelled a semi-complex refinery. A simple refinery cannot produce better than a simple yield, a semi-complex refinery can produce simple and semi-complex yields, and a complex refinery can produce all three types. Naturally every refinery will try to maximize the value obtained from its actual operations by producing in priority the optimum amount of the best type of yield attainable.

Thus every refinery will produce one or several types of yields. The nature and combination of these yields depend on:

(a) the type and capacity of the processing units available to the refinery;
(b) the extent to which each of them is used; and
(c) the type of feedstocks processed.

The combination of yields produced (the average yield) is unique to each refinery, and is likely to vary at different times, since the types and capacities of processing units in a refinery can be combined in many different ways, and the rates of capacity utilization and the feedstock mix can be varied according to circumstances.

For the purposes of identifying the marginal yield and estimating the potential yields in the European refinery system, it is not enough to define types of yield and to characterize refineries by the most valuable type of yield they can produce. We need to know how much of each type of yield a given refinery can produce under certain assumptions about the mode and rate of utilization. This introduces the concept of capacity by type of yield.

Simple, semi-complex and complex capacities refer to the amounts of crude *distilled in the refinery* that can be converted to these respective types of yield in that same refinery. The following example illustrates the definition.

Consider a complex refinery with 20,000 tonnes per day (t/d) of crude distillation capacity, a thermal cracker of 2,000 t/d and a catalytic cracker of 2,000 t/d. Distilling a common type of Middle Eastern crude will give 50 per cent atmospheric residue on crude, which will give 25 per cent vacuum gas oil and 25 per cent short residue (on crude). The catalytic cracker, which must be fed with vacuum distillates, is needed to make a complex yield. As it has a capacity of 2,000 t/d, it can make a complex yield from only 8,000 t/d of the 20,000 t/d of crude passing through the CDU. The refinery therefore has only 8,000 t/d of complex capacity.

Having used 4,000 t/d of residue to make 2,000 t/d of catalytic

Table 6.1: Breakdown of Capacity of Specimen Complex Refinery by Type of Yield. Tonnes per Day.

Yield Type	Volume
Simple	8,000
Semi-complex	4,000
Complex	8,000
Total	20,000

cracker feed, the CDU can produce a further 6,000 t/d of residue. The thermal cracker converts 2,000 t/d of this residue and therefore gives a semi-complex yield on 4,000 t/d of crude intake (the residue yield being 50 per cent on crude). Therefore, this refinery would have the capacities per yield as shown in Table 6.1.

Measures of capacity by type of yield can be combined with either an ordinal or a cardinal measure of yields by type to draw 'production possibility curves'. The ordinal measure merely ranks the complex yield as more valuable than the semi-complex and the semi-complex yield as more valuable than the simple. A possible cardinal measure is the GPW of each type of yield at a given date.

A two-dimensional graphical representation of the production possibility curve will have on the vertical axis the measure of yields (ordinal or cardinal), and on the horizontal axis the quantity variables – capacity and throughput.

Production possibility curves may be drawn for single refineries or for a group of refineries, e.g. the European system as a whole. They usually have the shape of a step-wise function. Since one of our purposes is to identify the marginal yield at given dates, this can be done by reading the type of yield (e.g. semi-complex) that corresponds to actual throughput at those dates on the production possibility curve for Europe as a whole.

In the next sections we describe the steps involved in constructing production possibility curves for the European refining system, estimate the yields and capacities available to it, construct the production possibility curves, and finally attempt to identify changes in the yield of marginal refineries in 1976–86. In Section 6.2 we describe the characteristics of the refinery technologies that produce the three different types of yield; in Section 6.3 we analyse the changes in the feedstock of European refineries (because product yields depend on the nature and composition of the feedstock mix); in Section 6.4 we estimate capacity by the type of yield in Europe; and in Section 6.5 we estimate and draw the production possibility curves.

6.2 Refinery Processes and Types of Yield

(*a*) *Topping and Simple Refineries.* The process unit common to almost all refineries is the crude distillation or topping unit, which splits the crude oil into a number of fractions by distillation at atmospheric (or near-atmospheric) pressure. Ignoring facilities for the production of special products such as lubricating oils and bitumen, a topping refinery has only a crude distillation unit and some treating in the processing train. There were thirty-four topping refineries in operation at end-1976 and fourteen at end-1986.

A simple (or hydroskimming) refinery has crude distillation (CDU), catalytic reforming (CRF) and hydrotreating (HDT) in the processing train. It may also have hydrodesulphurization (HDS) for gas oil and kerosine. A simplified flow scheme for a simple refinery is given in Figure 6.1.

The simple configuration is more widely used than the topping, because it enables the refinery to make motor gasoline and greatly assists in the treating of sour crude components. There were sixty-eight simple refineries in operation in 1976 and fourteen in 1986.

We do not distinguish in the remainder of this chapter between topping and simple refineries, for several reasons. Topping capacity has normally been used to meet the need for petrochemical feedstock naphtha, and this has not been sufficient to make topping the marginal yield in Europe in the period considered. Furthermore, it is technically difficult to distinguish between the capacities of the topping and simple yields at the same refinery.

(*b*) *Semi-complex Refineries.* The next step in complexity is to add thermal cracking (THC) to the simple refinery. This process converts residue, principally into gas oil, and for the first tranche of residue

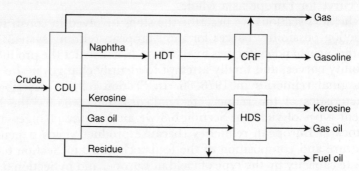

Figure 6.1: Flow Scheme for a Simple Refinery.

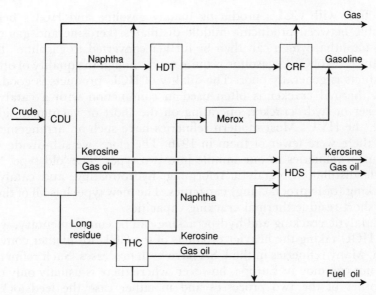

Figure 6.2: Flow Scheme for a Semi-complex Refinery.

conversion it is considerably cheaper than either catalytic cracking or hydrocracking.

There are many varieties of this process but none of them is very selective. Therefore, although gas oil is the main product, gas, naphtha and kerosine are also produced. For most purposes the products are of poor quality and need to be treated. Thermally-cracked kerosine, for instance, cannot be used as aviation fuel. Figure 6.2 shows a simplified diagram for a semi-complex refinery.

For a medium-gravity Middle Eastern type of crude, thermal cracking can reduce the fuel oil yield by about 15 per cent by weight on crude. A further extension of thermal cracking is to use a coking unit, which continues the cracking process until the residue is converted to solid coke, but this is not very widely used in Europe.

(c) Complex Refineries. Our definition of a complex refinery is one that has catalytic cracking (CCU) or hydrocracking (HCU) in the processing train. Both of these processes commonly use a vacuum gas oil as feedstock and therefore a high-vacuum distillation unit (HVU) is normally also required.[1] The conversion achieved in both these processes is much higher than in thermal cracking. They are also more

---

[1] Some more modern CCUs can use a proportion of atmospheric residue as feedstock.

selective, with CCUs producing mainly gasoline and HCUs being flexible between producing middle distillates (kerosine and gas oil) and naphtha, which can then be further converted to gasoline. The octane level of CCU gasoline is quite good, though the quality of other products is generally poor. The quality of HCU products is good.

A thermal cracker is often used in conjunction with a catalytic cracker or hydrocracker, operating on the short or vacuum residue from the HVU. Most modern refineries have such an arrangement, but there were fewer of them in 1976. Therefore, we sub-divide the complex refineries in our sample into two types. The 'old type' has crude distillation, catalytic reforming, hydrotreating, and catalytic cracking (or hydrocracking) capacities. The 'new type' has all of these *and* short-residue thermal cracking capacities.

Catalytic cracking and hydrocracking can be complementary, with the HCU taking the heavier products of the CCU for further conversion. Many refineries in the USA have both processes. Such refineries are not common in Europe, however, where there is usually only one or other of the two processes and in either case the feedstock is normally vacuum gas oil. For a medium-gravity Middle Eastern crude, a new-type complex refinery can reduce the fuel oil yield by 20–25 per cent (by weight). A simplified flow diagram for a typical complex refinery (of the new type) is given in Figure 6.3.

6.3 Changes in the Feedstock of European Refineries

Crude oil is the main feedstock to all major refining systems, but certain other feedstocks such as NGLs or residues, though small in volume, have a significant influence on refinery output. There are many varieties of crude oil with widely varying characteristics, and it is necessary to make some fairly drastic simplifications to reduce the complexity of the analysis of changes to manageable proportions. Therefore changes in crude oil characteristics are considered in terms of the average API gravity of the crude oil intake of European refineries. There was a substantial rise in the production of NGLs between 1976 and 1986. A large proportion of these NGLs, though not all, entered the refining system. Where separate information on NGLs use is available, their effect on refinery yields has been estimated by calculating their effect on the average API gravity of the crude diet. Residue feedstocks are discussed separately.

(*a*) *Crude Oil Use in Europe.* The major change in the pattern of crude use in Europe during 1976–86 was the development of the North Sea fields. In 1976 indigenously produced crude accounted for only 6 per

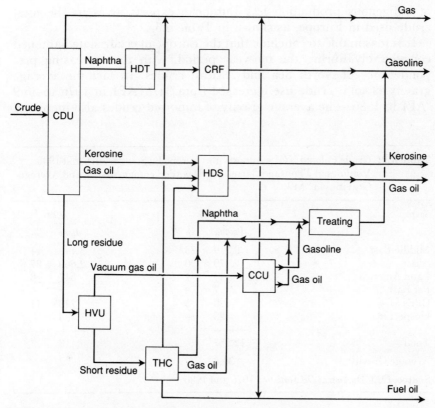

Figure 6.3: Flow Scheme for a Complex Refinery (New Type).

cent of the total crude used in Europe; while by 1986 this share had increased to 31 per cent. The main benefit to refiners of having crude on their doorstep was that they now had the opportunity to reduce their risks by increasing the amount of short-haul crude they purchased. This became particularly advantageous in the 1980s when prices began to fall and long-term contracts were no longer an attractive option.

Because North Sea production was increasing, European refiners began to change the pattern of their overseas crude supply. Middle Eastern crudes constituted 73 per cent of total imports into Europe in 1976, but during the next ten years, as OPEC production fell and volatile prices increased the risk to refiners of buying long-haul crude, this share fell to only 44 per cent. Table 6.2 shows European crude and NGLs imports by source. By 1986, 56 per cent of these imports were coming from the CPEs, Africa and Latin America. The addition of indigenous production less European exports gives us the total crude used in Europe, as shown in Table 6.3.

It is reasonable to conclude that the European crude slate lightened considerably during the ten-year period, with the increasing pre-ponderance of North Sea and African crudes. In fact the average gravity of total crude use increased from 34.7 °API in 1976 to 36.9 °API in 1986. The average gravity of imported crudes also increased

Table 6.2: Crude Oil and NGLs Imports into Europe by Source. 1976 and 1986. Volumes in Thousand Barrels per Day, Percentage Shares, and Average Gravities in °API.

Source	1976		1986	
	Volume	*%*	*Volume*	*%*
Middle East	9,219	73	3,149	44
Africa	2,570	20	2,660	37
Latin America	143	1	547	8
Far East	7	–	1	–
CPEs	590	5	748	11
Unspecified	28	–	8	–
Total	12,557		7,113	
Average Gravity	34.8		37.2	

Source: OECD, *Annual Oil Statistics*, 1976 and 1986.

Table 6.3: European Crude Oil and NGLs Use by Source. 1976 and 1986. Volumes in Thousand Barrels per Day, Percentage Shares, and Average Gravities in °API.

Source	1976		1986	
	Volume	*%*	*Volume*	*%*
Europe	805	6	3,247	31
Middle East	9,219	69	3,149	30
Africa	2,570	19	2,660	26
Latin America	143	1	547	5
Far East	7	–	1	–
CPEs	590	4	748	7
Unspecified	28	–	8	–
Total	13,362		10,360	
Average Gravity	34.7		36.9	

Source: OECD, *Annual Oil Statistics*, 1976 and 1986.

over the period, and in both years was slightly higher than the average gravity of total crude used (see Table 6.4).

The role of NGLs in lightening the crude barrel is important if we look at the volumes of NGLs that are included in European imports (as reported by the OECD). To the extent that some NGLs may be included in the crude oil import statistics, NGLs figures are likely to be underestimated. However, they allow us to make some estimate of the effect on refinery input. In 1976, only 28 thousand b/d of NGLs were reported as imports into Europe, a mere 0.2 per cent of total imports. There was also some local production of NGLs, however, bringing the total volume to 74 thousand b/d, or 0.6 per cent of total use. Even this small percentage could increase the overall gravity by 0.3–0.4 °API. In order to calculate the average gravity of crude that was run in refineries, we first subtract the amount used directly without further processing. This has generally been small in Europe, amounting to only 8 thousand b/d of NGLs and 3 thousand b/d of crude in 1976. Refinery intake in Europe (including intake from crude stocks) was therefore around 13,285 thousand b/d of crude and 66 thousand b/d of NGLs, with an estimated average gravity of 34.2 °API.

The same calculation for 1986 shows that the total use of NGLs had increased to 209 thousand b/d, of which 83 thousand b/d were imported. Some 77 thousand b/d of NGLs were used directly, mainly in the UK, leaving refinery input of 10,149 thousand b/d of crude and 132 thousand b/d of NGLs. The average gravity of refinery throughput is estimated at 36.6 °API. These estimates of average API gravities are shown, together with those calculated for other major regions,

Table 6.4: Average Crude Gravities by Region. 1976 and 1986. °API.

Region	1976	1986
Total World Production	35.5	37.2
WOCANA Production	34.1	36.5
OPEC Production	34.4	37.0
European Imports	34.8	37.2
Europe – Total Use	34.7	36.9
– Refinery Intake	34.2	36.6
North America – Total Use	n.a.	40.0
– Refinery Intake	n.a.	35.8
Japan/Australasia – Total Use	n.a.	37.8
– Refinery Intake	n.a.	36.4

in Table 6.4. This shows that there was an overall lightening of crudes produced and traded world-wide.

Table 6.5 shows the variation in the sources and average gravities of the crude used in the five main European refining areas in 1986. Taken together, the UK, France, Italy, Germany and the Benelux area accounted for 79 per cent of OECD Europe's refinery intake in 1976 and 74 per cent in 1986. The UK and Italy stand at opposite ends of the spectrum in their use of European crudes. In 1986, indigenous European crude accounted for 73.6 per cent of crude consumption in the UK whereas it accounted for only 6.5 per cent in Italy. Some 82 per cent of crude used in Italy came from Africa and the Middle East, the producing areas to which it is geographically much closer than are the countries of North West Europe. Despite the differences in their sources of crude, the average gravities of crudes used in the UK and Italy were very similar in 1986, lying above the total European average at 37.3 and 37.2 °API respectively.

The geographical spreads of crudes consumed in France, Germany and the Benelux area lay somewhere in between those of the other two countries, with around 50–60 per cent coming from the Middle East and Africa and between 20 and 40 per cent from European sources. The French crude slate turned out to be rather heavier on average, with a gravity of 36.0 °API, owing to the import of heavier rather than lighter Middle Eastern crudes.

(*b*) *Feedstock Imports.* We have estimated that the average gravity of crude oil and NGLs feed to European refineries changed from 34.2 °API in 1976 to 36.6 °API in 1986 (see Table 6.4). This change would imply a reduction of just under 5 per cent (by weight) in the yield of atmospheric residue produced from crude distillers.[2]

The proportion of distillate yield relative to residue is an important property of crude oils. Usually, the capacity of a crude distillation unit is mainly related to the amount of distillate product produced, i.e. any given crude distillation unit will usually be able to process a light (higher distillate yield) crude only at a lower rate than a heavier crude. As the residue part contains most of the cracker feed, it follows that a lighter crude will normally produce cracker feed at a lower rate than a heavier crude.[3] Therefore, the change in crude and NGLs gravity should affect the balance of cracking capacity and crude distillation capacity.[4]

---

[2] There is no precise correlation between API gravity and atmospheric residue yields, since crudes with the same API gravity can have quite widely differing residue yields, but 5 per cent by weight is a reasonable approximation.

[3] This is not true of all crudes and all refineries, but it is a fair generalization for a system as large as the European one.

[4] In such a case, the ratio of cracking to distillation capacity effectively increases.

Table 6.5: Total Crude Used in Major European Countries by Source, and Average Gravities. 1986. Volumes in Thousand Barrels per Day. Gravities in °API.

Source	UK		France		Italy		Germany		Benelux	
	Volume	%	Volume	%	Volume	%	Volume	%	Volume	%
Europe	1,085	73.6	328	23.5	100	6.5	565	37.3	489	32.2
Africa	146	9.9	371	26.7	628	41.1	474	31.3	312	20.6
Middle East	165	11.2	519	37.2	626	40.9	285	18.8	616	40.6
Latin America	39	2.6	72	5.2	29	1.9	114	7.5	37	2.4
Asia/Australasia	–	–	104	–	–	–	1	0.1	–	–
CPEs	40	2.7	104	7.5	146	9.5	77	5.1	63	4.2
Total	1,475		1,394		1,529		1,437		1,518	
Average Gravity	37.3		36.0		37.2		37.7		36.9	

Source: OECD, *Annual Oil Statistics*, 1986.

However, during the period 1976–86, imports of other feedstocks to the European refining system rose from an insignificant amount in 1976 to 35.9 million tonnes in 1986. Unfortunately neither the type nor the use of these feedstocks is shown in the OECD statistics. Nevertheless, it is known that a large proportion was imported residue, mainly from Eastern Europe; and some refiners have suggested to us that most of this residue was processed initially in crude distillation units.

The other main constituent of these feedstock imports was naphtha, which was processed primarily in chemical plants and only to a limited extent in refineries' crude distillers.

Assuming that about 25 million tonnes of residue was imported in 1986, this would constitute about 5 per cent of the total refinery feed of 500 million tonnes. Admittedly, not all of the imported residue would turn out as atmospheric residue, since one of the reasons for processing imported residues in crude distillers is to extract some gas oil. However, a high proportion of the imported residue would have been equivalent to atmospheric residue.

Although the data are not precise, we assume here that the increased importation of residues into the European refining system between 1976 and 1986 roughly counter-balanced the lightening of the crude oil and NGLs intake and, for the purposes of this chapter, that there was little change in the average gravity of total refinery intake between 1976 and 1986.

6.5 Refinery Capacities by Type of Yield

(a) *Refinery Capacity*. For the purpose of estimating the potential yields in the European refining system we have estimated the volumes of capacity by type of yield available to the system, and an illustrative example was given in Section 6.1. It is useful, however, to begin with a note on the definition of capacity. In general the capacity quoted for a refinery is taken to mean the rate at which it can process crude oil. However, this capacity is affected by several factors and can be expressed in a number of ways.

Capacity can be expressed as a number of barrels or tonnes per stream day. This is the maximum amount of crude oil that the refinery can process in one day (twenty-four hours), when all equipment is operating normally. This number is affected by the type of crude oil processed, so capacity on a design or nominal crude oil is often used, usually without specifying which crude is referred to; and it may well be that the refinery actually runs quite different crude and feedstocks, on which its capacity will be different.

Refinery equipment cannot run at 100 per cent capacity every day of every year. Shut-downs or slow-downs for maintenance and other reasons are inevitable. Therefore, capacity can also be expressed as the maximum amount of crude (usually design or nominal crude) that can be processed in an average year. The 'average year' is used because major planned refinery maintenance shut-downs are seldom as frequent as once per year. The capacity can be expressed in tonnes per year or divided by 365 and called tonnes or barrels per calendar day (bpcd).[5]

The amount of crude actually processed will only be as high as average annual capacity when there is insufficient refinery capacity to meet demand, since product demand is not exactly uniform, and there are peaks and troughs of demand over time for the various products, for seasonal or other reasons. In Europe the refinery system would be considered to be approaching full loading if the actual crude and feedstock processing reached 85–90 per cent of the annual average capacity. The definition of capacity is therefore not as precise as might be thought. In this chapter we use capacity to mean average annual capacity, whether expressed per year or per day. As we estimate that there has been little change in the overall crude/feedstock quality in the European system between 1976 and 1986, the variation of capacity due to changes in feedstock quality can be ignored.

(*b*) *Yields*. The main product yields that can be expected from each type of capacity are given in Table 6.6. For simplicity these have been calculated from Arabian Light crude oil. This crude has a gravity of about 35 °API, and was typical of European refinery feedstock in 1976. We argue that the quality of feedstock to the system in 1986 was similar to that in 1976, and therefore that the yields of atmospheric residue and vacuum gas oil, the two principal feedstocks for conversion processes, did not change much. However, with a much larger proportion of North Sea crudes in the system in 1986, the sulphur content of products is certainly lower.

It will be seen from Table 6.6 that the yields are not identical for the two years quoted. One reason for this is that the octane requirements for gasoline rose substantially between 1976 and 1986, making the yield of finished motor gasoline lower. Another reason is that, in the complex yield in 1986, there was more thermal cracking of short residue.

---

[5] It will usually be found that the relationship between capacity per stream day and capacity per calendar day gives between 330 and 345 stream days per year.

Table 6.6: Specimen Yields of Final Products from Arabian Light.[a]
1976 and 1986. Percentage Shares by Weight of Input.

	1976	1986
Simple		
C_1–C_4	2.2	2.3
Naphtha	–	3.4
Gasoline	16.5	13.5
Kerosine	11.2	11.2
Gas Oil	20.8	20.8
Fuel Oil	46.5	46.5
Fuel and Losses	2.8	2.3
Semi-complex		
C_1–C_4	4.0	3.9
Naphtha	–	4.4
Gasoline	19.4	15.7
Kerosine	11.2	11.2
Gas Oil	31.4	31.4
Fuel Oil	30.6	30.6
Fuel and Losses	3.4	2.8
Complex		
C_1–C_4	5.0	5.2
Naphtha	–	4.5
Gasoline	29.5	26.3
Kerosine	9.4	11.2
Gas Oil	25.5	26.4
Fuel Oil	25.9	21.8
Fuel and Losses	4.7	4.6

Note: (a) Maximum gasoline mode of operation.

(c) *Capacities of European Refineries by Type: 1976 and 1986.* Using the method described in Section 6.1 above, the capacities of all European refineries have been split into simple, semi-complex and complex. Table 6.7 presents a summary of the results.

Our procedure depends on the following assumptions:

(a) In a complex refinery a thermal cracker or delayed coker is fed by vacuum residue. If both types of plant are present, the thermal cracker is filled first.

(b) In a semi-complex refinery, thermal crackers and cokers are fed by atmospheric residue. The same applies in the semi-complex part of a complex refinery.

(c) If both a catalytic cracker and a hydrocracker are present at the

Table 6.7: Total Capacities by Yield Type in Europe. 1976 and 1986.
Thousand Barrels per Calendar Day.

Yield	1976		1986	
	Volume	*%*	*Volume*	*%*
Simple	13,900.6	67.7	4,249.4	29.4
Semi-complex	1,192.3	5.8	1,746.3	12.0
Complex	5,433.9	26.5	8,353.0	57.6
Ultra-complex	–	–	147.2	1.0
Total	20,526.8	100.0	14,495.9	100.0

    same site, the two types of capacity are added together and treated as a single cracking unit. This is possible because in Europe vacuum gas oil is commonly the feedstock to them both. The final product yield from complex capacity will vary, however, depending on whether the plant is a catalytic cracker or a hydrocracker, since hydrocrackers in Europe yield mainly middle distillates. Only six sites in Europe have hydrocrackers, and this assumption, although a simplifying one, should not lead to any gross errors on an aggregate basis.

(d) A few refineries have thermal cracking capacity but no reforming capacity. For simplicity, these have been treated as if they were semi-complex. In practice, the yields they produce will not be the same as those shown in Table 6.6, since there is no conversion of naphtha to reformate.

(e) Feedstock for each unit comes only from primary crude distillation and vacuum distillation.

    The overall breakdown of European refining capacity by type is shown in Table 6.7. The change in capacities between 1976 and 1986 illustrates clearly both the increase in thermal and catalytic cracking capacities and the closure of crude distillation capacity in the period. Total crude distillation capacity fell by 6,031 thousand bpcd, from 20,527 to 14,496 thousand bpcd. During the same period the combined capacity of catalytic cracking and hydrocracking almost doubled, from 1,046 to 1,894 thousand bpcd, and thermal cracking capacity tripled, from 500 to 1,528 thousand bpcd.

    It should be noted that not only did many refineries add conversion capacity for the first time between 1976 and 1986, but also those that already had it in 1976 greatly increased their percentages of complex and semi-complex yields. This is illustrated in Figures 6.4, 6.5 and 6.6.

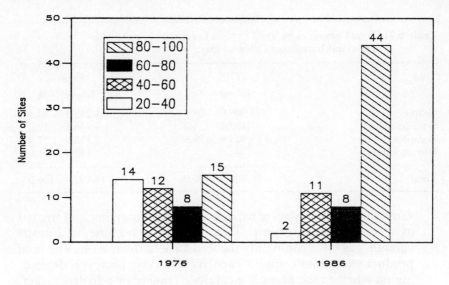

Figure 6.4: Distribution of Sites by Percentage Shares of Complex Yields in Total Capacity. 1976 and 1986.

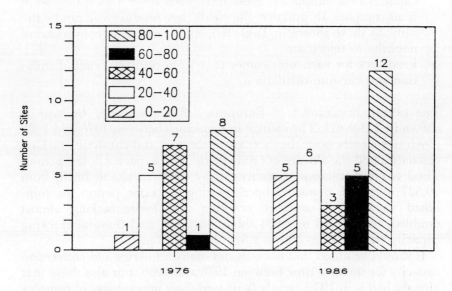

Figure 6.5: Distribution of Sites by Percentage Shares of Semi-complex Yields in Total Capacity. 1976 and 1986.

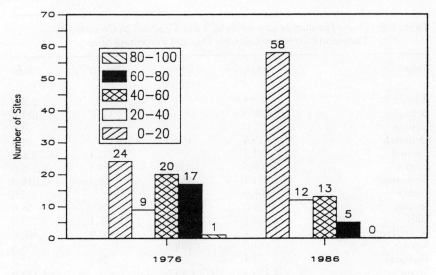

Figure 6.6: Distribution of Sites by Percentage Shares of Simple Yields in Total Capacity (Upgraded Sites Only). 1976 and 1986.

(*d*) *Distribution of Capacities by Country.* The total capacities by type of yield for each country considered in 1976 and 1986 are shown in Tables 6.8 and 6.9 respectively. These figures are simply the sums of refinery capacities by type and take no account of feedstock trade or transfers between refineries.

The picture varies significantly from country to country. In 1976, the Finnish refineries were by far the most sophisticated, producing a 71 per cent complex yield. Of the six largest refining countries,[6] only the UK produced more than a 30 per cent complex yield. By 1986 four of the top six had significantly shifted their yields to over 60 per cent complex.

Although a large number of its refinery sites are complex, France is still notably less upgraded in terms of its output than the other major refining countries. In 1986, 32.5 per cent of its yield was simple, compared with 7.2 per cent in the UK and 12.4 per cent in Germany. Italy also appears to have invested less in shifting its yield. However, many Italian refineries upgraded to the semi-complex rather than the complex level, as did refineries in Denmark and Norway.

Table 6.10 shows the changes in the percentage shares of capacities by type in Europe between 1976 and 1986. The most striking change

---

[6] Germany, France, the UK, Italy, the Netherlands and Belgium.

Table 6.8: Crude Distillation Capacities by Yield Type and by Country. 1976. Thousand Barrels per Calendar Day and Percentage Shares.

Volume	Simple	Semi-complex	Complex	Total
Austria	189.4	–	76.6	266.0
Belgium	729.9	–	357.7	1,087.6
Cyprus	15.0	–	–	15.0
Denmark	115.5	104.3	–	219.8
Finland	93.2	–	233.1	326.2
France	2,466.3	38.6	1,074.6	3,579.6
Germany	1,844.4	431.7	740.7	3,016.8
Greece	408.0	–	–	408.0
Ireland	56.0	–	–	56.0
Italy	2,852.7	120.8	1,266.1	4,239.6
Netherlands	1,462.1	20.7	403.2	1,886.0
Norway	151.0	108.5	–	259.5
Portugal	107.4	27.5	36.6	171.5
Spain	1,129.4	43.5	–	1,172.9
Sweden	317.0	79.7	–	396.7
Switzerland	79.0	58.0	–	137.0
Turkey	171.4	–	151.6	323.0
UK	1,712.7	159.0	1,093.7	2,965.4
Total	13,900.6	1,192.3	5,433.9	20,526.8
% Share				
Austria	71.2	–	28.8	
Belgium	67.1	–	32.9	
Cyprus	100.0	–	–	
Denmark	52.5	47.5	–	
Finland	28.6	–	71.4	
France	68.9	1.1	30.0	
Germany	61.1	14.3	24.6	
Greece	100.0	–	–	
Ireland	100.0	–	–	
Italy	67.3	2.8	29.9	
Netherlands	77.6	1.1	21.4	
Norway	58.2	41.8	–	
Portugal	62.6	16.0	21.3	
Spain	96.3	3.7	–	
Sweden	79.9	20.1	–	
Switzerland	57.7	42.3	–	
Turkey	53.1	–	46.9	
UK	57.8	5.4	36.9	
Average	67.7	5.8	26.5	

Table 6.9: Crude Distillation Capacities by Yield Type and by Country. 1986. Thousand Barrels per Calendar Day and Percentage Shares.

Volume	Simple	Semi complex	Complex	Ultra-complex	Total
Austria	70.6	–	140.0	–	210.6
Belgium	150.4	24.2	538.4	–	713.0
Cyprus	16.0	–	–	–	16.0
Denmark	12.2	169.6	–	–	181.8
Finland	–	–	255.0	–	255.0
France	697.8	18.0	1,430.0	–	2,145.8
Germany	204.8	270.8	1,171.7	–	1,647.3
Greece	288.0	–	100.0	–	388.0
Ireland	56.0	–	–	–	56.0
Italy	793.0	607.0	1,362.6	–	2,762.6
Netherlands	349.9	91.4	697.9	147.2	1,286.4
Norway	79.2	179.3	–	–	258.5
Portugal	246.6	–	91.5	–	338.1
Spain	582.3	228.9	552.6	–	1,363.8
Sweden	208.9	108.8	129.0	–	446.7
Switzerland	88.7	48.3	–	–	137.0
Turkey	283.0	–	307.6	–	590.6
UK	122.0	–	1,578.7	–	1,700.7
Total	4,249.4	1,746.3	8,355.0	147.2	14,497.9

% Share					
Austria	33.5	–	66.5	–	
Belgium	21.1	3.4	75.5	–	
Cyprus	100.0	–	–	–	
Denmark	6.7	93.3	–	–	
Finland	–	–	100.0	–	
France	32.5	0.8	66.6	–	
Germany	12.4	16.4	71.1	–	
Greece	74.2	–	25.8	–	
Ireland	100.0	–	–	–	
Italy	28.7	22.0	49.3	–	
Netherlands	27.2	7.1	54.2	11.4	
Norway	30.6	69.4	–	–	
Portugal	72.9	–	27.1	–	
Spain	42.7	16.8	40.5	–	
Sweden	46.8	24.3	28.9	–	
Switzerland	64.7	35.2	–	–	
Turkey	47.9	–	52.1	–	
UK	7.2	–	92.8	–	
Average	29.3	12.0	57.6	1.0	

Table 6.10: Changes in Percentage Shares of Crude Distillation Capacity by Yield Type and by Country. 1976–86. Percentage Points.

	Simple	Semi-complex	Complex	Ultra-complex
Austria	−37.7	–	+37.7	–
Belgium	−46.0	+3.4	+42.6	–
Cyprus	–	–	–	–
Denmark	−45.8	+45.8	–	–
Finland	−28.6	–	+28.6	–
France	−36.4	− 0.3	+36.6	–
Germany	−48.7	+2.1	+46.5	–
Greece	−25.8	–	+25.8	–
Ireland	–	–	–	–
Italy	−38.6	+19.2	+19.4	–
Netherlands	−50.4	+6.0	+32.8	+11.4
Norway	−27.6	+27.6	–	–
Portugal	−10.3	−16.0	+5.8	–
Spain	−53.6	+13.1	+40.5	–
Sweden	−33.1	+4.2	+28.9	–
Switzerland	+7.0	−7.1	–	–
Turkey	−5.2	–	+5.2	–
UK	−50.6	−5.4	+55.9	–
Total	−38.4	+6.2	+31.1	+1.0

is the increase of 56 percentage points in the share of complex capacity in UK refineries, which rose to over 90 per cent in 1986 (the remainder being due to the continued operation of two small bitumen plants). Other notable changes were the increases in complex capacity in Belgium and Germany, in semi-complex yield in Denmark, Italy and Norway, and in both types of yield in Spain. Portugal appears to have actually 'downgraded' its yields in the period.

6.5 The Production Possibility Curve of the European Refining Industry

In this section we attempt to estimate the potential production – volume and composition – of petroleum products by the European refining system under a variety of assumptions. The central concept used is that of a production possibility curve, which plots capacities by type (complex, semi-complex, etc.) against either an ordinal or a cardinal measure of yields by type. We begin with a definition of the production possibility curve for a single refinery, and then proceed to define and estimate production possibility curves for the whole of the European refining industry under two different assumptions:

(a) that the whole system is operated as a single giant refinery; and
(b) that each refinery is a self-contained entity.

Case (a), therefore, allows for transfers of intermediate products between European refineries, while case (b) assumes that each refinery can only use crude and the feedstocks processed in its own CDUs. These are the two polar cases that together define a range for the actual production possibility curve. Case (a) is the upper limit and case (b) is the lower limit. We then compare throughputs and the production possibility curve in order to identify the marginal yield for different throughput levels, and summarize our results.

(a) The Production Possibility Curve for a Single Refinery. Not every barrel of a given crude run through a refinery necessarily produces the same mix of products. The relative sizes and technical characteristics of the units within a single refinery determine the capacities by type of yield, i.e. the volumes of crude producing complex, semi-complex and simple yields, which enable us to draw a production possibility curve. A two-dimensional graphical representation can be obtained by ranking the various types of yield ordinally, under the assumption that the complex yield is more 'valuable' than the semi-complex, and the semi-complex yield more valuable than the simple. This assumption may be tested by taking the GPW of a product barrel as a common measure, or 'numeraire', for comparing different types of yield. The hierarchy of complex, semi-complex and simple yields would be established if the differences between the GPWs of complex and semi-complex, and semi-complex and simple, were always positive. Monthly average GPWs can be calculated for the period 1976–86 using the final product yields shown in Table 6.6 and monthly average Rotterdam barge prices. We found that there was an invariant hierarchy between complex, semi-complex and simple yields, because all the differences in the GPWs of relevant pairs of yields were positive (i.e. there were no reversals of sign).

This invariant ranking of GPWs enables us to draw the production possibility curve as a step-wise function. The horizontal axis plots the *quantity* variable (capacity or throughput); and the vertical axis can be used to plot *either* an ordinal ranking of the yields (complex higher than semi-complex, etc.) *or* the actual GPW values, which give a cardinal ranking. The production possibility curve for a complex refinery is shown in Figure 6.7.

With throughput at point x, all crude produces a complex yield. Between x and y, the marginal yield is semi-complex, producing more fuel oil and less distillate. When throughput increases beyond point y,

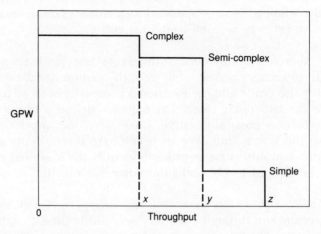

Figure 6.7: Production Possibility Curve for a Complex Refinery.

there is a large increase in fuel oil production at the margin, as the yield moves into the simple range. At point z, the total capacity is fully utilized.

If a refinery has a lubricants or bitumen plant, or makes naphtha for a petrochemicals plant, these units will generally be loaded first, since the value of special products (especially lubricants) is high. Thus the curve can be altered to show special products yields at the front end of crude throughput as shown in Figure 6.8. A shift in the production possibility curve between the two dates, due for example to investment in additional cracking capacity and the closure of crude distillation capacity, is shown in Figure 6.9.

(*b*) *Production Possibility Curves for Total Europe.* The production possibility curve for the whole European refining system cannot be determined without making some assumptions about refinery-by-refinery throughputs and inter-refinery flows of feedstocks. We can, however, define two limiting cases. The first assumes that the system operates optimally as a single refinery (i.e. that all intermediate products flow freely between refineries); the second assumes that each refinery is completely self-contained (i.e. that there are no flows between refineries). We shall refer to the first as the 'aggregated' case, and the second as the 'disaggregated' case. In practice the system will operate at some level between these two extremes.

Our estimates of total capacity by type for Europe were used to calculate the potential supply curve for the first polar case. European refineries were assumed to behave as one big refinery with no

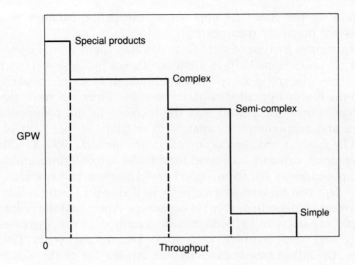

Figure 6.8: Production Possibility Curve for a Complex Refinery with Special Products Production Capacity.

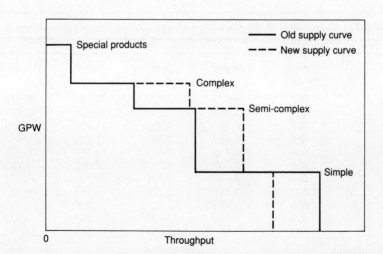

Figure 6.9: Old and New Production Possibility Curves for 'Improved' Complex Refinery.

restriction on the flow of components (except for vacuum residue which is not normally transported).

The capacities by type of yield from Arabian Light for the *aggregated* case for all years from 1976 to 1986 are shown in Table 6.11, which clearly shows the trend away from predominantly simple capacity in 1976 to the highly upgraded capacity in 1986. Thus, the most significant change over the period was the increase in the proportion of complex and semi-complex capacity from 34 to 90 per cent of the total. The biggest changes occurred in the period 1980–82 during which complex capacity increased from 6,753 to 8,640 thousand bpcd and simple capacity fell from 10,537 to 5,168 thousand bpcd.

This effect can be seen more clearly in Table 6.12, which lists the year-on-year changes in aggregate capacities. Almost all the reduction in simple capacity in 1979–80 can be ascribed to the increases in complex and semi-complex capacities. During the years 1981–5, however, the fall in simple capacity was largely due to the closure of crude distillation capacity.

The total capacities by type for the *disaggregated* case, in which each refinery is assumed to be self-contained, were found by adding the refinery-by-refinery yields from Arabian Light as calculated in Section 6.4. These estimates of total capacities by type of yield for 1976 and 1986 are shown in Table 6.13.

The production possibility curves under both assumptions for 1976 and 1986 are shown in Figures 6.10 and 6.11 respectively. Figure 6.11

Table 6.11: European Refinery Capacity by Type of Yield from Arabian Light: Aggregated Case. 1976–86. Thousand Barrels per Calendar Day.

	Special Products[a]	Complex[b]	Semi-complex	Simple	Total
1976	864	5,623	1,329	12,711	20,527
1977	864	5,742	1,283	12,494	20,383
1978	864	6,301	1,399	11,926	20,490
1979	864	6,349	1,483	11,791	20,487
1980	868	6,753	2,085	10,537	20,243
1981	854	7,737	2,292	8,872	19,755
1982	812	8,640	2,754	5,168	17,374
1983	847	9,366	2,780	3,353	16,346
1984	838	9,755	2,920	1,900	15,416
1985	874	9,935	2,928	1,134	14,871
1986	841	10,183	2,857	615	14,496

Notes: (a) Lubricants and bitumen at specialist refineries only; some naphtha for petrochemical feedstock.
(b) Includes ultra-complex.

shows that there were marked differences in the shapes of the curves for the two cases in 1986. Complex capacity in the aggregated case was 10,183 thousand bpcd, compared with 8,298 thousand bpcd in the disaggregated case. The 1,885 thousand bpcd discrepancy was due to cracking capacity that was left unused at refineries that did not have big enough distillation units to load their crackers. In the aggregated case it is assumed that this cracking capacity will be filled by feedstock from other refineries. In 1976 the discrepancy in complex capacity between the two cases was much smaller – only 307 thousand bpcd.

The effect on the production possibility curve (in the aggregated case) of the change in the relative capacities of upgrading and distillation plant is illustrated in Figure 6.12, which shows the potential output of products from Arabian Light feedstock in 1976 and 1986.

Table 6.12: Year-on-Year Changes for Refinery Capacity by Type of Yield from Arabian Light: Aggregated Case. 1976–86. Thousand Barrels per Calendar Day.

	Special Products	*Complex*	*Semi-complex*	*Simple*	*Total*
1976–7	–	+119	−46	−217	−144
1977–8	–	+559	+116	−568	+107
1978–9	–	+48	+84	−135	−3
1979–80	+4	+404	+602	−1,254	−244
1980–81	−14	+984	+207	−1,665	−488
1981–2	−42	+903	+462	−3,704	−2,381
1982–3	+35	+726	+26	−1,815	−1,028
1983–4	−9	+392	+140	−1,453	−930
1984–5	+36	+177	+8	−766	−545
1985–6	−33	+248	−71	−519	−375

Table 6.13: European Refinery Capacity by Type of Yield from Arabian Light: Disaggregated Case. 1976 and 1986. Thousand Barrels per Calendar Day.

Yield Type	*1976*	*1986*
Special Products	904	880
Complex	5,316	8,298
Semi-complex	1,163	1,711
Simple	13,144	3,606
Total	20,527	14,495

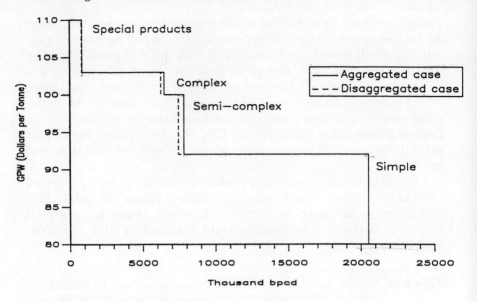

Figure 6.10: Production Possibility Curves for European Refineries. 1976.

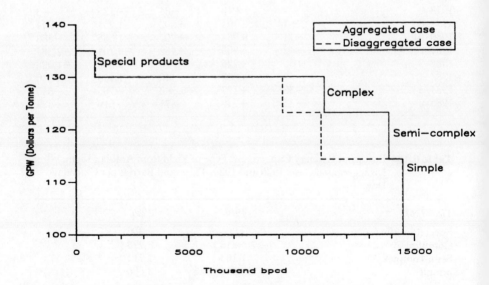

Figure 6.11: Production Possibility Curves for European Refineries. 1986.

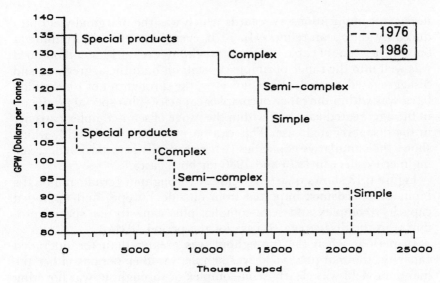

Figure 6.12: Effects of Changes in Capacity on the Production Possibility Curve of European Refineries (Aggregated Case).

The change in the structure of output here is therefore due to investment and disinvestment in refinery plant as described above.

Complex capacity from Arabian Light crude rose in absolute terms from 5,623 thousand bpcd in 1976 to 10,183 thousand bpcd in 1986, and increased as a proportion of total capacity from 27 per cent in 1976 to 70 per cent in 1986. Approximately half of this increase was due to the closure of crude distillation capacity and half to investment in new cracking capacity. Semi-complex capacity also rose, from 1,329 thousand bpcd (6.5 per cent) to 2,857 thousand bpcd (19.7 per cent). Simple capacity from this feedstock fell to a very low level, dropping from 12,711 thousand to 615 thousand bpcd, and just over half of this reduction was due to the closure of distillation capacity and the remainder to the increase in upgrading plant.

(c) Potential Output and the Marginal Yield. Refinery throughput in Europe fell almost continually during the period, from around 13.5 million bpcd in 1976 to an all-time low of 9.5 million bpcd in 1985, rising again in 1986 to 10.5 million bpcd. Under the assumption that refinery capacity is run sequentially in decreasing merit order of configuration, this reduction in crude throughput, combined with the changes in the structure of the potential output discussed above, had

important implications as regards which was the marginal yield produced by European refiners. In 1976, even with refineries running at only 64 per cent of capacity, the throughput level of 13.5 million bpcd was well into the range of simple capacity in both the aggregated and disaggregated cases. In 1986, however, the throughput of 10.5 million bpcd was within the range of complex capacity (plus special products) in the aggregated case and within the range of semi-complex capacity in the disaggregated case. This can be seen from Table 6.14, which shows the cumulative capacities (where capacity is ranked in decreasing merit order) in 1976 and 1986 for both cases.

Figure 6.13 shows quarterly refinery throughput (crude and NGLs input plus feedstock imported from outside Europe) and upgraded capacity (complex and semi-complex plus capacity for special products) in the disaggregated case for the period 1979–87.

In periods when the throughput was greater than the upgraded capacity, the marginal yield was simple; in other periods either the marginal yield was clearly semi-complex or throughput was hovering close to the semi-complex/simple boundary.

During the period 1979–81, throughput, although declining, was still unequivocally in the simple zone at the margin. By 1982, however, upgraded capacity had increased to over 10 million bpcd and refinery input had fallen to just below this level for the first time.

The period 1983–5 was marked by low refinery throughputs, with semi-complex clearly being the marginal yield. During the first quarter of 1984 throughput rose briefly in response to the UK miners' strike, but quickly returned to previous levels as refiners found that refining margins could not justify the increase in output. The continued demand for residual fuel oil during the strike (1984: Q1 until 1985: Q2) kept distillates/fuel oil price differentials low; refining

Table 6.14: Cumulative Refinery Capacity by Type of Yield from Arabian Light: Aggregated and Disaggregated Cases. 1976 and 1986. Thousand Barrels per Calendar Day.

	1976		1986	
	Aggregated Case	Disaggregated Case	Aggregated Case	Disaggregated Case
Special Products	864	904	841	880
+ Complex	6,487	6,220	11,024	9,178
+ Semi-complex	7,816	7,383	13,881	10,889
+ Simple	20,527	20,527	14,496	14,495

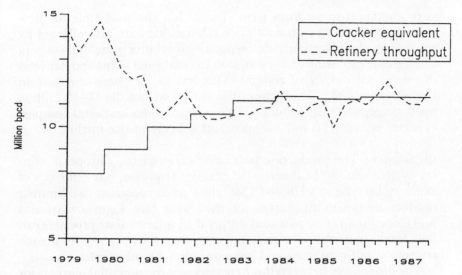

Figure 6.13: Upgraded Capacity and Actual Throughput of European Refineries. 1979–87.

margins were also low and throughput dropped to an all-time low of 10 million bpcd in the second quarter of 1985. Refinery input in this three-year period oscillated between 10 and 11.5 million bpcd, close to or below the semi-complex/simple yield boundary.

The era of netback deals, which began towards the end of 1985, allowed refining margins to rise and pushed refinery throughput up to 12 million bpcd in the third quarter of 1986, its highest level since 1980 and probably close to the real capacity of the European system. Simple and topping capacity, which had been out of operation for some time, were brought on stream again as it became profitable to run them. An examination of the price ratios reveals not only that the distillates/fuel oil price ratio was high in 1986 but also that the gasoline/naphtha ratio price also rose significantly (see Chapter 8 below), indicating that there was a substantial surplus of naphtha on the market in relation to gasoline. This is most easily explained by the fact that topping capacity was being run in preference to some simple capacity at the margin.

The longer-term effects on product price differentials of the changing relationship between throughput and upgraded capacity operate through the change in the *average* yield of distillates and residual fuel oil. The large decrease in the amount of simple capacity run in the refining system during the 1970s and early 1980s, as shown in Figure 6.13, resulted in a rise in the average yield of distillate from just under 60 per cent in 1976 to over 70 per cent in 1986.

In the short-to-medium term (i.e. within the lead time for new refinery investment), product price relationships are also affected by changes in the marginal yield, especially if relatively small swings in throughput can bring about a shift in the marginal plant and hence in the marginal output of residue. This has in fact been the case in Europe since 1982. Throughput has stayed within the 10–12 million bpcd range, while the combined volume of complex and semi-complex capacity is now 11.5 million bpcd and is likely to rise further.

(*d*) *Summary*. The production possibility curve for the European refining system can not be determined exactly. However, our estimates of capacity by type in 1976 and 1986 allow us to construct two limiting production possibility curves for each year (see Figures 6.10 and 6.11), one illustrating potential supply if all intermediate products can flow freely between refineries, and the other showing supply if each refinery is self-contained and has no trade with other refineries.

The differences between these curves show the potential markets for the transfer of feedstock within Europe. This was equivalent to 339 thousand bpcd of catalytic cracker feedstock in 1986 but only 74 thousand bpcd in 1976.

Between 1976 and 1986, two main changes occurred, both of which affected the pattern of product output. First, the production possibility curve 'shifted' to the right, owing to the change in the relative capacities of upgrading and distillation plant, and secondly refinery throughput fell by 3 million bpcd. The result of these changes was that throughput in 1986 was very close to the boundary between semi-complex and simple capacities. This is illustrated in Table 6.14, which shows that the 1986 throughput of 10.5 million bpcd would have used up most of the cumulative special products/complex/semi-complex capacity of approximately 10.9 million bpcd (in the disaggregated case). An increase in throughput of just 400 thousand bpcd would have brought utilization into the range of simple capacity. Table 6.14 also indicates that in the aggregated case the marginal capacity of European refining would have produced a complex yield. Considering that the aggregated and disaggregated cases describe two polar cases, we may safely conclude that the marginal capacity in 1986 was semi-complex.

7 The Relationship between Product Prices and Crude Prices

Robert Bacon

7.1 Introduction

The dominant element of current costs in the refining of products is the cost of the crude oil itself. Given the nature of refining technology we expect that, in a competitive market, the extra revenue from refining a barrel of oil should be equal to the cost of refining this incremental barrel. In long-run equilibrium, the extra cost includes capital costs as well as the current cost, but once over-capacity develops, as was certainly the case during 1976–87, then the price can be much lower than the *total* incremental cost. Conventional analysis suggests that the normal lower limit to the price is the incremental current cost, but the existence of substantial shut-down and exit costs means that the price can remain below running costs for a considerable period of time.

These shifting relationships between prices and costs have the very important implication that the revenue from an extra barrel of oil output (the gross product worth) and the price per barrel of the major input, crude oil, need not be in a constant relationship. Previous studies have focused on the stability of this relationship,[1] but with the longer period of reliable data now available it is possible to consider a more flexible specification.

In order to explore the links between crude prices and product prices, we need to establish a reference set of data, and this is done in Section 7.2. The basic behaviour of these series and their relationships to each other are presented in Section 7.3. Finally, more sophisticated statistical tests of the behaviour of the margin between product prices and crude prices are undertaken in Section 7.4. The important conclusions are summarized in Section 7.5.

---

[1] See Bacon, R., 1984, *A Study of the Relationship between Spot Product Prices and Spot Crude Prices*, Working Paper WPM5, Oxford Institute for Energy Studies, and Himona, I., 1987, *Crude Oil and Product Prices: An Investigation*, Surrey Energy Economics Centre Discussion Paper SEEDS No. 36, University of Surrey, Guildford.

7.2 Data and Definitions

Although we focus on a given set of product prices (Rotterdam barge prices reported by *Platt's*), the need to link such prices to input costs requires that we consider the yields of the various products that result from the refining of a barrel of oil. Since these are joint products, their total value is constrained by the type of refinery used (as well as by the type of crude). There were a number of distinct types of refinery process in operation in Europe during the period under study (see Chapters 4, 5 and 6 above), and the performance of a typical category itself changed over this period. Accordingly we have used four types of yield for the initial investigation:

(a) topping;
(b) simple;
(c) semi-complex;
(d) complex.

However, the yields for a given type of refinery have changed over time for three distinct reasons:

(a) the type of crude run through the refinery has changed;
(b) the product specifications have changed;
(c) the efficiency of a given type of plant has changed.

Two sets of yields and a mix-of-crudes variable have been made available to us by an industry source. These yields are based on Arabian Light as input with 1976 yields, and Ninian as input with 1986 yields. We also know how the typical use of crude in Europe changed over this period, so we can construct a set of weighted average yields that attempts to reproduce the way in which the yields of a typical refiner in Europe evolved. These yields are available for the five principal end-products for each type of refinery, and can be combined with the prices of the products (Rotterdam barges low) to give the gross product worth resulting from a unit input of crude oil in each case. These values make allowance for the amounts of crude or products used up as refinery fuel (and for volume changes), but make no allowance for any crude used to produce special products (e.g. bitumen).

The yields used are defined in terms of the five basic products, but in fact the output of fuel oil from topping or simple refineries (straight-run fuel oil) is usually valued more highly than that from semi-complex or complex refineries (cracked fuel oil). We have estimated the premium for straight-run fuel oil to obtain alternative series for the gross product worths for topping and simple refineries, by collating all references to the straight-run premium for high-sulphur fuel oil in North West Europe appearing in *Weekly Petroleum Argus*.[2]

In order to compare revenues with costs, we would ideally like to have time-series available for all current and capital costs for each type of refinery. Such data are not available and we only have series for crude prices f.o.b., and for the costs of transport into the North West European market. This allows us to construct a c.i.f. crude price series. Since crude prices are usually quoted in dollars per barrel and products prices in dollars per tonne, it is necessary to convert the crude prices into dollars per tonne. The conversion factor used depends on the crude being considered.

Two different monthly crude price series are used. The first is for an Arabian Gulf light crude (an average of Arabian Light, Dubai and Oman), for which we have data from 1976 onwards. The second is for a North Sea crude (an average of Brent, Ninian and Forties), for which data are available from mid-1980. This reflects the fact that in the earlier period not enough North Sea crude was traded for a continuous price series to be established. Data for both series are taken from *Petroleum Argus*. The two series are also weighted together to represent the shifting typical pattern of crude use by European refiners (using the same weights as were used for the gross product worth calculations). However, since prices are not available for all months until mid-1980 for the North Sea crudes, all calculations based on them are limited to the shorter period.

The two groups of crudes used to calculate these average prices are both very homogeneous, and are hence close in their technical characteristics to the crudes used to generate the gross product worth series. The advantage of using *average* prices is that they moderate the effects of any special temporary features that may have affected the price of any one crude. Comparisons of these average crude prices and the gross product worth series are not accurate enough to represent the day-to-day situations faced by individual refiners, but they will certainly show the principal movements of the series.

---

[2] Note, however, that the market in *straight-run* fuel oil had not been established at the beginning of the period, so that these data were available only from January 1981.

Table 7.1: Mean Gross Product Worths. 1976–87. Dollars per Tonne.

Yield by Type	*Gross Product Worth*		
	Arabian Light (1976)	*Ninian (1986)*	*Weighted Average*
Topping	171	177	174
Simple	176	183	180
Semi-complex	192	195	193
Complex	194	204	200
(Mean Crude Value c.i.f.)	180	n.a.	n.a.

Table 7.2: Mean Gross Product Worths. May 1980–January 1987. Dollars per Tonne.

Yield by Type	*Gross Product Worth*		
	Arabian Light (1976)	*Ninian (1986)*	*Weighted Average*
Topping	191	197	195
Simple	196	204	201
Semi-complex	213	216	215
Complex	215	225	222
(Mean Crude Value c.i.f.)	204	211	209

7.3 Simple Behaviour of Gross Product Worths and Crude Prices, 1976–87

The means of the various series over the period are shown in Tables 7.1 and 7.2. The gross product worths are arranged in ascending order for the refining technologies we have described, i.e. *on average* topping is lower than simple, simple lower than semi-complex, and semi-complex lower than complex.[3]

For an input of Arabian Light the biggest gap is between the simple and semi-complex yields, with an average increment of $16 per tonne. The increment of the complex yield over the semi-complex is only $2

---

[3] It should be noted that the mean crude values given in these tables are the average values for the 'Arabian Gulf' and 'North Sea' crudes as specified in Section 7.2 above, *not* the values for the individual crudes on which the yields used to calculate the GPWs are based.

per tonne. For an input of Ninian crude, the increments between the yields are rather different: that from simple to semi-complex is \$12 per tonne and that from semi-complex to complex is \$9 per tonne. Thus, with a pattern of crude inputs, product specifications and efficiencies such as existed in 1976, the advantage of running a complex yield instead of a semi-complex yield was very small. By the end of the period, however, the gap had opened up considerably to give refiners a clear preference for the complex yield.

The differences in GPWs for the different crudes and levels of efficiency but using the same type of technology always favoured the use of Ninian with 1986 costs and product specifications. This difference is least marked for the semi-complex yields and most marked for the complex. In essence the system and the use of crude evolved so as to leave semi-complex GPWs virtually unchanged on average but to improve complex yields so that, whereas they had been very similar to semi-complex under 1976 conditions, they were clearly superior by the end of the period. These two technologies had always enjoyed a substantial average margin over simple and topping yields and this remained the case throughout the period.

Finally, the statistics for the GPWs allowing for a premium on straight-run fuel oil for topping and simple refineries are shown in Table 7.3. It can be seen that the straight-run fuel oil premium improves average GPWs by around \$4 per tonne. The variability of the GPWs calculated on the two bases is virtually identical, which indicates that shifts in the premium largely reflect general product price shifts and do not smooth out GPWs. The advantage of using semi-complex yields rather than simple is still substantial, although it is reduced when allowance is made for the premium.

Table 7.3: Mean Gross Product Worths and Crude Values c.i.f. using Weighted Average of Crudes: With and Without Straight-run Fuel Oil Premium. January 1981–January 1987. Dollars per Tonne.

Yield by Type	*Gross Product Worth*	
	With Premium	*Without Premium*
Topping	194.3	190.4
Simple	200.4	196.6
Semi-complex	–	209.2
Complex	–	216.4
(Mean Crude Price c.i.f.)	–	203.0

For the period as a whole, it is also meaningful to compare the GPWs calculated using Arabian Light with the Arabian Gulf crude price (see Table 7.1). On average, the crude price was above the topping and simple GPWs but below the semi-complex and complex GPWs. Given that there were other running costs, as well as capital costs, it is immediately apparent that any simple or topping refinery operating throughout the period, on the basis of 1976 crude inputs and costs, would not merely have been failing to make an overall profit: it would have failed to cover even its running costs. This is still true when we allow for the straight-run fuel oil premium.

Turning to the sub-period from May 1980 to January 1987, we see from Table 7.2 that a very similar picture emerges. All the averages are higher, but their relative positions are virtually unchanged. The ordering of the GPWs resulting from the use of different refining technologies remains as before, so that again for Arabian Light the benefit of using complex in preference to semi-complex is minimal, while for Ninian (on a 1986 basis) the difference is substantial.

For the shorter period it is meaningful to look at GPWs based on a weighted average input (and yields) of both Arabian Light and Ninian. These GPWs show the same ordering as before, but a less even spread between the average values than those for the longer period. The increment of the semi-complex GPW over the simple is particularly strong. The GPWs based on the mixture of crudes are combined to give new series of differentials as reported in Table 7.4.

The relatively low coefficients of variation suggest that the ranking of the GPWs was undisturbed throughout the period, and a month-by-month check reveals that there were indeed no negative values, so that complex dominated semi-complex throughout, which in turn dominated simple, which dominated topping.

Table 7.4: Summary Statistics for Differentials between GPWs based on a Mixture of Crude Inputs. May 1980–January 1987. Dollars per Tonne.

Difference	Mean	Standard Deviation	Coefficient of Variation (%)	Standardized Range
Complex/ Semi-complex	7.16	2.82	39	4.8
Semi-complex/ Simple	13.28	5.34	40	3.8
Simple/Topping	6.38	2.47	39	3.5

These differential values do vary, however, and show that the relative advantages of the different refining processes measured solely in terms of revenue *did* change a great deal during the period. To put these results in perspective we must compare them with those in Table 7.2, where the corresponding mean GPW is between $195 and $222 per tonne, while the mean crude price is $209 per tonne. Not only are the differences in the mean GPWs important, but also their variability is clearly large relative to the margin over crude costs. The choice of refining technique appears to be crucial in determining the degree of profitability. Complex refining would always have given the largest GPW, however, albeit sometimes by a very small amount, while the jump from the simple to the semi-complex GPW is altogether more significant.

Comparing GPWs with the associated crude prices c.i.f. gives a uniform picture. *Neither* for Arabian Gulf crudes taken against a yield based on their performance as at 1976 *nor* for North Sea crudes against a yield based on their performance as at 1986 do topping or simple refining on average cover the costs of crude c.i.f., while semi-complex and complex refining *do* on average cover crude costs. This implies, as Table 7.2 shows, that the weighted average yield also covers the cost of the weighted average crude for semi-complex and complex refining, but *not* for simple or topping refining.

The relationship between the GPW and the c.i.f. crude price lies at the heart of understanding how the general level of product prices is determined. If this relationship were very stable, a certain predictability would enter the system, and this would suggest that the levels of refinery throughput and of demand for the various products adjust so as to preserve some margin against the principal cost. We first examine this margin by analysing the simple differences between the GPWs and the prices of the associated crude types. Summary statistics for these differences are presented in Table 7.5.

Presenting the information in this way, we see that the standard deviations of the differences are very similar for the different types of refinery, but that they differ to some extent with the choice of crude input and of time-period. Semi-complex refining shows (marginally) less variation in the margin than the other types of plant. The margin using Arabian Gulf crudes shows the greatest variation (particularly when the whole period is included), but the degree of variability is reasonably similar for the different crude types. Since the standard deviations of this difference are of the same order of magnitude as the mean differences, the coefficients of variation are universally large, and this is particularly so for simple and semi-complex refining. If the standard deviation of the differential were *exactly* equal to the mean

Table 7.5: Summary Statistics for Differences between GPWs and Mean Prices of Associated Crude Types. Dollars per Tonne.

	Mean	Standard Deviation	Coefficient of Variation (%)	Standardized Range
1976–87 (Arabian Gulf)				
Topping	−9.0	12.56	−140	5.8
Simple	−4.2	12.19	−290	5.8
Semi-complex	11.5	11.94	104	6.9
Complex	13.6	12.45	92	6.6
1980–87 (North Sea)				
Topping	−14.38	9.23	−64	7.5
Simple	−7.53	8.41	−112	7.7
Semi-complex	4.46	7.67	172	7.0
Complex	14.12	8.58	61	5.0
1980–87 (Weighted Average)				
Topping	−14.00	8.73	−62	6.8
Simple	−7.62	8.27	−109	7.0
Semi-complex	5.66	7.78	137	6.8
Complex	12.82	8.63	67	5.7
1980–87 (Arabian Gulf)				
Topping	−12.38	10.68	−86	6.8
Simple	−7.04	10.43	−148	7.0
Semi-complex	9.13	10.10	111	6.8
Complex	10.86	10.45	96	5.9

differential (and this were positive), then, assuming that the observations were normally distributed, *about one-sixth* of the observations should be expected to be negative (i.e. the GPWs would not even be sufficient to cover crude costs). For the case where the standard deviation is only two-thirds of the (positive) mean, negative values of the differential should be expected on 7 per cent of occasions. In fact, for the weighted average price case with semi-complex refining there were twelve months out of ninety-two with negative margins, and for complex refining there were just three such months. The standardized ranges, although large, are not excessively so, so that the picture is one of margins fluctuating strongly but not abnormally.[4] Conversely, simple refining covered crude costs in only twelve months and topping covered crude costs in only three months. In terms of this variability,

[4] For tables of the distribution of the standardized range, see for example Owen, D. B., *Handbook of Statistical Tables*, Pergamon Press, London, 1962.

Table 7.6: Regressions of GPWs less Crude Margins on Trend.
May 1980–January 1987.

Yield by Type	Constant	Trend	R^2	SEE	DWS
Topping	−29 (3.8)	0.17 (0.03)	0.43	7.1	0.69
Simple	−22 (3.9)	0.14 (0.03)	0.33	7.3	0.65
Semi-complex	6 (4.3)	−0.01 (0.03)	0.07	8.05	0.52
Complex	13.2 (4.7)	−0.03 (0.03)	0.09	8.84	0.43

Note: All regressions are based on yields for a mixture of crudes and on average
prices. Values in brackets are standard errors.

however, March 1986 was quite exceptional.[5] Even topping had a
GPW some $20 per tonne greater than the crude price (while for
complex refining the margin was $38 per tonne). For topping this
margin was nearly four standard deviations from the mean, and is so
aberrant compared with all other values that it must be regarded as
an outlier. The fact that these are monthly averages serves to emphasize that, on occasion, the lags between crude price shifts and the
resulting product price shifts produce a very great widening of the
contemporaneous margin between them.

Given that fuel and transport costs are included in the margin
between the GPW and the price of the associated crude type, it is
important to see the extent to which this margin is random or systematic. A random margin would indicate that no other systematic
variable linked input costs and output prices month by month. There
would be no evidence of other cost factors being involved, while at the
same time all autonomous crude price changes would be fully and
instantly passed on into product prices (and vice versa). A simple test
of these ideas is undertaken by regressing the differential between the
GPW and the price of the associated crude type on a constant, a trend
and seasonal variables. The results are shown in Table 7.6.

These results show that for topping and simple refining the margin
steadily increases over the period (there is a significant positive

[5] The various crude and product markets became severely dislocated in this month. Arabian Gulf crude
prices fell very quickly as the netback deals for Arabian Light were signed with Japanese refineries, and
although the forward structure of Brent held up the prices of North Sea crudes temporarily, they too fell
sharply. Product prices did not fall at the same moment as crude prices, which produced a very large but very
short-lived differential of a sufficient magnitude to allow even topping to cover crude costs by a large margin.

coefficient on the trend in each case), while this is not the case for semi-complex or complex refining. In all cases the very low Durbin–Watson statistic suggests that some factor is omitted from the relationship, which has a strongly serially correlated pattern. None of the monthly seasonal dummy variables was significant in any of the regressions and these are therefore not reported.

To summarize the findings on the basic behaviour of the gross product worth series we note:

(a) The mean and month-by-month values of the four types of GPW are always in the same order, but the differences between them vary a great deal relative to the mean difference;
(b) The largest jump in the average GPW is from simple to semi-complex refining;
(c) Complex and semi-complex refining had GPWs that nearly always covered crude costs c.i.f., while simple and topping GPWs rarely covered crude costs;
(d) The margin of the GPW over the crude price varies a great deal relative to the mean size of the margin;
(e) Temporary shocks produce abnormally high values of the margin, suggesting that crude and product prices are not instantaneously linked;
(f) Tests suggest that the margin is not random, even allowing for the presence of a trend for topping and simple refining margins. There is no evidence of seasonality in the behaviour of margins, nor of a trend in semi-complex or complex margins.

7.4 Theoretical and Empirical Relationships between Gross Product Worths and Crude Prices

The relationship between GPWs and crude prices is critical to our understanding of the behaviour of product prices. If cost changes are fully and instantly reflected in output prices, and if no other factor disturbs the relationship between them, then a simple link between the supply of crude and the product market is established.

In equilibrium, i.e. when refining covers all its costs but there is no incentive to new entrants into the industry, and there is a simple technology of a fixed input–output type, we would expect the prices of products to settle when the extra revenue resulting from refining one more barrel of oil exactly covered the total costs of its production, including capital costs. Since there is no substitution between capital and raw material input, the incremental cost would then be the sum of crude costs, fuel costs, other current costs and capital costs.

Out of equilibrium, when there is excess capacity, we would expect marginal revenue to be equal to incremental running costs, unless demand were to fall so much that shut-down costs were also brought into the equation.

This account suggests that over a period such as the one under study, during which there was excess capacity (as shown in Chapter 6), the GPW of the marginally viable technology would be related to crude costs. Our results so far suggest that semi-complex refining was the marginal technique for much of the period. At no point was it in excess supply, while its GPW was sufficiently above that of simple (and topping) refining to make them very much less viable. Complex refining, with its even higher GPW, was in shorter supply still, so it was clearly intra-marginal.

This suggests a basic hypothesis that for the period 1976–87 semi-complex refining was marginal and simple refining was extra-marginal but kept in play by the magnitude of shut-down costs. If this hypothesis is correct, then the margin between the GPW for semi-complex refining and the price of the associated crude type c.i.f. is the focal point. Several points must be made about this margin:

(a) The difference between the GPW and the c.i.f. price of the crude is *not* expected to be zero even in the long run, since it omits capital costs as well as other current costs (labour, etc.);
(b) If the omitted current costs are relatively constant (as is likely to have been the case), then we might expect this margin to be fairly constant;
(c) If markets clear rapidly (i.e. in considerably less than the observation interval of one month), then we might expect crude price shifts and product price shifts to be co-incident (whichever moves exogenously);
(d) If the assumptions about the nature of the markets and technologies are correct, then the margin should be a random variable. Any predictable or systematic feature observed in the behaviour of this margin would suggest that the basic hypotheses are incorrect.

Given this appreciation of the nature of this margin it is useful to recapitulate the assumptions we have used in constructing it:

(a) Semi-complex refining was the marginal technique over the period (i.e. it covered its running costs);
(b) The yields and crude mix used in our analysis correctly reflect those faced by the marginal firm;

204   *Robert Bacon*

(c) The crude prices and transport costs correctly represent purchasing costs;
(d) All cost and price shifts are transmitted within the month;
(e) Other current costs did not change rapidly or substantially during the period.

The preliminary testing of the margin for semi-complex refining shows that it had an average value of $5.66 per tonne with a standard deviation of $7.78 per tonne (see Table 7.5). Regressing this margin on a trend and on seasonal dummy variables revealed no systematic influence from either of these, but the Durbin–Watson statistic was so low that it strongly suggests that there is some other systematic factor linking these two series.

Our detailed examination of the behaviour of this margin begins with the time-series plot given in Figure 7.1. This shows that the margin was indeed positive for most of the period but that for two episodes (October 1980–April 1981 and November 1986–March 1987) it was negative. For the period January–April 1986, the margin was clearly abnormally high. Finally, the typical values in 1980 and 1981, excluding the negative-margin period, seem to be a little higher than those thereafter. It is clear that semi-complex refining was certainly not covering current costs during the low-margin periods, but these were sufficiently short lived not to encourage exit and hence make complex refining the truly marginal technique. The high-margin periods are also important: in the early 1980s simple and topping plants still did not cover even their crude costs (apart for a couple of months when simple refining showed a small positive margin). In early 1986 both simple and topping plants could have covered their running costs and at that time semi-complex was not the marginal technique. Topping was probably the marginal technique for a three-month period, so that we would expect an abnormal value for the semi-complex margin (caused purely by the superiority of its yields relative to topping yields). This is the same phenomenon as the observed trend in topping and simple margins over the period as a whole.[6]

---

[6] Suppose there are two products with prices X and Y ($X > Y$) and the input price is P. The yields on the marginal type of refining are a and $1 - a$, while those for an extra-marginal refinery are $a - b$ and $1 - a + b$. In short-run equilibrium, where running costs are just covered, we have for the marginal refinery:

$$aX + (1 - a)Y = P$$

(with a zero margin). For the extra-marginal refinery the margin is:

$$(a - b)X + (1 - a + b)Y - P$$

which is equal to $b(Y - X)$. As the gap between X and Y increases or decreases, the margin, although negative, can show a trend.

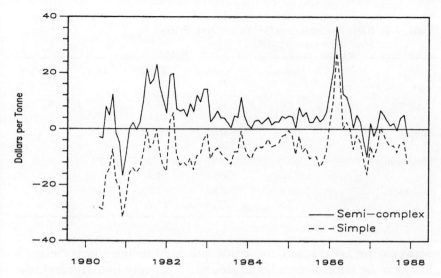

Figure 7.1: Refiners' Margins for Semi-complex and Simple Refining. Rotterdam GPWs against Crude Prices c.i.f. May 1980–December 1987.

Thus, although the margin on semi-complex refining does vary considerably, its behaviour does not appear to show any cyclical pattern. This is a very important finding, since it means that even when relative product prices altered, presumably because of shifts in the pattern of demand, the market worked well enough to keep the weighted average product price steady in relation to the crude price. This first confirms the strongly competitive nature of the market and secondly suggests that the same type of refinery remained the marginal one for much of the period. If this had not been so, then the margin for semi-complex refining would have jumped more often at times when a type of plant with a lower GPW had become truly marginal. This phenomenon appears to have occurred only in early 1986.

(a) Basic Regressions. Rather than regressing the difference between the GPW and the crude price on a constant and a trend (as in Table 7.5 above), it is a valuable starting-point to regress the GPW on the crude price, as well as on the constant and trend. The former procedure imposes the restriction of a dollar-for-dollar instantaneous passing-on of changes in crude prices to product prices, while the latter does not. The results are shown in Table 7.7.

These results show very clearly that, even for the period after the 1979 price rise, there is not just a simple contemporaneous link

Table 7.7: Basic Regressions of GPWs on Crude Prices.
May 1980–January 1987.

Yield by Type	Constant	Crude Price	Trend	SEE	DWS
Topping	5.8 (0.5)	0.91 (34)	−0.007 (0.1)	6.7	0.71
Simple	28 (2.7)	0.88 (35)	−0.09 (1.8)	6.3	0.71
Semi-complex	57 (5.0)	0.87 (30)	−0.26 (4.2)	7.1	0.56
Complex	69 (5.3)	0.87 (27)	−0.29 (4.2)	8.0	0.47

between the GPWs and the crude price. Although the correlation between the series is very high (around 98 per cent in each case), the standard error of the estimate is substantial (over $6 per tonne in each case), while the low Durbin–Watson statistic implies that some systematic factor is not being captured by the basic specification. This point is dramatically illustrated by the coefficients on the crude price, which are all significantly less then unity. If the model were accepted as reflecting actual behaviour, it would imply that only around 90 cents of every dollar change in crude prices was passed on in product price changes.

These results confirm the findings of the previous section that the systematic relationship between crude and product prices can not be fully explained by concentrating solely on the margin of the GPW over the corresponding crude price.

The presence of significant trends in the relationship may well in part reflect the absence of some other more important variable from the specification.

(*b*) *Dynamic Adjustment.* The first detailed investigation of the behaviour of the margin between GPWs and crude prices (c.i.f.) focuses on the dynamics of the relationship between the two. Previous studies have found evidence that the transmission of shocks from one side of the market to the other is not instantaneous.[7]

We would expect a shock in demand to be felt first in product prices and afterwards in crude prices, while the reverse would be true if the

[7] See Bacon, 1984; Himona, 1987.

shock originated on the supply side. Given that crude oil markets are international, it seems clear that any supply shock would be felt in *all* markets and hence felt by refiners in the European market. Looking at the reverse link, a shock of a given percentage magnitude in European demand would affect product prices in the European market. The feedback to world crude prices would be weaker, however, since Europe is only one outlet for crude. Only by product arbitrage between the European and other markets would the full impact of the demand shock be felt, and this might well take longer to be established. Thus, a *temporary* local shock to European product prices might disappear before it affected product prices world-wide. If this were so, then for most of the time world crude prices would predominantly be seen to lead European product prices, while very short-run demand-side shocks would not feed back on to crude prices.

These ideas are tested by means of general dynamic regressions for all the yield patterns using the weighted average crude input series. These regressions are of the form:

$$GPW(t) = f[\text{Constant, Crude Price } (t + m, \ldots t, \ldots, t - n),$$
$$GPW \ (t - 1, \ldots, t - p)]$$

The presence of both lags and leads in the crude price term allows for the presence of causality in both directions, while the lagged values of the GPW series allow for more flexible patterns of dynamic response.

The first important result is the negative one that the *lead* of the crude price on the GPWs is *not* significant for any of the regressions. There is no evidence that, over the period as a whole, demand-side shifts that affected product prices then took time to feed through to crude prices. Any effect from this side of the market must therefore have been felt *within* the period if it had any effect on world crude prices.

In all regressions of this form, considerable variations in the lag structure were tried, but the best-fitting model, with all coefficients significant, invariably included a single lag on the GPW and the current and single-lagged crude prices. The trend variable was not significant. The results are shown in Table 7.8. All the models fit very well and the standard error is much reduced (to around $4.5 per tonne) from the levels reported in the basic results in Table 7.7. In order to test for misspecification, Durbin's *h*-statistic is calculated and this shows that there was no systematic pattern in the residuals.

The dynamic structure of the system is first used to generate the total impact of a change in crude prices on product prices (the long-run price effect). For topping and simple refining this is less than

Table 7.8: Dynamic Models for the Regression of GPWs on Weighted Average Crude Prices. July 1980–October 1987.

	Topping	Simple	Semi-complex	Complex
Constant	−1.06	2.28	0.89	1.8
	(0.13)	(1.1)	(0.4)	(0.8)
Price	0.74	0.73	0.78	0.80
	(19.2)	(19.8)	(19.3)	(18.6)
Lagged price	−0.37	−0.36	−0.47	−0.55
	(5.0)	(4.8)	(6.2)	(7.2)
Lagged GPW	0.61	0.60	0.70	0.75
	(8.8)	(8.4)	(10.7)	(12.1)
R^2	0.992	0.993	0.993	0.992
SEE	4.50	4.32	4.71	5.05
DWS	2.17	2.18	2.20	2.14
h-statistic	−1.06	−1.12	−1.20	−0.79
Long-run price effect	0.94	0.94	1.01	1.02
Mean lag (months)	0.54	0.55	0.78	0.88

unity, but for semi-complex and complex refining there is effectively dollar-for-dollar passing-on. The average speed of passing on price changes is important: for the more acceptable results from semi-complex and complex refining the *average* lag between a crude price increase and the corresponding GPW increase is 0.8 months.

This last result is important because the lag in the response of product prices to changes in crude prices means that, when crude prices start to climb, a margin calculated on the difference between contemporaneous GPWs and crude prices will temporarily narrow. Correspondingly this margin will widen if crude prices fall. This does not mean that a smaller actual margin was being made: to the extent that it takes time for crude to be transported to the refinery, stored and then processed, the products coming out are in a sense based on a rather earlier crude price, and the current margin is therefore misleading as a guide to actual market behaviour. The gradual shift from Middle Eastern to North Sea crudes, as a result of which the transportation factor decreased substantially in importance, may be associated with a shortening of the average lag of product prices behind crude prices.

Finally the sign of the constant term indicates whether the GPW would have covered crude costs on average over the period as a whole. The actual constant gives the average margin in the short run, before all crude prices have been absorbed, and a 'long-run' constant can be derived by dividing this value by the difference between the coefficient on the lagged GPW term and unity. This calculation is not likely to be helpful for topping or simple refining, since the relationship is inconsistent with their being the marginal refinery types for the period as a whole. For semi-complex refining the long-run constant is about $3 per tonne, while for complex refining it is $7.2 per tonne. These results, together with earlier evidence, support the view that *on running costs alone* complex refining was more profitable than semi-complex. The issue of whether either type was covering *all* running costs over the long run cannot be settled decisively from the available data. However, for semi-complex a margin of $3 per tonne is likely to have covered all the other running costs that we have not identified.

At this stage, it appears that the GPWs for semi-complex and complex refining are tightly tied to crude prices, but that the GPWs for simple and topping refineries are related to crude prices only indirectly and hence imperfectly. If, for example, no topping capacity had been run during the period (because of its lack of profitability), a hypothetical yield based on it would nevertheless be strongly correlated with the crude price because the differences in yields of the specific products (relative to those from semi-complex refining) are not so great as to offset the generally similar movements in all product prices.

In carrying out this analysis, we have so far focused on the GPWs and the prices for the weighted average of crude inputs. This is the most representative calculation but it limits our analysis to a period from 1980 onwards since there are no price data available on a continuous basis for North Sea crudes before this time. However, one important feature of the European market is the shifts in refining capacity that were taking place over the longer run. In order to analyse the data with a view to investigating the stability of this relationship, it is necessary to use GPWs and crude prices based solely on Arabian Gulf crudes. These are fully representative of the beginning of the period but are very much less so by the end. The regressions for the whole period are as shown in Table 7.9.

The results from these regressions are uniformly indicative of some misspecification. All the long-run coefficients on the crude prices are so far below unity that it is clear that the long-run margin was not constant for any single type of refining. There are three possible reasons for these results:

(a) The mismeasurement of GPWs and crude prices towards the end of the period biases the estimates from the whole period;
(b) There is some other factor affecting the margin which has been

Table 7.9: Dynamic Models for the Regression of GPWs on Arabian Gulf Crude Prices. February 1976–December 1987.

	Topping	*Simple*	*Semi-complex*	*Complex*
Constant	4.28	4.81	4.35	4.22
	(2.5)	(2.7)	(2.3)	(2.2)
Price	0.73	0.74	0.81	0.82
	(17.4)	(17.8)	(16.7)	(16.9)
Lagged price	−0.49	−0.52	−0.64	−0.66
	(8.1)	(8.8)	(10.5)	(11.4)
Lagged GPW	0.72	0.75	0.82	0.84
	(11.7)	(12.5)	(15.2)	(16.5)
R^2	0.990	0.990	0.989	0.989
SEE	6.24	6.20	7.19	7.15
DWS	1.80	1.84	1.88	1.89
h-statistic	1.86	1.41	0.90	0.80
Long-run price effect	0.86	0.87	0.93	0.93
Mean lag (months)	0.57	0.61	0.71	0.73

omitted, and which varied in such a way as to bias the coefficients on prices;

(c) The relationship between GPWs and crude prices shifted during the period.

The first factor is undoubtedly present, but is unlikely to be large enough to explain the results observed. The second factor is investigated later (see Section (*c*) below). The shift in the relationship between GPWs and crude prices could come, for example, from a change in the type of marginal refinery.

The examination of the *current* margins of GPWs over crude prices for the *mixture* of crudes had some very important characteristics as we noted above (see Figure 7.1). The margin for semi-complex refining was mainly positive (but less so than for complex), while those for simple and topping refining were negative. This allows us to focus on semi-complex as the marginal technique. This assumption is supported by the results of Chapter 6 which related semi-complex capacity to throughput, showing that from the early 1980s onwards virtually all throughput could have been run through semi-complex capacity. However there were some short abnormal episodes:

(a) From the end of 1980 to early 1981, when the semi-complex margin was negative, only complex refining could have covered costs;

(b) During the early part of 1986, when the margin on all technologies was strongly positive, topping would have covered current costs and may have been the marginal technique;
(c) During late 1986, when the margin on semi-complex was again negative.

Since the argument is that the marginal type of technology will be determined by demand and hence that its GPW is related to the crude price, we should ideally use a 'switching regime' approach. The estimated relationship would switch between technologies as demand moved across capacity boundaries. However, there were so few months when techniques other than semi-complex were marginal that their relationships cannot be estimated *for the periods in which they were truly marginal.* Hence the appropriate solution is to work on the semi-complex GPW for just those periods when it appeared to be the marginal technique. Accordingly we omit all months in which:

(a) the semi-complex GPW was less than the *current* crude price;
   or
(b) the GPW for simple refining was greater than the *current* crude price.

This selection of observations on which to estimate the dynamic relationship between crude prices and GPWs is not quite ideal for two reasons:

(a) If there is indeed a lag in the passing through of prices, the correct criteria would be to compare the GPWs with the appropriately lagged crude prices;
(b) Any mismeasurement of the GPWs could change the selection of points to be included.

Neither of these problems can be completely overcome, but the selection of points will be fairly robust against the likely magnitude of these errors.

The final regression for the period in which it appears that semi-complex refining was genuinely marginal is:

$$GPW = -1.43 + 0.926\ P - 0.343\ P_{(-1)} + 0.438\ GPW_{(-1)} \qquad (4.4.1)$$
$$(0.68)\ (19.4) \qquad (4.2) \qquad\quad (5.3)$$

$$R^2 = 0.995, \quad SEE = 3.1, \quad DWS = 2.21, \quad h = -1.16$$

where P is the c.i.f. price of crude oil.

The overall performance of this equation is, not surprisingly, very good: the average error in fitting GPWs to crude prices is only $3 per tonne. The mean lag for the equation is 0.2 months and the long-run coefficient on prices is 1.03. The equation shows no evidence of any other systematic influences on GPWs. Its long-run price coefficient is slightly greater than unity, but given the problems of measuring the GPW exactly the result is near to the unity coefficient expected. We can formally test hypotheses about the long-run coefficients (which are non-linear functions of the estimated parameters) by the use of Fieller's method of constructing approximate confidence intervals.[8] At a 95 per cent confidence level we have:

$$-\$9.972 < \text{Margin} < \$5.235$$

$$0.983 < \text{Price coefficient} < 1.087.$$

The confidence interval for the price coefficient shows that the data is quite consistent with a long-run coefficient of unity on crude prices. The confidence interval for the margin is rather wide, but certainly includes positive values: the data would be consistent with a long-run margin of GPWs over crude prices of up to $5 per tonne.

This equation provides us with two crucial pieces of information:

(a) There is a short but distinct lagged reaction of product prices to crude prices. Experiments with unlagged models had a distinctly larger standard error of estimate and also showed evidence of misspecification with large values of the h-statistic;

(b) Once allowance is made for the lagged structure, and provided that demand shifts are not so large as to change the marginal type of refining, product prices are tied extremely closely to crude prices on the whole. Even with very large shifts in relative prices, such as those discussed in Chapter 8 below, the system was able to adjust product prices very rapidly so that changes in crude prices or external shifts in product markets resulted in new combinations of prices that just balanced extra costs against extra revenues. This can be taken as evidence that the product market is truly competitive. It also means that in analysing the effects of external forces on product price determination we do not have to stress the variability of the refining margin: the margin over current costs

---

[8] See, for example, Maddala, G. S., *Econometrics*, McGraw-Hill, 1977, pp. 101–2.

does indeed vary but the margin relative to the appropriately lagged crude prices is very stable except during those episodes when other techniques appear to have been marginal.

(*c*) *Other Variables*. The final aspect of the relationship between crude and product prices that is explored here is the impact of other factors. Four factors were investigated:

(i)   The total throughput of European refining;
(ii) A measure of the degree of utilization of the European refining system;
(iii) Official (as opposed to spot) crude prices for Arabian Gulf crudes;
(iv) A measure of the average distance over which crudes used in European refining were transported.

These subsidiary factors are introduced as a check for systematic variability in the margin. The variables and results are introduced as alternatives at this stage.

(*i*) *Refinery Throughput*. One simple hypothesis on the behaviour of the refining system as a whole is that the more crude is processed the more the margins of GPWs over crude prices will change (even for a given technology). As extra plants are introduced in some rough order of merit, the *average* margin of GPWs over crude prices would need to rise in order to allow the costs of increasingly less efficient forms to be covered.

The throughput of European refining is measured as in Chapter 8 below from data given by the IEA. However, these are quarterly data so we have to extrapolate in order to obtain monthly data. This was done by assuming that the total throughput in each quarter was divided equally among the three months of the quarter in question. Such an approximation would not pick up all short-run links between the series but would show any important medium- and long-run effects.

Since the data based on the *mixture* of crudes are the most appropriate to the study, and since the effect of a declining average yield should show if present (even post 1979), the regression is estimated for the best-fitting model with throughput as an additional explanatory variable. The throughput did not make a significant difference to the relationship between crude and product prices. If the average yields (and hence the GPWs) were changing with the level of throughput, then the correlation with crude prices was too weak to be isolated.

The dominant factor still appears to have been the change in relative product prices.

(*ii*) *Degree of Semi-complex Capacity Utilization.* A more sensitive version of the previous hypothesis is tested by attempting to see whether the ratio of throughput to the capacity at which semi-complex plant was utilized is significant. Variations in this ratio around the 100 per cent mark could be important, since extra throughput would have to come from simple refining, thus generating a much lower marginal GPW and hence a steeper rate of decline of the average yield. The margin of a fixed yield over the crude price should widen as the average yield falls, and this variable is designed to be a more sensitive index of the average yield. The data is again the same as that used in the previous section and is based on monthly extrapolations from quarterly data. The analysis is conducted for Arabian Gulf crudes and for the weight-ed mixture of crudes, but in no case was the margin of the fixed yield found to be correlated with the percentage utilization of semi-complex capacity. This is perhaps not very surprising since the post-1980 index does not vary a great deal.

(*iii*) *Official Prices.* Earlier work showed the existence of a correlation of the GPWs with official as well as spot crude prices for Arabian Light during the period in which spot prices were above official prices (i.e. 1978–81).[9] That study used simpler and less satisfactory data for GPWs, so it is necessary both to check the results for the earlier period and also to see whether there is any evidence to support the hypo-thesis that *official* prices exerted an *independent* influence on product prices (once allowance is made for *spot* crude prices).

The basic regression is modified to include, as well as current and lagged spot crude prices and the lagged GPW, also the *current official* price of Arabian Light (taken as being representative of official prices). This series is found to be significant only for the period 1976–8 and then only for simple and semi-complex GPWs, but the effect of spot prices then seems to be very small. This in fact may well accord with reality, since purchasing at official prices was at its most important at the beginning of the period.

Experiments with lagged values of official prices reveal an unusual feature. The current GPW is related to the *change* in official prices in the period 1980–85. It appears that the relatively infrequent changes

9. See Bacon, 1984.

in official prices acted as a separate signal for product prices to rise *temporarily* but to fall back into line with spot prices thereafter until the next jump in official prices. The overall goodness of fit is almost unchanged so that this very short-run phenomenon, which is no doubt related to the role of expectations in price formation, can be seen as a purely historical event of relatively little significance.

(*iv*) *The Speed of Adjustment*. Since crude oil takes time to be transported from the point of its f.o.b. sale to the refinery (as well as time to be refined), the speed of adjustment of product prices might depend on the time taken to transport the crude. Since the period saw a shift from almost 100 per cent use of Middle Eastern crude to almost 100 per cent use of North Sea crudes, clearly the average transportation time fell sharply and hence the mean lag may have fallen over the period. This reason for a lag is essentially based on the assumption of a 'first in, first out' (FIFO) pricing policy. A 'last in, first out' (LIFO) policy would mark up product prices simultaneously with the rise in crude prices, even though the crude would not reach the refinery for some time.

In order to test this hypothesis, an index of the average transportation time was constructed weighting fixed time-periods for Arabian Gulf and North Sea crudes by the yearly averages estimated to correspond to European refinery throughput (using the same weights as were used for constructing the average GPWs for the mixture of crudes). This index was multiplied by the lagged dependent variable (whose coefficient measures the speed of adjustment), and the new variable was added to the regressions. Over the period 1980–87 this variable made no significant additional contribution to the model for any type of refining.

7.5 Interpretation and Conclusions

The analysis of the margin of GPWs over crude prices is based on the assumption that, if the variables (prices, yields and costs) are correctly measured and the marginal technology is correctly identified, then the long-run relationship between input costs and the GPW will be dollar for dollar.

Hence the properly specified dynamic regression of the appropriate GPW on the crude price should show a long-run coefficient of unity and the residuals show no non-random behaviour. Once such a relationship is identified, other aspects of the GPWs' behaviour can be derived.

The first matter to be investigated was the evidence as to which of the refining techniques was the truly marginal one. It was shown that the ordering between techniques never varied, and that for most of the post-1980 period complex and semi-complex refining techniques covered their c.i.f. crude costs while simple and topping techniques did not. Only for very short episodes was the simple GPW greater than or the semi-complex GPW smaller than crude prices. Furthermore, the gap between the GPWs for semi-complex and for simple refining was substantial on average, thus making for a very clear boundary between the two. Whenever the two techniques were already in existence and thus came into competition, the advantage seems to have been decisively with semi-complex refining.

Tests on a simple current relationship between the GPW and the crude price were universally unsatisfactory, indicating clearly that the current GPW was systematically affected by something other than the current crude price.

Our investigation of a general dynamic adjustment model produced much better results. However, for tests based solely on Arabian Gulf crude prices and the associated GPWs, the results were still not acceptable, thus indicating a misspecification.

Since the typical crude input mix for European refineries shifted over the period studied, from one based almost entirely on Middle Eastern crudes in 1976 to one based on North Sea crudes in 1987, it was clearly likely that the use of GPWs and prices based on the weighted averages would better represent the genuinely marginal situation than the use of the corresponding figures based on Arabian Gulf crudes alone. Tests of this model produced much better results and the long-run price coefficient for semi-complex refining was not significantly different from unity (and was also closer to unity than the corresponding coefficients for the other technologies). There was no evidence of misspecification and the *average* lag of product prices behind crude prices was around six days.

Tests on the stability of the margin against movements in certain other variables were carried out. There was some evidence that in the earliest period (1976–8) the *official* price of Arabian Light also affected the margin calculated for Arabian Gulf crudes. This is plausible, since companies were still buying some crude at official as well as at spot prices during that period. For the period for which the best regression is established (post 1980) this factor was not important except that there was a minor and transient shock whenever the official price changed.

A second factor that might have affected the relationship between the GPW calculated for a fixed set of yields and the price was the extent to which yields varied between refineries. At higher levels of demand, the less efficient plants, whose GPWs would be less (at the same prices), might come into operation. Since their GPW would be the one equated to crude prices, the fixed GPW would appear better against crude the greater the total throughput of the refinery system. There was in fact no measurable variation of the margin, either with throughput or with the degree of utilization of semi-complex and complex capacity combined. However, this variable did not change substantially after 1980 (the period for which the most reliable price data were available), so it is perhaps not surprising that we were unable to detect evidence of a strong gradient of efficiencies between refineries.

Further tests revealed no significant lead of barge product prices (as incorporated into the GPWs) over crude prices. Whatever lags there were on the demand side must have occurred at stages nearer to the consumer.

The primary hypothesis that changes in crude prices are fully passed on into product prices (with a lag) is thus fully supported by the model. This result has several important implications:

(a) The product market is highly competitive: there is no evidence, for example, that falls in crude prices were not reflected in falls in product prices, nor that product prices rose when crude prices were not doing so.

(b) The adjustment of product prices to crude prices over the post-1980 period was very rapid, but not instantaneous. The *average* delay was of the order of 0.2 months (six days). This implies that *part* of crude price changes are passed on immediately (i.e. that pricing is at least partly on a LIFO basis), but that a fair part of the change takes some time to be reflected in product prices.

The lag of GPWs behind crude prices implies that the *current* margin will not in general be constant. For example, during a steady fall in crude prices (driven by supply shifts), the current margin will appear to be larger than normal, and the opposite will apply when crude prices are rising. Demand-side shifts did not apparently produce such variations in the margin.

(c) The behaviour of the difference between non-marginal GPWs and crude prices is related to the relative movements of the GPWs. If a rise in GPWs is accompanied by an increase in the price of high-value products relative to that of low-value products, then the GPWs of the output from the 'low-technology' plant will fall relative to crude prices (and the GPWs of the output from a 'higher-technology' plant will rise).

A regression of GPWs on crude prices, during a period in which rises in GPWs are positively correlated with rises in relative product prices, will produce an apparent 'long-run coefficient' of less than unity for extra-marginal technologies and greater than unity for intra-marginal technologies.

If, however, rises in GPWs were associated with a fall in the relative price ratio, then the extra-marginal technology would appear to have a coefficient greater than unity and the intra-marginal technique a coefficient less than unity.

(d) The margin of GPWs over crude prices was apparently unrelated to throughput levels in the post-1980 period. If there were substantial differences in the efficiencies of refineries of the same type in different parts of Europe, then the throughput did not vary enough to make this effect felt. The margin of a refinery with the yields we have used in the above analysis would have stayed remarkably constant once due allowance is made for lags.

(e) This general stability of the relationship between GPWs and crude prices means that relative product prices are constrained to fall within a certain range. Only when throughput changes to such an extent that a different refining technique becomes the marginal one will the relationship between the GPWs for semi-complex refining and crude prices change. When this happens, the relationships between relative product prices and the crude price will shift, and attempts to explain product prices in terms of the relationship between the semi-complex GPW and the crude price will be misleading.

8 Relative Product Prices

David Long

8.1 Introduction

In this chapter we aim to provide an explanation of the movements in relative product prices in the European market over the longer term. Before we can do this, however, we must first describe what happened to relative prices. The differentials and ratios between them are not constant, nor even random about a given margin: they show, rather, systematic patterns of behaviour that require explanation, so we must identify and evaluate the major sustained variations in relative prices to enable us to concentrate on the key shifts that are likely to have affected investment decisions in the European refining industry.

Changes in relative prices are important for two main reasons. First, they affect refiners' operating decisions since they alter the optimum mix of joint products that can be produced from existing refinery plant. Secondly, if sustained, they can create incentives for investment in new plant or disinvestment of old plant. In either case, shifts in relative prices will bring about changes in the supply of refined products which can, in turn, affect the prices themselves.

Our analysis will focus on the five main refined products: gasoline, naphtha, kerosine, gas oil and fuel oil. We use monthly average prices based on *Platt's* quotations for the various products f.o.b. Rotterdam barges low.

8.2 Relative Price Behaviour

Relative price movements can be described in different ways depending on the objectives of the analysis. As may be seen from Figure 8.1, the general pattern of peaks and troughs in product prices is very similar for the four distillate products (gasoline, naphtha, kerosine and gas oil) and differs from that displayed by fuel oil prices. This is not to say that there is no variation in the relative prices of distillate products, since they are clearly subject to independent variations as well, but simply that there appears to be less variation in the relationships among the four distillate prices than there is between the prices of any of the distillates and fuel oil.

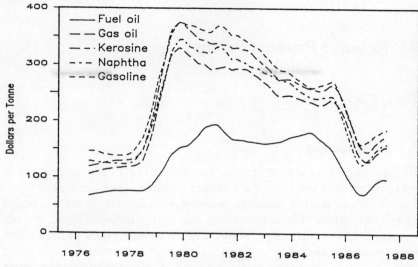

Figure 8.1: Moving Average Prices for Five Products. July 1976–July 1987.

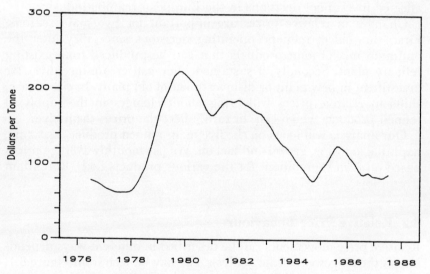

Figure 8.2: Moving Average Price Differential: Gasoline versus Fuel Oil. July 1976–July 1987.

The most common method of describing changes in relative prices is to use price differentials. These have a practical appeal in that they can be directly related to both operating and investment decisions, since they constitute a measure of the benefits of converting one

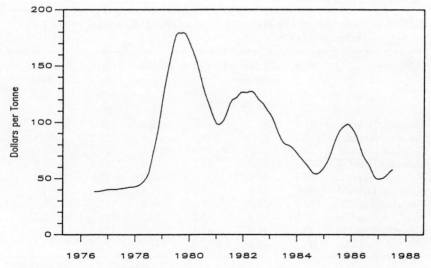

Figure 8.3: Moving Average Price Differential: Gas Oil versus Fuel Oil. July 1976–July 1987.

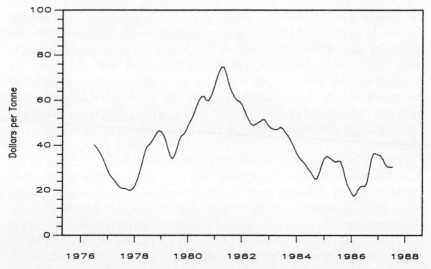

Figure 8.4: Moving Average Price Differential: Gasoline versus Gas Oil. July 1976–July 1987.

product into another. As can be seen from Figures 8.2–8.4, which show the changing differentials over the period 1976–87 between the moving average prices of gasoline, gas oil and fuel oil, the range of the moving average price differentials between pairs of products is considerable.

Table 8.1: Basic Statistics for Rotterdam Product Price Differentials. 1976–87. Dollars per Tonne.

Differential	Mean	Standard Deviation	Coefficient of Variation (%)	Maximum	Minimum	Standardized Range
Gasoline/Naphtha	27.2	14.2	52.2	72.0	4.3	4.8
Gasoline/Kerosine	13.1	20.7	158.0	58.8	−52.4	5.4
Gasoline/Gas Oil	39.8	21.7	54.5	103.4	−27.3	6.0
Gasoline/Fuel Oil	125.9	54.3	43.1	251.4	45.7	3.8
Kerosine/Naphtha	14.1	20.1	142.6	86.2	−23.6	5.5
Kerosine/Gas Oil	26.6	14.3	53.8	71.4	2.9	4.8
Kerosine/Fuel Oil	112.8	54.4	48.2	246.6	45.0	3.7
Naphtha/Gas Oil	12.6	19.3	153.2	48.7	−62.1	5.7
Naphtha/Fuel Oil	98.7	46.8	47.4	218.9	25.3	4.1
Gas Oil/Fuel Oil	86.1	44.8	52.0	217.7	34.7	4.1

It can be seen from Table 8.1 that the mean differentials between the simple monthly average prices of distillate products and residual fuel oil lie between $126 per tonne for gasoline/fuel oil and $86 per tonne for gas oil/fuel oil, and are much greater than those between pairs of distillate products, which vary between $40 per tonne for gasoline/gas oil and $13 per tonne for gasoline/kerosine or naphtha/gas oil. This pattern of differentials is not unreasonable given that both the capital and operating costs of converting fuel oil to distillates are much greater than those of converting one type of distillate to another.

What is more striking, however, is the extent of the variation in the monthly average price differentials over the period. The price differential between gasoline and residual fuel oil, for example, varied between a maximum of $251 and a minimum of $46 per tonne. Furthermore, it is evident from the size of the standard deviation ($54 per tonne) that this wide range of variation can not be ascribed to the influence of a few 'extreme' months during the period: indeed the average variation of the gasoline/fuel oil differential for the period as a whole (as measured by the coefficient of variation) is 43 per cent. Other pairs of price differentials exhibit similar behaviour. As can be seen from Table 8.1, the coefficients of variation are also around the 50 per cent mark for all pairs except gasoline/kerosine, kerosine/naphtha and naphtha/gas oil, where the coefficients of variation are larger because the mean differences are so small. This variability of the price differentials indicates that it would be dangerous to attempt to forecast any product price solely by adding a constant factor to another, already known, product price. For example, the set of product prices should not be forecast from the price of heavy fuel oil (based on, say, a fixed relationship with the prices of competing fuels), simply by adding a given set of differentials. In both the short and the medium run, the set of figures given in Table 8.1 makes clear that the differentials diverge considerably from their average values.

Although they provide a useful practical measure of changes in relative product prices, and are frequently used in determining investment decisions, price differentials do not necessarily provide the best indicator of structural changes in price behaviour, since at least part of the variation in these differentials is due to changes in the *overall* level of prices, for reasons unconnected with the supply of and demand for individual refined petroleum products in a given market. Such limitations, which are largely a question of scaling, can be overcome by using price *ratios* rather than price *differentials*. Furthermore, the use of ratios rather than differentials can be justified on the grounds that refining costs (which must be a factor in determining the differentials between prices) will tend to vary in line with the overall level of oil prices, since fuel is the major component of variable operating costs. Since changes in the overall level of oil prices will dominate changes in the prices of specific products, these ratios will remain fairly constant against such shifts while differentials will widen or narrow with the general price level. Since we are interested *at this stage* in identifying features revealing predictability, we focus our attention on price ratios.

It can be seen from Figures 8.5 and 8.6 that the range of the moving average price ratios between pairs of products is also considerable. However, the behaviour of the ratios between the prices of the four distillate products and those for fuel oil is rather different from that of the ratios between the prices of the pairs of distillate products. The distillates/fuel oil price ratios all display a similar cyclical pattern: there was an increase from mid-1978 to a peak in early 1979, then a steady decline from 1979 to early 1985 (apart from an abrupt dip in late 1980/early 1981), followed by a sharp rise from early 1985 to an extreme peak in mid-1986, and finally a sharp fall to mid-1987 followed by a further sharp rise.[1] By comparison distillate/distillate price ratios are much less cyclical, although they also display variability in the shorter term.

---

[1] A similar but less clear-cut pattern was displayed in Figures 8.2 and 8.3 for the differentials between gasoline, gas oil and heavy fuel oil prices.

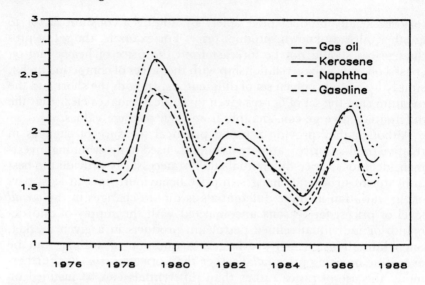

Figure 8.5: Moving Average Price Ratios: Distillates versus Fuel Oil.
July 1976–July 1987.

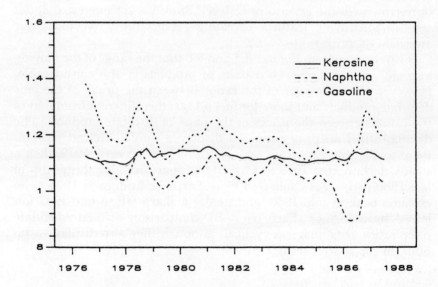

Figure 8.6: Moving Average Price Ratios: Distillates versus Gas Oil.
July 1976–July 1987.

Table 8.2 shows that the mean ratios for the simple monthly average prices of the four distillate products against those of fuel oil, which range between 1.70 for gas oil/fuel oil and 2.05 for gasoline/fuel oil, are much higher than those between pairs of distillate products, which range between 1.06 for kerosine/naphtha and 1.21 for gasoline/gas oil. The coefficients of variation provide further confirmation that the price ratios between distillate products and fuel oil are much more variable than the price ratios between pairs of distillate products. These coefficients of variation lie between 17 per cent for naphtha/fuel oil and 20 per cent for gasoline/fuel oil, and between with 4 per cent for kerosine/gas oil and 10 per cent for kerosine/naphtha.

Both these simple comparisons of relative price behaviour support the idea that distillate prices as a whole have followed a different path from residual fuel oil prices, and that as a result the correlations between the movements of distillate and fuel oil prices are weaker those between the movements of prices of pairs of distillates.

This hypothesis obtains further support from the results of a series of ordinary least squares regressions designed to evaluate the relationships between the prices of pairs of products in the Rotterdam barge market (using monthly averages), the results of which are shown in Table 8.3. The highest correlations were found within the light distillates (gasoline/naphtha) and within the middle distillates (kerosine/gas oil), which yielded R^2 coefficients of between 0.97 and 0.99. The next highest were the correlations between the light and middle distillates (gasoline/kerosine, gasoline/gas oil, naphtha/kerosine and naphtha/gas oil), which yielded coefficients of around

Table 8.2: Basic Statistics for Rotterdam Product Price Ratios. 1976–87.

Differential	Mean	Standard Deviation	Coefficient of Variation (%)	Maximum	Minimum	Standardized Range
Gasoline/Naphtha	1.13	0.08	7.1	1.46	1.03	5.4
Gasoline/Kerosine	1.07	0.10	9.3	1.32	0.75	5.7
Gasoline/Gas Oil	1.21	0.12	9.9	1.50	0.85	5.4
Gasoline/Fuel Oil	2.05	0.40	19.5	3.61	1.24	5.9
Kerosine/Naphtha	1.06	0.11	10.4	1.72	0.83	8.1
Kerosine/Gas Oil	1.12	0.04	3.6	1.25	1.01	6.0
Kerosine/Fuel Oil	1.91	0.35	18.3	3.06	1.36	4.9
Naphtha/Gas Oil	1.07	0.10	9.3	1.36	0.66	7.0
Naphtha/Fuel Oil	1.81	0.30	16.6	2.74	1.20	5.1
Gas Oil/Fuel Oil	1.70	0.31	18.2	2.78	1.22	5.0

0.95. The lowest were the correlations between distillates and fuel oil, which yielded coefficients of only 0.72 for gasoline/fuel oil and 0.78 for naphtha/fuel oil. In other words, the price series for the four distillates are much more highly correlated with each other than they are with the series for residual fuel oil. However, the low values obtained for the Durbin–Watson statistic (DWS) indicate that some other systematic factor is involved in the relationships between pairs of prices for the different products. The regressions were therefore repeated using seasonal dummies in order to test whether seasonality plays a role in the relationships. These were found to be significant in only three cases, all of which involved gasoline (gasoline/gas oil, gasoline/naphtha and gasoline/gas oil). This result is probably attributable to the fact that gasoline prices exhibit a different seasonal pattern from the prices of other products.

Nevertheless, despite the significant seasonal pattern observed in the ratios of gasoline prices to those of other distillates, there was no real improvement in the values obtained for the Durbin–Watson statistic and one is forced to conclude, first, that the relationships between prices for the different products are also determined by other factors that vary over a period of years rather than within the year, and, secondly, that these factors play a greater role in determining the variations in the prices of the distillate products relative to the price of fuel oil than in the variations of the prices of distillates relative to each other.

The strongly cyclical pattern in the distillates/fuel oil price ratios (or differentials) suggests that some systematic factors were involved. If we are able to isolate such factors, then we will have achieved an important step towards the understanding of product price behaviour. Our investigation begins with the most promising relationship (that between distillates and heavy fuel oil), but is then extended to inter-distillate price ratios.

8.3 Factors Affecting Relative Product Prices

Our investigation of relative price movements has shown that these differ depending on the choice of products considered. On the one hand, the relationship between distillate prices as a whole and residual fuel oil prices has not only varied considerably during the period under study but also displayed large and sustained cyclical movements. Such behaviour indicates that the factors determining the relative prices of distillates and fuel oil are slow to adjust to changes in these prices; this usually occurs when adjustment requires investment. On the other hand, the ratios of the different distillate prices to

Table 8.3: Regressions of Rotterdam Product Prices on Each Other, 1976–87.

Dependent Variable	Constant	Gasoline	Naphtha	Kerosine	Gas Oil	R^2	SEE	DWS
Fuel Oil	12.49 (1.99)	0.45 (19.34)	–	–	–	0.725	24.8	0.14
Fuel Oil	13.75 (2.56)	–	0.50 (22.47)	–	–	0.781	22.1	0.13
Fuel Oil	18.30 (3.19)	–	–	0.45 (20.21)	–	0.742	24.0	0.10
Fuel Oil	17.01 (2.98)	–	–	–	0.52 (20.52)	0.748	23.7	0.11
Gas Oil	–6.11 (1.32)	0.87 (50.04)	–	–	–	0.946	18.3	0.41
Gas Oil	4.21 (0.95)	–	0.93 (49.91)	–	–	0.946	18.4	0.36
Gas Oil	3.12 (1.43)	–	–	0.88 (102.62)	–	0.987	9.1	1.18
Kerosine	–8.89 (1.69)	0.98 (50.15)	–	–	–	0.947	20.7	0.43
Kerosine	2.13 (0.45)	–	1.05 (52.95)	–	–	0.952	19.7	0.37
Gasoline	14.67 (4.48)	–	1.06 (77.55)	–	–	0.977	13.5	0.48

each other are much less cyclical and also tend to fluctuate more rapidly around a constant level. Such behaviour indicates that the factors determining the relative prices of distillates adjust more quickly (and that the shifts in their relative levels of demand are smaller); and therefore suggests that these adjustments may have been achieved without the need for additional investment.

Simple economics dictate that relative product prices must depend on the relative levels of supply of and demand for the different refined products. What complicates the picture is the fact that supply and demand also depend, in part, on changes in product prices, and that this adjustment is not always instantaneous since both the refinery plant, which determines the relative supply of the different products, and the stock of oil-consuming equipment, which determines the levels of demand, cannot always adapt without investment. If investment is required, then the required adjustment takes longer, and therefore prices will necessarily bear the brunt of the adjustment in the short run.

These considerations, therefore, determine the framework for our investigation of the factors affecting relative product prices. Given that the supply of refinery products is jointly determined, we will focus on price ratios and consequently the relative supply of and demand for the different products. Four types of factors are likely to be important: the relative levels of demand for the different products, the factors affecting their supply, the levels of their stocks, and the nature of the adjustment process.

If the demand for one product increases relative to that for another at existing prices, then refiners as a whole can react in several ways. First, they can put up the relative price some or all of the way required to keep *actual* demand constant. In the extreme case we would observe no changes in actual relative demands and large changes in relative prices. Secondly, they could, if supply flexibility made it possible, change their production pattern so as to satisfy the new demand completely at existing prices. This full quantity adjustment would not then change the price ratio, while a partial quantity adjustment would require some offsetting price movement. The less flexible the refining system, the larger the price shift would be. Thirdly, they could meet the extra demand solely from stocks. The larger the stock level of the product strongly in demand, the easier this would be, and the less the refiners would have to rely on production or price movements. Hence we can see that large relative demand shifts are certainly likely to be associated with relative price movements. The magnitudes of such shifts will depend on the relative supply flexibility and relative price elasticities of the various products, and the willingness to use stocks.

In deciding how to meet any change in demand from the range of options available, the refiners' initial reaction to the change may be different from their reaction over a longer period. If it is costly to adjust prices (e.g. if it is thought to be bad for business to adjust them too often, or to have to reverse them if the demand shift is not sustained), then we would expect there to be a certain inertia in the behaviour of relative product prices (given the variability of the other factors). This can be modelled by the lagged price ratio, and a 'speed-of-adjustment' factor can be estimated.

In order to test these ideas we carried out a number of regressions using supply and demand data for OECD Europe taken from the *Quarterly Oil and Gas Statistics* series published by the OECD. Monthly data are not available for the full period. Prices and price ratios (PRIRAT) were therefore calculated on a quarterly basis also. In the case of the ratios of distillate prices to fuel oil prices, we used aggregate price, supply and demand data in order to simplify the analysis: the price of 'distillates' was calculated using a simple average of the gasoline, naphtha, kerosine and gas oil prices; and the supply of and demand for 'distillates' were calculated by subtracting the figures for 'heavy fuel oil (residual)' from those for 'total products'.

Choosing an appropriate measure for demand is fairly straightforward: for these regressions the ratios of the demand for one product type to the demand for the other (DEMRAT) have been calculated from the gross observed consumption levels for each product type. These are defined by the OECD as deliveries into final consumption from refineries and other primary storage facilities, and should be regarded as a measure of demand *as perceived by refiners* rather than one of *actual* demand by consumers.

Choosing an appropriate measure for the flexibility of supply is not so easy, so several different proxy variables were tried. The first, and simplest, measure we used is observed refinery throughput for OECD Europe (OBSRUNS), as reported in the *OECD Quarterly Oil and Gas Statistics*. This can be regarded as a proxy for the average yield of products which, as we have shown earlier, will change as refinery capacity utilization changes.

A more precise measure of the changes in the average product yield can be obtained by comparing refinery throughput with available upgrading capacity. Given the large differences between the product yield from upgrading plant and the yield from distillation, we would expect the product supply mix to reflect the changing proportion of upgrading plant being used. We therefore used the ratio of refinery input to upgrading capacity (CATRAT) (see Chapter 6). An alternative measure was a dummy variable (CATDUM) which took the value 1 when the upgrading capacity was fully loaded (CATRAT ≥ 1) and 0 when it was not. This enabled us to test whether the supply flexibility had a sharply different effect on prices when no more upgrading capacity was available.

A more direct measure of supply based on net refinery output (NETREF) was also tried. This was calculated as gross refinery output less fuel consumed by refineries, as reported by the OECD, and provides a measure of what the refiners were actually producing in any period.

Finally, we allowed for the relative stocks of the different products by including the ratio of opening product stocks held in primary storage (mainly) by refiners (STKRAT), which can be regarded as a measure of what is actually available to meet demand at any given moment.

The regressions fall into two groups; those for the average distillate versus heavy fuel oil, and those between distillates.

8.4 Distillates/Fuel Oil Price Ratios

Our analysis so far has indicated that the relationship between distillates and fuel oil prices is not constant. The correlation between the distillates price and the fuel oil price is only about 75 per cent; and the differences between them are due to non-seasonal variations in other factors that have yet to be identified. We expect these to include changes in the supply of and demand for distillate products relative to fuel oil.

The behaviour of each of these possible explanatory variables is illustrated by Figures 8.7–8.9, which show the ratios of demand and opening stocks for the aggregate of distillates against those for fuel oil and the level of observed refinery runs for 1976–87. It is worth commenting on two aspects of these graphs. First, they demonstrate the very substantial shift in the relative importance of distillates and fuel oil to the refiner that has taken place over the period. The ratio of distillates demand to fuel oil demand increased from around 2.0 at the beginning of the period to over 5.0 at the end, with the most rapid change occurring from 1985 onwards once the short-run effect of the UK miners' strike had ended. This shift towards distillates is mirrored by the ratio of their opening stocks to fuel oil stocks, which also increased over the period. Secondly, these graphs reveal that the demand and stocks ratios exhibit a pronounced seasonal pattern, which is clearly not reflected in the behaviour of the quarterly distillates/fuel oil price ratio which is shown in Figure 8.10. This disparity between the seasonal variation in demand and the non-seasonal variation in prices suggests that refiners do not generally respond to seasonal shifts in demand by changes in prices: rather they use stocks to smooth out those variations.

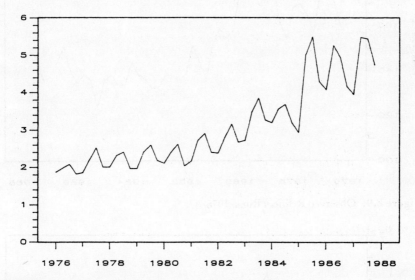

Figure 8.7: Distillates/Fuel Oil Demand Ratio. 1976–87.

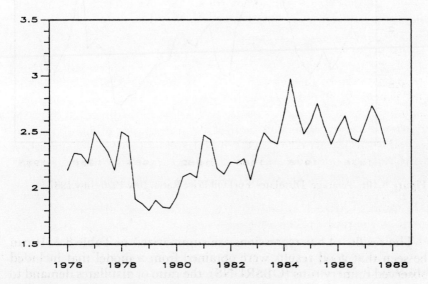

Figure 8.8: Distillates/Fuel Oil Stocks Ratio. 1976–87.

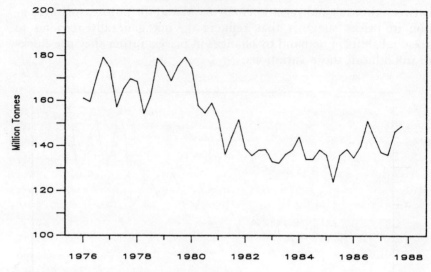

Figure 8.9: Observed Refinery Runs. 1976–87.

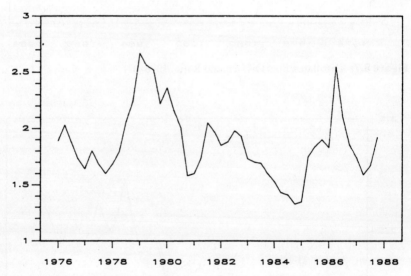

Figure 8.10: 'Average' Distillates/Fuel Oil Price Ratio. July 1976–July 1987.

The results of our regressions are summarized in Table 8.4. It can be seen that good results were obtained from a model that included observed refinery runs (OBSRUNS), the ratio of distillates demand to fuel oil demand (DEMRAT), the ratio of opening stocks of distillates to opening stocks of fuel oil (STKRAT), the ratio of distillate prices to fuel oil prices (PRIRAT) in the previous period, and quarterly seasonal dummies. As can be seen from the correlation coefficient ($R^2 = 0.883$), this equation now explains just over 88 per cent of the variation in the distillates/fuel oil price ratios, and the residual error (SEE $= 0.114$) is low in relation to the mean value of the price ratio (1.87), indicating an average error of 6 per cent. Furthermore, the Durbin h-statistic (0.88) indicates that there is no strong systematic factor missing from the equation, since this is well below its critical value of 1.64. Finally, each of the parameters estimated by the regression displays the expected sign, and has coefficients significantly different from zero (except for two of the seasonal dummies). The results were obtained using a data set that excluded the very sharp increase in the distillates/fuel oil price ratio in the second quarter of 1986, since this was an extreme movement that could not be accommodated in the model and was probably associated with the general dislocation of markets observed during this period.

These results can be interpreted in the following manner. The positive sign on the coefficient for DEMRAT indicates, as might be expected, that an increase in the demand for distillates relative to fuel oil will lead to an increase in the price of distillates relative to fuel oil. This happens because the supply of distillates relative to fuel oil is not sufficiently flexible to adjust fully to the increase in demand, whose impact is therefore partly moderated by the change in prices. The price increase then acts as a signal to both wholesalers (who lift products from primary storage) and refiners (who supply the products), thus simultaneously depressing demand and stimulating supply. In the short run, a unit change in the demand ratio produces about a 0.1 unit change in relative prices. The long-run effect is still below 0.2 units (see below).

The negative sign on the coefficient for STKRAT indicates that, if a higher opening level of primary stocks of distillates relative to fuel oil is held by refiners, then this will reduce the price of distillates relative to fuel oil. This happens because, for most companies, stocks provide an important direct way of changing the balance of supply and demand. Each company will have its own operational targets for the stocks of different products, and will adjust its supply in order to try to maintain these. A higher level of opening stocks will also allow a greater proportion of any demand increase to be met from stocks and thus reduce the pressure for a price increase. The coefficient on STKRAT indicates that a unit increase in the stocks ratio is associated with slightly less than a unit fall in the price ratio. Since the typical stocks ratio is of the same magnitude as the corresponding

Table 8.4: Regressions of Distillates/Fuel Oil Price Ratio on Supply Variables; Demand, Stocks and Lagged Price Ratios; and Dummy Variables. 1976: Q2–1987: Q4.

Constant	Supply Variable	$DEMRAT_t$	$STKRAT_t$	$PRIRAT_{t-1}$	Seasonal Dummies			R^2	SEE	Durbin's h-statistic
					$Q2$	$Q3$	$Q4$			
	$OBSRUNS_t$									
2.748	0.004	0.131	−0.961	0.232	0.066	−0.099	−0.22	0.883	0.114	0.88
(5.79)	(2.22)	(4.74)	(7.31)	(2.56)	(1.29)	(1.80)	(4.10)			
	$NETREF_t$									
2.852	0.003	0.107	−0.930	0.264	0.064	−0.083	−0.22	0.885	0.114	0.74
(6.27)	(1.77)	(3.86)	(6.92)	(2.84)	(1.24)	(1.49)	(4.10)			
	$CATRAT_t$									
3.000	0.134	0.118	−0.922	0.287	0.043	−0.098	−0.23	0.885	0.114	0.81
(7.03)	(1.79)	(3.86)	(6.87)	(3.22)	(0.83)	(1.92)	(4.16)			

Note: Observations for 1986: Q1, and 1986: Q2 were excluded as they represented extreme fluctuations in the price ratio between distillates and fuel oil, and produced exceptional residuals if included in the regression.

demand ratio, this points to the very substantial role of stocks in moderating relative demand shifts.

The positive sign on the coefficient for OBSRUNS indicates that higher levels of refinery runs are associated with a higher price of distillates relative to fuel oil. This is true for a combination of reasons. As explained earlier, refineries produce joint products, so that increases in the output of one product may lead to an increase in the output of the others. Although this is not always the case, it will certainly be true for distillates as a whole and fuel oil, where the ability of the refiner to vary the mix of product types is limited by the inflexibility of the refinery plant. In these circumstances the effect of an increase in refinery runs will be felt through the changing shares of distillates and fuel oil in the total output from the refining system. If an increase in refinery runs leads to a decrease in the share of distillates relative to fuel oil, then the distillates/fuel oil price ratio should rise (and vice versa). Our results indicate that increased runs yield progressively less distillates per unit of output, necessitating an increase in their relative prices to maintain a given demand ratio. This is consistent with the structure of the supply curve described in Chapter 6 above.

Seasonality was detected in the third and fourth quarters. As can be seen from Table 8.4, the seasonal dummy was strongly significant in the fourth quarter, and almost significant in the third quarter. Since we did not observe any seasonality in the behaviour of the ratios of distillate prices to fuel oil prices, it appears that the seasonality in this model derives from the behaviour of the other explanatory variables.

The fact that the distillates/fuel oil demand ratio has a strong seasonal component (see Figure 8.7) presents the refiner with a choice. At one extreme, he can vary his output mix or stock and destock to track the changes in relative demand; while at the other he can keep his output mix constant and allow relative prices to move instead. Since relative prices clearly do not change in a regular seasonal pattern, it seems that refiners adjust their output or stocks instead. However, it is also clear from the seasonal variation in the relative stock levels of distillates and fuel oil that refiners are not able to vary their output sufficiently to meet the change in demand, since stocks are being built up and run down in a counter-seasonal fashion.

It is this mismatch between the seasonal variation in relative demand and the seasonal variation in stocks and refinery output that generates the seasonal pattern observed in the regressions as reported in Table 8.4. As might be expected, the pattern is strongest in the winter quarter when the change in relative demand is most marked. This implies that refiners are prepared to smooth out what would otherwise be a higher relative price for their fuel oil output in the winter and a lower relative price in the summer.

Finally, since the regression also includes the lagged value of the price ratio (PRIRAT), it is possible to estimate the speed with which relative prices respond to changes in refinery throughputs, and to relative demand and stock levels. This can be calculated from the coefficient on the lagged value of PRIRAT. This coefficient is quite small (0.232), which means that adjustment takes place fairly rapidly within the time-period used for estimation. In this model, which uses quarterly data, the full adjustment takes 0.30 of a quarter on average, or just under one month. The ratio of the short-run to long-run effect of the various factors on the price ratio is 76.8 per cent, indicating again that the adjustment process is rapid.

The relative contributions of these various factors to the variation in the price ratio are shown in Figure 8.11. This uses the coefficients established in the regression to calculate the contribution of each variable to the determination of the price ratio:

(a) Line (1) is the contribution of the constant plus the demand variable (DEMRAT);
(b) Line (2) adds the contribution of the throughput (OBSRUNS), dynamic adjustment, and seasonal factors;
(c) Line (3) adds the contribution of the stocks ratio;
(d) Line (4) is the *actual* price ratio.

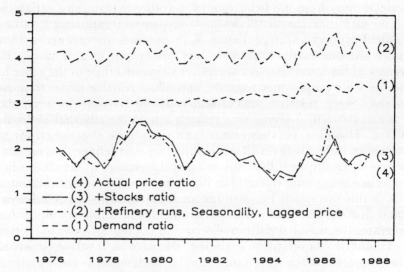

Figure 8.11: Distillates/Fuel Oil Price Model. July 1976–July 1987.

We can see from line (1) that the movements in the demand ratio have quite a small effect on relative prices and are mainly responsible for generating an upward trend component. The refining output, seasonal and dynamic adjustment factors add some variation to the effect of demand. The key to explaining the pattern of this variation is the ratio of opening stocks. Its movement over time is the factor that best matches the substantial variation of relative prices. This is an extremely important result: a shortage of stocks forces prices to rise, and a surplus will damp down price movements. Refiners will not then be able to alter their production to adjust to shifts in the levels of relative demand for distillates and fuel oil, but will have to rely largely on changes in stocks.

We repeated the regression using the two alternative measures of refinery utilization described above: refinery input net of indigenously produced refinery feedstocks (NETREF), and the ratio of net refinery input to total upgrading capacity (CATRAT). As can be seen from Table 8.4, we found that there was very little difference in the results obtained using from those OBSRUNS: in each case the correlation coefficient, the standard error and the values of the coefficients remained fairly similar. The dummy variable that was intended to differentiate between periods in which the marginal yield was simple refining and periods in which it was semi-complex (CATDUM) was not found to be significant, indicating perhaps that the *average* yield of products that matters rather more than the *marginal* yield.

The overall performance of this equation is highly satisfactory. As shown above, there has been substantial variation in the distillates/fuel oil price ratio, which neither moved at random around a constant, nor followed a simple trend. Rather it was cyclical, with cycles of differing magnitude. Our model has managed to explain nearly 90 per cent of the variation, and clearly improves on the null hypothesis that the price ratio was constant. The unexplained average error in the distillates/fuel oil price ratio was 0.11, which compares well with its mean value of 1.87. We have also shown not only that shifts in relative demand levels alter relative prices, but also that the effects of such shifts will be different at different levels of refinery throughput. This confirms the view that refinery throughput is not 'neutral' as far as product prices are concerned. Finally, our results show the great extent to which product price changes are smoothed out by refiners' management of their stocks whenever these are available. This smoothing factor is confirmed by the low level of seasonal price movement in comparison with the substantial level of seasonal demand variation.

8.5 Distillate/Distillate Price Ratios

As we have seen above, the relationships between the prices of pairs of distillates are already quite strong: indeed we have used this result to justify the use of an average price for distillates in our above investigation of the relationship between the prices of distillates and those of residual fuel oil. The ratios of the prices of the different distillates to each other are much less variable than those for the 'average' distillates price to the fuel oil price (see Table 8.2), and the correlation coefficients are correspondingly much higher (see Table 8.3). In other words there is far less unexplained variation in the ratios of distillate prices to one another than there was in the ratios of distillate prices to fuel oil prices. Nevertheless, the correlations are not perfect and the statistical evidence suggests that there is still some systematic factor missing from the relationship.

Although refiners undoubtedly have greater short-run flexibility in varying the proportions of the different distillate products in their output, since they can substitute (some) kerosine for gas oil or (some) naphtha for kerosine by blending, this flexibility is limited in practice by the need to meet a variety of product quality standards. In addition, substituting gasoline for naphtha requires additional catalytic reforming capacity, and this may not be available without additional investment. In these circumstances we would also expect the relationships between pairs of distillate prices to be affected by changes in the relative supply of and demand for pairs of distillate products as we found in the case of 'average' distillate and fuel oil prices. Their role might be rather diminished, however, because of the greater opportunities to match output to demand.

In order to test this hypothesis, we regressed the ratios of the prices of the distillate products to each other (PRIRAT) on the factors that we found to be most effective in explaining the variation in the distillates/fuel oil price ratio: the ratios of demand for pairs of distillate products (DEMRAT), the ratios of their opening stocks (STKRAT), the ratios of their prices (PRIRAT) in the previous period, the observed level of refinery throughput (OBSRUNS) and quarterly seasonal dummies. The behaviour of each of these variables is similar to that of the corresponding variables in the distillates/fuel oil model (e.g. the demand and stocks ratios for all pairs of distillate products are strongly seasonal). The results of the regressions are summarized in Table 8.5.

We found it necessary to exclude a few exceptionally large fluctuations in these price ratios, which fell well outside the normal range of variation of the ratios and seriously distorted the results of our

Table 8.5: Regressions of Distillate/Distillate Price Ratios on Refinery Throughput; Demand, Stocks and Lagged Price Ratios; and Dummy Variables. 1978: Q2–1987: Q4.

Price Pair	Constant	$OBSRUNS_t$	$DEMRAT_t$	$STKRAT_t$	$PRIRAT_{t-1}$	Seasonal Dummies			R^2	SEE	Durbin's h-statistic
						Q2	Q3	Q4			
Gasoline/Naphtha[a]	−0.609 (0.29)	0.002 (2.32)	0.060 (3.21)	0.030 (2.00)	0.510 (5.54)	0.047 (2.30)	−0.010 (0.42)	−0.006 (0.29)	0.632	0.042	0.034
Gasoline/Kerosine[b]	1.330 (2.56)	−0.003 (1.82)	0.028 (0.78)	−0.151 (3.59)	0.536 (4.56)	0.125 (4.70)	0.011 (0.39)	−0.010 (0.039)	0.700	0.054	1.18
Gasoline/Gas Oil[c]	0.269 (0.60)	0.001 (0.48)	0.784 (2.00)	−0.600 (2.90)	0.560 (4.95)	0.044 (0.59)	−0.121 (1.22)	−0.052 (1.17)	0.636	0.067	−0.61
Naphtha/Kerosine[d]	0.368 (2.51)	0.001 (1.27)	0.052 (1.15)	−0.112 (1.73)	0.528 (5.46)	0.050 (2.26)	−0.006 (0.22)	−0.035 (1.58)	0.582	0.048	1.47
Naphtha/Gas Oil[e]	0.509 (2.57)	0.001 (1.21)	0.469 (0.93)	−1.413 (1.56)	0.433 (3.78)	0.049 (1.18)	0.018 (0.53)	−0.040 (1.39)	0.450	0.064	0.68
Kerosine/Gas Oil[f]	1.181 (6.30)	0.0001 (0.46)	0.241 (0.29)	−0.522 (1.01)	−0.038 (0.26)	−0.025 (1.04)	0.007 (0.19)	−0.005 (0.32)	0.293	0.029	n.a.

Notes: (a) 1986: Q2 excluded
(b) 1986: Q2, Q3 excluded
(c) 1978: Q3, 1986: Q2, Q3 excluded
(d) 1986: Q1 excluded
(e) 1978: Q4, 1986: Q1 excluded
(f) 1978: Q4, 1986: Q4 excluded

regressions. These large fluctuations were only found in the second half of 1978 and during 1986, both of which were periods of rapid changes in the overall level of oil prices, which can therefore reasonably be regarded as instances of temporary market failure or extreme distortion in relative price levels.

As can be seen from Table 8.5, the correlation coefficients R^2 are all quite low (particularly in comparison with those in the distillates/fuel oil case). They range from 0.29 for kerosine/gas oil to 0.70 for gasoline/kerosine, with the majority falling between 0.50 and 0.70. This is not unexpected, however, since, as explained above, the total variation in these price ratios is comparatively small. Consequently this lower degree of correlation is just as good as a larger correlation when there is more variation to be explained. Furthermore the standard errors for all these regressions (SEE) are now very low, and the residual error (measured in relation to the mean price ratio) is now under 6 per cent in every case. This compares with a coefficient of variation for the price ratio of between 7 and 10 per cent for all pairs of distillate products except kerosine/gas oil (4 per cent) before we introduced our additional explanatory variables (see Table 8.2). It is because the kerosine/gas oil price ratio already had a very low coefficient of variation that its correlation coefficient in this regression is so low (since there is very little left to explain), and this probably accounts for the generally poor performance of the equation as a whole.

Our four explanatory variables met with mixed success. If we exclude the results obtained for kerosine/gas oil for the reasons given above, it can be seen that the ratios of opening stocks (STKRAT) are significant (or very close to being significant) in all the remaining equations. Furthermore the estimated value of the coefficient has the expected (negative) sign for all but one of the pairs (gasoline/naphtha).

The demand ratios were less successful in explaining price variations, and were found to be significant in only two of the five remaining equations (gasoline/naphtha and gasoline/gas oil). In the other cases they fell well below the level required to indicate they were playing an effective role, although all the signs on the estimated coefficients were positive as expected. Similarly, the level of refinery throughput (OBSRUNS) was found to be significant in only two cases (gasoline/naphtha and gasoline/kerosine), but the signs on the coefficients were negative in the latter case.

As we explained earlier, increases in refinery throughput do not necessarily have the same impact on the price ratios for all pairs of products. We expected higher runs to increase distillate prices relative to those of fuel oil, because the share of distillates in refinery output falls as throughput increases. The same relationship should also apply to gasoline and naphtha, since gasoline yields typically fall relative to naphtha yields as throughput increases and less sophisticated plant is brought on stream. This view is supported by the positive coefficient observed for OBSRUNS in the gasoline/naphtha regression. If, however, gasoline yields were to increase in relation to those of some other product as throughput increased, then the opposite effect would be observed, as seems to be the case for gasoline/kerosine. This is a result of joint production, which means that although an increase in the share of one product inevitably leads to a decrease in the share of the other products as a group, it can also lead to an increase of one other individual product.

Seasonality was detected for only three pairs of prices (gasoline/naphtha, gasoline/kerosine and naphtha/kerosine); and in each case it was in the second quarter that the ratio was found to be significantly different from its first-quarter base level.

Finally, it is interesting to observe that the coefficients estimated for the *lagged* ratio of prices of pairs of distillates are consistently larger than those obtained for the lagged aggregate distillates/fuel oil price ratio. This indicates that the speed of adjustment is much slower, lasting approximately one period, or three months, compared with about one month for the distillates/fuel oil case. At first sight this appears to be a counter-intuitive result, since it suggests that refiners have greater flexibility in responding to changes in the demand for distillates relative to fuel oil than they have in responding to changes in relative levels of demand for the different distillates. There is, however, another interpretation which explains this difference in speeds of adjustment. It is clear from the relative sizes of the mean price ratios, as shown in Table 8.2, that the economic benefits of responding to shifts in the distillates/fuel oil price ratio are much greater than those of responding to changes in the ratio of one distillate price to another. Furthermore, the fact that shifts in the price of distillates relative to fuel oil tend to be sustained, while shifts in the relative prices of distillates to each other are more quickly reversed, increases the incentive for refiners to follow and respond to changes in the distillates/fuel oil price ratio. Moreover, given that such adjustments cannot be made costlessly, it is likely that refiners will opt more quickly for the route that is more likely to yield sustained benefits.

These regressions for the inter-distillate price ratios indicate that some improvement can be made to a model that assumes that they are essentially constant. Any divergence from their long-term levels is put right only slowly, and again stocks play some role in smoothing out initial shocks. For certain products demand is important but for others it is not, which suggests that the larger part of demand shifts is met by supply shifts rather than price shifts, which are slow and sticky. The insignificance of the variables related to refinery technology suggests that, over the range of variation in output experienced, the relative yields of the products did not change much, and therefore did not interfere with the relative prices.

Putting the results together, we see that shifts in the relative demand for distillates and fuel oil are met substantially and rapidly with price increases, unless stocks are adequate to smooth them out; while shifts in the relative demands for the different distillates are met largely by shifts in refinery output, so that prices are slower and stickier to respond. In the latter case, changes in stocks ratios modify the price changes that would otherwise have taken place and act as a first line of adjustment, whether the second line is via price or quantity adjustments.

9   The Taxation of Petroleum Products

Robert Bacon

9.1 Introduction

Throughout Europe petroleum products are subject to substantial levels of taxation, and this drives a large wedge between the prices received by refiners and the prices paid by consumers. Variations in the tax payable will affect refiners' margins (if they absorb some or all of the change) and hence their profitability, or the price paid by consumers thus affecting demand for the products (to the extent that this is price sensitive) and hence the volume of products sold; and in general they will affect both. Since, as is well known, taxation is very high on certain products, changes in tax schemes or tax rates can be major factors affecting the refining sector.

We begin by first describing the tax systems used and computing average tax rates for 1978 and 1986. This is followed by a more detailed analysis of the way in which European governments have altered their tax rates in response to changes in product prices. This section suggests that tax rates have changed by large amounts, and in a systematic way over time. Hence shifts in product prices for reasons not directly associated with taxation changes have tended to be followed by taxation changes that have amplified the effects of the original shocks.

9.2 Taxation Systems in Europe

All the major petroleum products are taxed in most European countries. The tax levied generally consists of two elements:

(a) An excise element which is a fixed amount per unit of the product concerned, invariant with respect to variations in the net-of-tax price, until a new rate is determined by legislation. Such changes will often be annual, and the excise collected per unit of output may therefore remain constant despite wide price variations in the short run.
(b) A proportional element, usually a Value Added Tax (VAT), which is levied on the retail price *including* the excise duty.

The tax systems for 1986 are summarized for all the OECD European countries (except Iceland and Turkey) for the main products in Table 9.1, which shows the levels of excise duty per thousand litres or per tonne in local currencies. In order to reach a standardized format, we first work out the levels of tax that would be paid at the average product prices charged during the year (as given in the IEA publication *Energy Prices and Taxes*). These amounts, which include both excise and VAT elements, are presented as percentages of the price ex tax (excise and VAT) in Table 9.2.

It can be seen immediately that the rates of tax levied on the various products vary tremendously from one country to another. For example, the highest rate charged on gasoline (359 per cent, in Italy) is more than twice that charged in many of the other countries. The rates charged on other products – although not nearly so high – are even more variable, since some countries have effectively no taxation on certain products while other countries tax the same products heavily. Moreover, it is clear that countries differ in the extent to which they tax the various products relative to one another. For example, of the seventeen countries considered, the UK has the tenth-highest rate of taxation on gasoline, the fourth on commercial diesel, the eleventh on industrial gas oil, the sixteenth on residential gas oil and the ninth on heavy fuel oil. Other countries have similarly varied patterns of taxation.

It is clear from Table 9.1 that *within* countries tax rates vary greatly between products, so that the gap between the retail product price and the price received by the refiner varies enormously between products.

9.3 Taxation Policy and Tax Changes

The figures given in Section 9.2 above for the average rates of taxation on petroleum products are only a 'snapshot' of what is in fact a dynamic process. Product prices have generally changed each year by greater or lesser amounts, and European governments have altered their tax regimes in response to these changes. If they had not increased the excise duties levied in line with the rise in net-of-tax prices, then the revenue raised from the fixed excise duties would have fallen as a percentage of the net-of-tax prices. Furthermore, the VAT element would also have fallen as a percentage of the net-of-tax price, since VAT is charged not only on the price ex tax, but also on the excise duty.

The tendency to change the excise duty every year (and occasionally the VAT rate as well) has meant that the average tax collected per

Table 9.1: Taxes Levied on Principal Petroleum Products.[a] 1986. Local Currencies.

	Gasoline		Automotive Diesel			Gas Oil		Heavy Fuel Oil
	Excise	Excise & VAT	Excise	Excise & VAT	Excise (Industrial)	Excise & VAT (Residential)	Excise (Industrial)	Excise (Industrial)
Austria	3,850	5,522	3,820	5,391	1,058	1,837		0
Belgium	11,200	16,316	5,250	8,849	0	1,235		0
Denmark	3,426	4,562	0[b]	2,035	0[b]	2,000		0[b]
Finland	1,468	1,468[c]	901	901[c]	198	198[c]		110
France	2,750	3,484	1,650[d]	2,226	629[e]	685		297
Germany	530	666	442	569	17	73		15
Greece	54,459	54,459[c]	17,053	17,053[c]	17,053	17,053[c]		13,470
Ireland	277	390	211	254	18	36		8
Italy[f]	806	1,001	207	300[g]	207	288		10
Luxembourg	9,070	11,206	4,300	5,109	n.a.	510		100
Netherlands	738	993	221	360	35	147		15
Norway	2,050	2,702	52	413	52	363		86[h]
Portugal	66,000	74,000	33,879	39,067	33,880[c]	36,373		5,288
Spain	27,500	56,355[i]	11,000	22,035[i]	17,279[i]	20,660[i]		7,628[i]
Sweden	2,350	2,350[c]	529[j]	529[cj]	529	529[c]		563
Switzerland	549	621	626[k]	626	30	30[c]		36
UK	194	238	161	208	10	10[c]		8

Notes:
(a) Values given are per thousand litres for gasoline, diesel and gas oil; per tonne for heavy fuel oil.
(b) Excise refunded to commercial and industrial users.
(c) VAT not levied.
(d) VAT only partly refunded to commercial users.
(e) VAT not reimbursed to industrial users.
(f) Thousand lire per unit.
(g) Does not include supertax for diesel-engined vehicles.
(h) Additional excise payable for every 0.5 per cent sulphur above 0.5 per cent.
(i) Includes 'renta'.
(j) Does not include mileage tax for diesel-engined vehicles.
(k) VAT not refundable to commercial users.

Table 9.2: Average Taxes Paid, as Percentages of the Net-of-Tax Prices for Principal Products. 1986.

	Gasoline	Automotive Diesel		Gas Oil		Heavy Fuel Oil
		Commercial	Domestic	Industrial	Residential	Industrial
Austria	132	95	134	34	54	0
Belgium	176	57	97	0	17	0
Denmark	246	0	111	0	126	0
Finland	85	67	67	21	21	16
France	270	114	154	48	52	47
Germany	151	63	85	4	19	7
Greece	235	80	80	80	80	98
Ireland	188	97	118	10	22	7
Italy	359	67	103	85	118	8
Luxembourg	115	47	56	n.a.	6	2
Netherlands	201	44	72	5	33	6
Norway	135	3	23	3	23	10
Portugal	190	109	126	109	117	26
Spain	206	40	54	78	89	45
Sweden	133	28	28	41	40	61
Switzerland	183	144	144	9	9	18
UK	178	106	137	8	8	11

Note: (a) Two sets of data are given from here onwards for 'automotive diesel'. The tax rates given for 'commercial' diesel include *only* the excise duty element of the tax, since VAT on diesel for commercial use is refundable. The tax rates given for 'domestic' diesel include both excise duty *and* VAT.

unit has been controlled by positive government action in recent years. Table 9.3 shows the changes in the percentage tax rates charged on the various products between 1978 and 1986, and reveals that there were substantial switches even in the percentage of the price ex tax that was collected as tax. Average tax rates for gasoline rose in most countries, while for diesel the picture was more mixed. For heavy fuel oil the picture was one of very disparate behaviour, with very large increases in a few countries and decreases in other countries.

The relationship between the average tax levied and the net price charged is of considerable significance. If some external influence (e.g. a rise in the price of crude oil) forces up the prices charged by refiners, the effects of this on demand and on the refining sector will depend on how such price rises are transmitted to consumers. The increment in the retail price will consist of three elements:

(a) the increment in the net price of the refined product;
(b) the increment in the tax payable on the product;
(c) the increment in other elements making up the margin between the retail and 'factory gate' prices (distribution costs).

If items (b) and (c) are zero, then the retail price will rise by the same absolute amount as the net price. However, if this 'tax plus margin' is large (as would certainly be the case for some products), then the percentage rise in the retail price will be much less than that in the factory gate price. For example, with a 'tax plus margin' equal to 200 per cent of the factory gate price, a rise in the latter of 30 per cent will cause retail prices to rise by only 10 per cent: the greater the 'tax plus margin' as a percentage of the price net of tax, the more shocks to factory gate prices will be 'damped down', and the less the percentage rise or fall in demand will be. In the case of heavily taxed products, such as gasoline, this phenomenon could lead an observer, taking just a 'snapshot' of taxes at a moment in time, to play down the importance of supply-induced product price shifts. He would see the price change as being passed on but with little resulting change in demand to feed back into the refining sector.

The key issue is how taxes are changed in response to 'factory gate' price changes. Of course the VAT element rises as quickly in percentage terms as the price itself (including excise). Excise duties do not change automatically, however, and this might lead to the conclusion that high levels of taxation damp down the effects of supply-induced price changes. However, as Table 9.3 makes abundantly clear, there were very large shifts in excise taxes over time, which implies that

Table 9.3: Changes in Percentage Tax Rates from 1978 to 1986.

	Gasoline	Automotive Diesel		Gas Oil		Heavy Fuel Oil
		Commercial	Domestic	Industrial	Residential	Industrial
Austria	+14	+20	+45	+2	+18[b]	0
Belgium	+15	−57	−52	−11	0	−4
Denmark	+70	0	+71	0	+93	0
Finland	−3	−10	−10	+19	+19	+13
France	+98	−5	−3	+18	+22	+47
Germany	+13	−50	−55	−1	+2	−1
Greece	+99	+55	+55	+58[a]	+70[a]	+93
Ireland	+66	+49	+70	+4	+16	0
Italy	+112	+46	+68	+68	+86	+7
Luxembourg	+31[a]	+19[a]	+21[a]	n.a.	−6[a]	+1[b]
Netherlands	+48	−11	−11	−8	+5	−2
Norway	−6	+2	+2	−11	+2	+7[a]
Portugal	−50	+89	+106	+89	+93	+53
Spain	+180	+88	+108	+65	+87	+54
Sweden	+25	+20	+20	+30	+29	+46
Switzerland	+11	+35[a]	+35[a]	+1	+2	+6
UK	+77	+24	+30	−1	−1	−1

Notes: (a) Calculated from prices and taxes starting in 1979.
 (b) Calculated from prices and taxes starting in 1981.
Source: Author's calculations from OECD/IEA, *Energy Prices and Taxes* (quarterly).

retail product prices may have risen more closely in line with 'factory gate' prices than would at first appear to be the case. The stronger this effect is, the more significant the sensitivity of final demand is to price changes following a supply shock.

In order to analyse how tax rates were changed by governments, we have related the total tax charged for a unit of product (yearly average) to the net price of that product, for the period 1978–86. (No comparable earlier data exist.) A regression of tax T on net price P of the following form is used:

$$T = a + bP \tag{1}$$

If the excise duty were fixed then the estimate of a would be the excise duty and the estimate of b would be the VAT rate. If excise duty were instead behaviourally related to price so that:

$$a(P) = cP \tag{2}$$

then the behavioural tax equation would be:

$$T = (b + c)P \tag{3}$$

giving effective proportionality and a situation in which retail prices would have the same percentage variability as 'factory gate' prices.

It is important to interpret correctly the hypothesis expressed by (2). It implies that, on (say) a yearly basis, excise duties are altered in order to maintain taxes in a fixed ratio to current net-of-tax prices, and that *during* the year the tax rate is not changed, so that the relation between the two prices will not be proportional if net prices change. Moreover this is purely a 'behavioural' relationship. The government does not bind itself to maintain this long-term relationship (as with the legislation for VAT rates), but merely behaves as if it wished to maintain the relationship.

The basic relationship (1) is estimated by ordinary least squares. However, plots of the data reveal a very important characteristic: the tax levied appears to be more strongly related to the previous year's price than to that of the current year. The shifts in excise rates, which are only periodic, in fact appear to be related to the recent history of prices. This result is not unexpected, since the planning and implementation of most changes take time. Accordingly, a second regression is run in the form:

$$T_t = a' + b'P_{t-1} \tag{4}$$

Table 9.4: Regressions of Taxes on Prices Net of Tax.

	Intercept	Standard Error	Slope	Standard Error	R^2
Gasoline					
Austria	2.08	0.39	0.57	0.12	0.78
Belgium	6.41	0.95	0.73	0.10	0.90
Denmark	1.38	0.41	0.85	0.22	0.71
Finland	0.68	0.09	0.26	0.06	0.76
France	0.79	0.36	1.04	0.25	0.75
Germany	0.41	0.02	0.38	0.06	0.89
Greece	−0.56	6.62	1.09	0.24	0.78
Ireland	−0.02	0.02	1.37	0.08	0.98
Italy	0.12	0.07	1.66	0.20	0.92
Luxembourg	2.71	1.10	0.63	0.16	0.76
Netherlands	0.43	0.08	0.63	0.17	0.63
Norway	0.99	0.10	0.63	0.07	0.94
Portugal	15.54	3.42	0.99	0.08	0.96
Sweden	0.71	0.25	0.56	0.15	0.69
Switzerland	0.55	0.01	0.09	0.02	0.73
UK	−0.02	0.01	1.31	0.09	0.97
Diesel (Commercial)					
Belgium	3.64	0.28	0.10	0.03	0.74
France	0.77	0.05	0.37	0.03	0.97
Germany	0.39	0.00	0.08	0.01	0.96
Greece	−3.57	3.53	0.61	0.20	0.61
Ireland	−0.03	0.01	0.79	0.07	0.95
Italy	−0.06	0.04	0.41	0.10	0.72
Luxembourg	−0.86	0.77	0.39	0.11	0.73
Netherlands	0.17	0.01	0.05	0.02	0.60
Portugal	−7.88	3.50	0.84	0.10	0.92
UK	0.02	0.00	0.67	0.04	0.98
Diesel (Domestic)					
Belgium	4.74	0.63	0.36	0.06	0.87
Denmark	0.10	0.34	0.44	0.18	0.51
France	1.00	0.07	0.58	0.04	0.96
Germany	0.47	0.02	0.17	0.04	0.74
Greece	−3.57	3.53	0.61	0.20	0.61
Ireland	−0.05	0.02	0.98	0.12	0.92
Italy	−0.05	0.03	0.64	0.08	0.91
Luxembourg	−0.66	0.88	0.45	0.12	0.73
Netherlands	0.26	0.16	0.15	0.03	0.79
Portugal	−7.88	3.50	0.84	0.10	0.92
UK	0.03	0.01	0.88	0.06	0.97

Table 9.4: (cont'd)

	Intercept	Standard Error	Slope	Standard Error	R^2
Gas Oil (Residential)					
Belgium	573.93	464.42	0.11	0.05	0.46
Denmark	172.16	342.54	0.43	0.18	0.48
France	147.83	56.80	0.26	0.04	0.90
Germany	65.48	14.62	0.06	0.04	0.26
Greece	−6,240.24	1,660.52	0.53	0.16	0.70
Ireland	−3.41	12.11	0.11	0.09	0.21
Italy	−52.86	34.85	0.64	0.10	0.86
Luxembourg	967.16	142.56	−0.20	0.02	0.18
Netherlands	95.24	19.61	0.11	0.04	0.55
Portugal	−8,343.32	3,906.60	0.85	0.11	0.91
UK	5.16	0.79	0.02	0.01	0.56
Heavy Fuel Oil (Industrial)					
Austria	−536.86	114.80	0.32	0.05	0.87
Belgium	109.31	31.72	−0.01	0.00	0.59
France	−106.50	72.59	0.17	0.06	0.58
Finland	−37.27	9.08	0.14	0.01	0.95
Greece	−3,511.84	2,581.06	0.62	0.16	0.72
Ireland	11.98	3.69	−0.02	0.03	0.05
Italy	2.92	3.40	−0.00	0.01	0.00
Netherlands	17.02	1.57	−0.01	0.00	0.49
Norway	5.78	12.91	0.04	0.02	0.54
Sweden	−88.85	45.80	0.40	0.04	0.95
Switzerland	13.40	4.94	0.06	0.02	0.55
UK	6.68	0.46	0.01	0.01	0.39

where the term T_t is the tax in year t, etc. These regressions fit better (in virtually all cases) and are the ones reported in Table 9.4. We were unable to carry out regressions for all products and all countries, however, because of limitations on the availability of data.

The regressions show that for gasoline and diesel, there is a clear link between the taxes levied and the previous year's net price. The fit is good, and in virtually all cases the coefficient on the price is much greater than the VAT rate (which is virtually always less than 25 per cent). There is strong evidence that during the period the governments of the European countries were increasing excise duties, after a delay, in line with factory gate prices. The intercept terms, which represent the 'permanent' part of excise duties, are usually small in absolute terms.[1] The evidence supports the view that governments

[1] These are in the same units as the price of the product, i.e. units of local currency per litre, except for light fuel oil which is per thousand litres and heavy fuel oil which is per tonne.

attempted to keep retail and factory gate prices in proportion, at least for gasoline and diesel (which were the most important products for tax purposes). For gas oil and heavy fuel oil, the relationship is much weaker in many cases, but since taxes were so much lower in general, as shown in Table 9.1, it mattered much less whether this small margin was or was not indexed. In these cases, changes in 'factory gate' prices would be largely passed on because the margin available to damp their impact in percentage terms was so small.

We may conclude from the above that supply-side shifts in product prices were reflected equally in retail prices (after a delay), so that the retail market faced the same magnitudes of price variation as were seen in the 'factory gate' prices. This observation points to the importance of the price elasticity of demand for the various products as a potentially crucial determinant of shifts in the 'demand barrel' (i.e. in the relative levels of demand for different products in a given market).

The analysis so far has concentrated on the period 1978–86 and used models with lagged prices, i.e. the latest prices to enter the regressions are for 1985. Although the prices of products were falling in dollar terms during this period, they did not fall in European local currencies until 1986 (because of offsetting currency movements), when there was a very substantial (supply-driven) price fall in net terms.

It is of interest to examine governments' fiscal responses to the fall in oil prices in 1986. While the increases in prices earlier on had generally been associated with increases in tax rates, as shown in Table 9.3 above, the fall in net prices in 1986 did not lead to a symmetrical reduction in tax rates. Only in a few cases were the tax rates (on net prices) kept constant to allow the fall in the net prices to be passed on to the final user. On the contrary, it is clear from Table 9.5 that, despite the very large decline in net product prices in 1986, most governments pushed up tax rates (on the net prices) on most products. This counter-price tax behaviour would have damped the net price falls very greatly and cancelled out the effect of lower crude prices on the demand for products. The refining sector in 1987 (and thereafter) gained less in throughput terms than might have been anticipated.

This asymmetry of tax changes, if continued (and not offset, say, by tax reductions in 1988), will potentially affect the size of European product demand and hence the size of the refining sector. An ever-increasing percentage 'take' by the governments of consuming countries, disguised by the insufficient tax cuts in weak markets, would keep the market smaller than might otherwise be anticipated.

Table 9.5: Taxes Paid on Principal Petroleum Products as Percentages of Net-of-Tax Prices. 1986 and 1987.

	Gasoline		Automotive Diesel		Light Fuel Oil (Residential)		Light Fuel Oil (Industrial)		Heavy Fuel Oil (Industrial)	
	1986	1987	1986	1987	1986	1987	1986	1987	1986	1987
Austria	134.2	149.4	88.0	92.7	54.3	47.7	33.9	n.a.	0.0	n.a.
Belgium	176.2	186.5	57.5	63.7	17.0	17.0	0.0	0.0	0.0	0.0
Denmark	244.8	n.a.	n.a.	n.a.	125.7	174.7	0.0	0.0	0.0	0.0
Finland	87.6	94.2	56.3	51.5	21.8	23.2	14.4	3.4	11.7	4.5
France	238.1	304.9	113.7	130.9	51.5	55.0	48.4	55.5	47.9	26.3
Germany	159.7	168.8	104.1	118.3	19.3	20.2	4.6	5.4	6.8	7.1
Greece	213.5	211.5	58.7	89.8	73.3	85.5	73.3	66.4	97.6	76.1
Ireland	192.4	209.6	100.8	110.1	22.0	35.5	10.7	24.2	7.5	6.7
Italy	358.7	358.7	66.7	93.4	118.3	154.5	85.2	115.5	8.1	6.6
Luxembourg	115.1	122.2	46.8	53.4	6.0	6.0	n.a.	n.a.	2.2	2.0
Netherlands	200.3	225.7	42.7	63.1	33.2	58.2	n.a.	n.a.	7.0	12.9
Norway	133.1	177.8	3.5	9.3	25.0	33.2	4.2	10.9	11.0	18.3
Portugal	208.6	188.2	117.9	124.7	126.2	133.1	117.9	124.7	26.4	−9.0
Spain	208.6	188.2	103.7	99.6	88.7	57.0	68.4	40.1	54.8	0.7
Sweden	130.9	143.3	29.4	41.4	42.0	69.2	43.5	72.4	62.3	91.6
Switzerland	158.4	171.7	154.5	168.8	9.4	7.9	10.4	8.7	18.6	13.9
UK	177.0	177.0	107.9	119.8	8.0	9.2	9.1	11.2	10.6	9.5